Philosophies of Race and Ethnicity

Philosophies of Race and Ethnicity

EDITED BY

PETER OSBORNE AND
STELLA SANDFORD

Continuum
The Tower Building, 11 York Road, London SE1 7NX
370 Lexington Avenue, New York, NY 10017–6503

First published 2002

British Library Cataloguing-in-Publication Data
A catalogue record for this book is available from the British Library.

ISBN 0-8264-5993-5 (hardback)
ISBN 0-8264-5994-3 (paperback)

Typeset by SetSystems Ltd, Saffron Walden, Essex
Printed and bound in Great Britain by Biddles Ltd, Guildford and King's Lynn

Contents

Notes on Contributors

Linda Martín Alcoff is Professor of Philosophy, Political Science, and Women's Studies at Syracuse University. Her books include *Feminist Epistemologies*, co-edited with Elizabeth Potter (Routledge, 1993); *Real Knowing: New Versions of the Coherence Theory of Knowledge* (Cornell University Press, 1996); *Epistemology: The Big Questions* (Blackwell, 1998); and *Thinking from the Underside of History*, co-edited with Eduardo Mendieta (Rowman and Littlefield, 2000). Her *Visible Identities: Race, Gender and the Self* is forthcoming with Oxford University Press.

Chetan Bhatt is Senior Lecturer in the Department of Sociology, Goldsmiths College, University of London. His publications include *Hindu Nationalism: Origins, Ideologies and Modern Myths* (Berg, 2001) and *Liberation and Purity: Race, New Religious Movements and the Ethics of Postmodernity* (UCL Press, 1997).

Rey Chow is Andrew W. Mellon Professor of the Humanities at Brown University and the author of *Woman and Chinese Modernity* (University of Minnesota Press, 1991), *Writing Diaspora* (Indiana University Press, 1993), *Primitive Passions* (Columbia University Press, 1995), and *Ethics after Idealism* (Indiana University Press, 1998). Her latest book, *The Protestant Ethnic and the Spirit of Capitalism*, will be published by Columbia University Press in 2002.

Rebecca E. Karl teaches in the East Asian Studies and History Departments at New York University. She is author of *Staging the World: Chinese Nationalism at the Turn of the Twentieth Century* (Duke University Press, 2002), and co-editor (with Peter Zarrow) of *Rethinking the 1898 Reforms: Political and Cultural Change in China* (Council on East Asian Publications, Harvard University, 2002); and (with Cesare Casarino and Saree Makdisi) of *Marxism beyond Marxism* (Routledge, 1996).

David Macey, a freelance writer and translator, was born in Sunderland and educated at University College London. He is the author of *Lacan in Contexts* (Verso, 1988), *The Lives of Michel Foucault* (Jonathan Cape, 1993), *Frantz Fanon: A Life* (Granta Books, 2000) and *The Penguin Dictionary of Critical Theory* (Penguin, 2000). He has translated numerous works from French.

Peter Osborne is Professor of Modern European Philosophy and Director of the Centre for Research in Modern European Philosophy at Middlesex University, London. He is the author of *The Politics of Time* (Verso, 1995), *Philosophy in Cultural Theory* (Routledge, 2000), and editor of *A Critical Sense: Interviews with Intellectuals* (Routledge, 1996). He is an editor of the British journal *Radical Philosophy*, and a member of the editorial board of *Traces*.

Naoki Sakai is Professor in the Departments of Asian Studies and Comparative Literature at Cornell University. His books include *Voices of the Past: The Status of Language in Eighteenth-Century Japanese Discourse* (Cornell University Press, 1991, Japanese translation forthcoming from Ibunsha), *Translation and Subjectivity: On 'Japan' and Cultural Nationalism* (University of Minnesota Press, 1997), *Nihon Shiso toiu Mondai: Honyaku to Shutai* [The Problem called Japanese Thought] (Iwanami Shoten, 1997), and (with Osamu Nishitani) *'Sekaishi' no Kaitai? Honyaku, Shutai, Rekishi* [Destruction of 'World History'?: Translation, Subjectivity, History], (Ibunsha, 1999). He is Senior Editor of *Traces, Multi-lingual Journal of Cultural Theory and Translation*.

Stella Sandford is Senior Lecturer in Modern European Philosophy at Middlesex University, London. She is the author of *The Metaphysics of Love: Gender and Transcendence in Levinas* (Continuum, 2000), and various articles on philosophies of sex and gender. She is an editor of the British journal *Radical Philosophy*, and the British *Women's Philosophy Review*.

Bill Schwarz teaches in the Department of Media and Communications at Goldsmiths College, University of London. He is an editor of *History Workshop Journal*, *New Formations* and *Cultural Studies*. His book, *Memories of Empire in Twentieth-Century England: Unfinished Histories of Decolonization* is forthcoming from Verso.

Denise Ferreira da Silva is Assistant Professor at the Department of Ethnic Studies, University of California, San Diego. Her forthcoming *Race and Nation in the Mapping of the Modern Global Space: A Critique of Sociology of Race Relations* will be published by Duke University Press.

Françoise Vergès is Lecturer in the Centre for Cultural Studies, Goldsmiths College, University of London. She has written widely on colonial psychiatry, postcolonial theory, slavery and the politics of reparation, and diasporic formations in the Indian Ocean and is the author of *Abolir l'esclavage: une utopie coloniale. Les ambiguités d'une politique humanitaire* (Albin Michel, 2001).

Robert J.C. Young is Professor of English and Critical Theory at Oxford University and a Fellow of Wadham College, Oxford. He is the author of *White Mythologies: Writing History and the West* (Routledge, 1990), *Colonial Desire: Hybridity in Culture, Theory and Race* (Routledge, 1995), *Torn Halves: Political Conflict in Literary and Cultural Theory* (Manchester University Press/ St Martin's Press, 1996), and *Postcolonialism: An Historical Introduction* (Blackwell, 2001). He is General Editor of *Interventions: International Journal of Postcolonial Studies* (Routledge).

Introduction: Philosophies of Race and Ethnicity

PETER OSBORNE and STELLA SANDFORD

'Race' is a concept with a disreputable past and an uncertain future, yet it continues to trouble the present, both politically and intellectually. It is politically troubling because of its enduring, and in many places increasing, practical significance as a hierachical mode of social differentiation and exclusion – that is, as a fundamental form of *social division*. It is intellectually troubling by virtue of the very fact of this endurance in the face of the widespread acknowledgement of its lack of objective validity as a principle for the classification of human differences – that is, in its character as *illusion*. For such illusion (rather than mere error)[1] would appear to restore to 'race' a quality of reality that critics of its scientific legitimacy are loath to accept. Yet it is precisely this quality of reality, in the lived experience of 'race' as social division, that, historically, has so often provided the basis of the solidarities and collective identities at the heart of anti-racist struggles by those most immediately subjected to racially discriminatory practices. How, then, can we maintain the merely illusory character of 'race' when its reality is existentially affirmed and normatively revalued, by those most subject to its oppressions? Would this not be, in some way, to deny the 'reality' of the racial character of the oppression itself? On the other hand, if the reality of race is acknowledged as an existential condition, might this not legitimize a new pseudo-scientific, culturalist conception of 'race as identity', thereby inaugurating the possibility of a politics of reverse racism, or racial competition, which is intellectually indistinguishable from racism itself?

'Race' thus troubles anti-racists in a way which is qualitatively distinct from the way in which 'empire' troubles anti-imperialists or 'war' troubles peace activists. For it remains hotly disputed whether and in what way such a thing as 'race' may (or should) be said to exist. This conflict has been the animating intellectual centre of anti-racist politics for several decades. It has recently acquired a more formal articulation in the philosophical debate between 'realist' and 'phenomenological' conceptions of race. One response to the apparent impasse of that debate has been to adopt a more historical approach to the construction of racial concepts, focusing on their diverse, contradictory and shifting explantory and social functions, rather than upon their more narrowly epistemological validity. Another, related response, reacting to current world-economic and geo-political developments dictating new patterns and types of migration, has been to broaden the intellectual horizon of the debate by displacing 'race' with 'ethnicity' and multiplying the disciplinary perspectives on its objects. Meanwhile, the political context of these debates has been changing from a politics of emancipation (collective self-determination of oppressed groups), predominant from the 1950s to the early 1980s, to the institutionalization of 'multiculturalism' as governmental, international NGO and corporate policy.

We may thus identify four distinct areas or, better, dimensions of current debates about race and ethnicity, in relation to which the chapters in this volume may be located: *philosophical ontology*, *conceptual genealogy*, *global comparativism* and *political context*.

PHILOSOPHICAL ONTOLOGY

The current state of the Anglo-American philosophical debate about the concept of race may be summarized in terms of responses to the thesis that 'there are no races: there is nothing in the world that can do all we ask "race" to do for us'. Formulated by Anthony Appiah in 1985,[2] this thesis was intended to do away with the concept of race as a means of human classification and, thereby, to abolish the intellectual basis of racism. The perceived problem with the formula, however, as already indicated, is that it destroys much of the intellectual basis of anti-racism along with that of racism, given the affirmation of the positive value of the beliefs and practices of racially identified social groups in anti-racist political struggles. In response to this concern, Appiah has amended his view to take account of 'race' not as nature or essence, but as identity, by which he understands a combination of self-identifications with ascriptions of identity by others – a 'dynamic nominalism'.[3] In acknowledging race as identity (which he now takes to be the best characterization of the views of W.E.B. Du Bois), Appiah has made a significant concession to the phenomenological view of race, which received its founding expression in the work of Frantz Fanon. This view is represented in the present volume by the opening chapter by Linda Martín Alcoff, which serves as a philosophical complement to David Macey's contribution in Chapter 2, a meditation on the socio-historical context of Fanon's articulation of the lived experience of race in the specific situations of French Martinique and Paris.[4]

Fanon's writings have had a profound effect on the philosophical aspect of critical race studies in both Europe and the USA. In critical dialogue with the negritude movement – associated most prominently with Aimé Césaire and Léopold Senghor – and the phenomenological ontology of Sartre's early work, their emphasis on the 'lived experience' of the Black (*le Noir*) became the basis for a distinct strand of black existentialism.[5] It is this tradition, now often inflected philosophically in the USA in the direction of pragmatism,[6] which underpins the idea of 'racial identities'. For some of Appiah's critics – notably Lucius T. Outlaw – this concession to racial identities is based on a conception of 'raciality and ethnicity' that is still too weak to account for what Outlaw calls the 'bio-social collectivities' which for him characterize human existence.[7] Appiah himself, on the other hand, still has worries in the other direction. He is not quite happy with race as identity (and identity politics more generally), for normative reasons, since he associates such identities with the expectations of fixed social roles and hence with the placing of constraints on individual freedom.[8]

This is a result of Appiah's political liberalism. Nonetheless, the character of the debate has been fundamentally transformed. For it is now plausible for those who wish to maintain a concept of race – against Appiah – to do so on strictly political grounds. The philosophical terms of the debate have shifted from 'realism' in the direction of what Gayatri Spivak called 'strategic essentialism'. But it should not thereby be considered to have been resolved. For not only might essentialism turn out in certain circumstances to be the *wrong* strategy – as Spivak herself subsequently argued – but, more fundamentally, the philosophical grounds of 'strategic' (as opposed to epistemologically 'realistic') thinking about race remain deeply obscure. After all, what is the character of the 'subjects' whose interests are to be strategically pursued? Once we dig a little deeper, all the 'old' ontological issues begin to reappear.[9] These are only held at bay by Appiah because his political liberalism is underpinned by a covert ontological individualism which makes social identities of secondary concern. For those who seek to think 'race' philosophically beyond liberalism, however, the turn in the debate from scientific realism to existential phenomenology is less a resolution than a further deepening of the issue. The phenomenological ontology of race is thus likely to remain a contested arena for some time.

CONCEPTUAL GENEALOGY

An alternative means of enriching the philosophical debate about 'race' has centred on the construction of genealogies of racial concepts that are attentive to their historical inscriptions and specific theoretical functions within the corpus of European philosophy. A large body of recent work has been devoted to uncovering and examining these histories, from the origins of racial classification in early European colonialism, via the first 'scientific' elaborations of the concept of race in eighteenth-century Europe, and their subsequent transformations and disseminations throughout the nineteenth century, to the socio-biological discourses of the 1970s and 1980s.[10] We shall not attempt to précis that complex history here, except to note the increasing recognition of the role of Immanuel Kant in formulating the first 'scientific' concept of race on the basis of a purported distinction between the 'natural description' of 'varieties' and the 'natural history' of 'permanent' forms of human diversity.[11] This growing sense of the *systematic* role of the concept of race in German idealist philosophy is reinforced in Chapter 3 by Chetan Bhatt's exploration of the pre-history of 'the Indian subject of postcolonial theory' in the Enlightenment philosophy of history, from Voltaire via Herder and Hegel to Schopenhauer. However, rather than merely uncovering within these texts a Eurocentric racism, Bhatt uses them to reflect critically upon the historical and philosophical dynamics of recent postcolonial theory itself.

The complexity of the task of genealogical construction is prodigious. Taken as a whole, the simultaneous and overlapping histories of the concepts of race and ethnicity that may be traced across various disciplinary traditions and in linguistic innovation and sedimentation do not form a neat or even continuous story. In chapter 4, Robert J.C. Young demonstrates that, even within the limited sphere of a single intellectual biography and its contiguous discourses, the emergence of a concept may be a contradictory and heavily – if not altogether visibly – invested business. In a consideration of race and language in the work of Ferdinand and his lesser known brother Léopold de Saussure, Young draws out the silent tensions in the former's attempt to avoid the identification of language and race with his invention of the concept of *ethnisme*. In suggesting that some of the difficulties encountered by Saussure remain in the post-war substitution of the concept of 'ethnicity' for 'race', Young also draws critical attention to a broad shift in terminology and emphasis, the implications of which are still being worked out.

As the title of this collection indicates, however, 'ethnicity' has not so much replaced 'race' as an object of conceptual analysis, genealogical construction and political critique, as supplemented and complicated it – displacing some dimensions of its meaning while reinforcing others.[12] However, the terminological shift is indicative of an important repositioning of theoretical interest and political commitment, in favour of the analysis of practices and identities, rather than anything like natures or essences. In narrating the move away from the concept of 'race', with its emphasis on immediately perceptible differences (such as 'colour'), to the study of ethnicities, it is tempting to suggest that, in the course of the past three decades of race studies, 'ethnicity' has come to stand to 'race' much as 'gender' stands to 'sex' within Anglo-American feminist theory. In both cases, sociology has been the primary disciplinary means for the new developments.

The Anglo-American sociology of race has its origins in the studies by the Chicago School during the 1930s of the effect of Black migration from the rural South to the industrialized North of the USA. An offshoot of urban studies as much as cultural anthropology, it was concerned with habituation, adaption and urban settlement, rather than the identification of fixed characteristics. These same studies may also have provided Simone de Beauvoir – whose work is often thought to mark the shift from the analysis of sex to that of gender – with a model for her detailed description of the lived experience of women in relation to the ideological structures and practical impediments of social sex discrimination.[13] This model was also imported into Britain in the years following the Second World War in the rather different context of labour immigration from ex-colonies. By the late 1960s, when 'race relations' in Britain were the subject of much public and political debate, this sociological approach had already begun to shift attention to broad questions of 'culture' and 'identity'. This move was consolidated during the 1970s by the emergence of the new discipline of cultural studies (perhaps the last British intellectual export to the United States), for which the politics of race in 'middle England' was a crucial formative context.[14]

Increasingly, in analyses of both gender and ethnicity, the broadly cultural (historico-political) and existential determinants of identities and subjectivities have been given explanatory priority over anything that might be thought as 'natural', to the extent that both 'sex' and 'race' are exposed as metaphysical fictions.[15] As in gender studies, the contemporary articulation of ethnicity – or ethnicities – is coincident with a shift in attention from the 'in-itself' of the object of study to the domain of representation, such that the construction of ethnicities is encountered as an epistemological, rather than an anthropological problem. As Stuart Hall remarks, in a brief essay noted for its marking of the move from 'race' (a concept conspicuous by its absence in Hall's essay) to 'ethnicity': 'The term ethnicity acknowledges the place of history, language and culture in the construction of subjectivity and identity, as well as the fact that all discourse is placed, positioned, situated, and all knowledge is contextual.'[16] However, as Hall is of course aware, even in its 'post-structuralist' guise, the concept of 'ethnicity' presents its own peculiar problems, not least regarding its mobilization in various discourses of colonial and postcolonial racism and zenophobia. In Chapter 5 Bill Schwarz focuses on what is perhaps the most egregious example of this constellation: the exclusive articulation of Englishness as white ethnicity in post-war Britain. In this respect, the identity politics of the Left in Britain, associated with cultural studies, is best understood, both historically and critically, as a counter-hegemonic response to a pre-existing racial politics of identity of the English Right.

Anglo- and Afro-American intellectual history dominates current philosophical debates on race and ethnicity in the USA and the UK (at least, insofar as there *are* such debates in philosophy in the UK), incorporating the 'European' phenomenological–existential tendency. To the extent that this incorporation – and, indeed, the initial constitution of the field – is an achievement of black US scholarship, often fostered in the black universities during and after segregation, it is a phenomenon deserving of its own cultural-intellectual history.[17] Too often in philosophy, however, the Anglo- and Afro-American axis dominates to the point of exclusion.[18] Yet there is not *one* conceptual genealogy of 'race' or 'ethnicity'. Other contributions to this volume – notably those by Rebecca Karl, Naoki Sakai and Rey Chow – raise the question of these conceptual genealogies – both general and specific – in entirely different forms, opening a multilingual and transcultural problematic of global scope.

GLOBAL COMPARATIVISM

In the 45 years from the end of the Second World War (1945) to the dismantling of the Berlin Wall (1989), the globally predominant geo-political imaginary was that of 'Three Worlds' theory, in which a hegemonic 'Western' capitalism confronted an embattled but independent socialist bloc, in competition over the developmental paths of a socio-culturally diverse and geographically diffuse array of de-colonizing and recently independent states. The conceptual unification of this latter group under the rubric of the Third World, in the early 1950s, gave rise to a paradigm of anti-colonial nationalism in which the pre-colonial 'cultures' of de-colonizing states became critically invested with an anti-imperialist potentiality, which promised to secure an independent national path to development. Third World anti-colonial nationalism was in this respect a form of *culturalist* (that is, racial and ethnic) nationalism from the outset; albeit always in conjunction with discrete economic and political projects – be they revolutionary socialist or modernizing capitalist in orientation. Such a unification of anti-imperialist culturalist nationalisms was a powerful ideological–political force, but, analytically, an 'extremely misguided notion'.[19] For not only did it lump together social forms of wildly differing kinds – not just 'culturally', but in their structural articulation of economic, political and cultural forms – but it presumed the existence and enduring significance of discrete pre-colonial 'cultures' articulated in some meaningful way with the spatial boundaries of the current struggles for political independence. Nonetheless, this was the dominant paradigm, both in the 'area studies' fostered in the USA during the Cold War, and in more radical circles elsewhere. Within this paradigm 'race' and 'ethnicity' were largely pre-givens of the enduring significance of the pre-colonial heritage to be affirmed or decried, depending upon one's political position.

It was the crucial transitional function of Edward Said's *Orientalism* (1978) to negotiate the passage from the Third-Worldist cultural nationalism of the 1950s and 1960s to the 'colonial discourse theory' of the 1980s and 1990s via the mediation of a broadly Foucauldian conception of knowledge as power. For if the *conceptual* unity of anti-imperialist cultural nationalisms could by that time no longer be sustained, even ideologically, on their own grounds (since it was a conjunctural *political* unity), it achieved here, from the standpoint of the post-colonial, an *external* totalization as an 'effect' of the discourses of colonialism. From the perspective of the 'post-colonial', the colonial itself achieved a retrospective *cultural* unification. Furthermore, and especially within subsequent versions of this argument influenced by deconstruction, the 'racial' and 'ethnic' aspects of the pre-colonial appeared now as cognitive constructions of colonialism itself. Hence the famous 'ambivalence' of colonial mimicry.[20]

Post-colonial theory, or colonial discourse theory, as it is alternatively known, has generated an immense amount of productive research into specific colonial histories. However, as a unified theoretical model it has inherited (indeed, exacerbated) many of the weaknesses of its predecessor, Third-Worldist culturalist nationalism. For it subjects cultural analysis to a typological development schema – pre-colonial/colonial/post-colonial – projected onto a geographical distribution of powers (First World/Third World, or more recently, the 'West'/'the Rest') which is largely imaginary, since it abstracts from the contingencies of history (and tends to forget the world-historical impact of the socialist experiment altogether). Two areas of the globe, in particular, (other than the so-called Second World) appear resistant to its simplifying gaze: Latin America and south-east Asia. Here, we are presented with regionally internal complexities that simply cannot be ignored. In this volume, we present three chapters from East Asian studies to represent the creative disturbance inflicted upon the paradigm of post-colonial studies by theoretical reflection upon a wider range of historical experiences than its restricted formation can accommodate.

Rebecca Karl in Chapter 6 traces the emergence of a discourse on 'race' in China at around the turn of the nineteenth into the twentieth century as a result of the insertion of China into global systems of signification and power relations. Naoki Sakai in Chapter 7 reconstructs the philosophical basis of the concept of the multi-ethnic state in Japanese imperialism in Tanabe's neo-Hegelian dialectics of genus and species. in Chapter 8 Rey Chow considers the construction of 'Chineseness' as an epistemologico-political problematic. In each case, the situation of concrete historical forms within a global perspective produces a form of transcultural analysis attentive to racialization and ethnicization as ongoing social *processes*, with only temporal historical forms of stabilization. For just as new routes and forms of migration provide new cultural materials to fuel the machine of racialization, so these new materials conflict with and undermine its existing patterns, to the point of throwing racialization itself into crisis, before themselves succumbing to new patterns and forms of stabilization. One is tempted to detect here a *historical dialectic of race and ethnicity* within which the racialization of relatively stable patterns of 'ethnic' difference is succeeded by periods of disruption in a contradictory dynamic, which current global patterns of migration are bringing once more to a crisis. The supposedly 'modular' form of ethnic nationalism (with its inherent tendency towards a racialization of cultural differences), based on 'print-capitalism', thus today finds its dialectical counterpart in the 'long-distance nationalisms' made possible by new communications technologies.[21]

POLITICAL CONTEXTS

A Third-Worldist nationalism dominated the politics of race, internationally, during the 1950s and 1960s. This was even so within the USA, where the history of slavery provided a narrative basis for the construction of a 'black nationalism', which became the main specifically racial oppositional political form. The racial and ethnic politics of that period were nonetheless overdetermined by the opposition between the socialist and capitalist 'camps'. In the wake of the geo-political dissolution of that opposition during the 1980s, and its accompanying world-economic and political developments, the political codings of previously racially construed ethnic differences have changed significantly. Nation–states remain the fundamental geo-political units of division, within an increasingly globally integrated, but nonetheless antagonistic, system of states subject to the hegemony of the USA. However, their perceived relations to ethnic divisions, which cut across national ones,[22] have become much more complexly politically mediated. The main and contradictory developments here have been an intensification of violent state-sponsored ethnic conflicts ('ethnic cleansing') and the institutionalization of 'multiculturalism' as policy within a wide array of international, national and corporate bodies. One consequence of the increasingly institutional recognition, and attempted mediation, of ethnic conflicts has been a series of demands for recompense for past wrongs.

Chapter 9 by Françoise Vergès sails critically against the winds of this trend, in its reflections on the UN negotiation of demands for material and symbolic reparation in the context of the Creole societies of the post-slavery French territories. It probes the continued reliance of reparation discourses on a Christian-inspired notion of guilt and an idiom of debt that implicitly ties those societes into a dependency over and beyond their already dependent political status as French Overseas Departments. In the final chapter Denise Ferreira da Silva similarly questions the assumption of certain discourses of authenticity within national and trans-continental histories of slavery and subjection. Specifically, Silva addresses the self-representation of the black Brazilian subject as a double-coded subject of resistance: the historical resistance or rebellion of slave ancestors and the contemporary resistance to elimination through 'whitening' and 'race democracy'.

The chapters in this collection are thus of two main, overlapping kinds: theoretical reflection on the historical constitution and logic of ethnic and racial categories (Part I); historical reflection on the political meanings and mobilizations of ethnic and racial categories in a variety of geo-political contexts during the twentieth century (Part II). Taken together they provide a sense of the ways in which the accumulated materials from a variety of disciplines, with a variety of specific concerns, can both instigate and inform more general theoretical reflection on questions of race and ethnicity, and of the continued necessity for philosophical reflection on the categories upon which these disciplines rely. The book presents a 'snapshot' of current work in a radically transdiciplinary field. It is in the maintenance of open links between the four approaches outlined above, in their diverse disciplinary articulations, we would like to suggest, that the most productive possibilities for theoretical work on the topic of race and ethnicity currently lie.

PART I

CHAPTER I

Philosophy and Racial Identity

LINDA MARTÍN ALCOFF

In the 1993 film *Map of the Human Heart*, an Inuit man asks a white engineer who has come to northern Canada to map the region, 'Why are you making maps?' Without hesitating, the white man responds, 'They will be very accurate.'

Map-making and race-making have a strong historical as well as conceptual relationship. The ordering and labelling of natural terrain, the classifying of natural types, and the typologies of 'natural races' emerged simultaneously in what Foucault called the Classical episteme. Arguing via Foucault, both Cornel West and David Theo Goldberg have attempted genealogies of modern racism – meaning here not contemporary racism so much as the racism of modernism – that link Western fetishistic practices of classification, the forming of tables, and the consequent primacy of the visible with the creation of metaphysical and moral hierarchies between racialized categories of human beings.[1] Given this genesis, the concepts of race and racial difference emerge as that which is visible, classifiable and morally salient. West argues that the application of natural history techniques to the study of the human species yields a comparative analysis 'based on visible, especially physical, characteristics . . . [which] permit one to discern identity and difference, equality and inequality, beauty and ugliness among animals and human bodies'.[2] Goldberg argues that the universal sameness that was so important for the liberal self required a careful containment and taxonomy of difference. Where rights require sameness, difference must be either trivialized or contained in the Other across a firm and visible border.

The result of these classification practices juxtaposed with liberal ideology is a paradox wherein 'Race is irrelevant, but all is race.'[3] Visible difference is the route to classification and therefore knowledge, and yet visible difference threatens the security of claims to know by challenging universal applicability and invoking the spectre of relativism. Classification systems can contain this threat and impede relativism by enclosing the entirety of difference within a taxonomy organized by a single logic. In this way the continuing hegemony of liberal discourse is ensured. But the resultant juxtaposition between universalist legitimation narratives that deny or trivialize difference and careful delineations of supposedly morally relevant phenotypic human difference is one of the greatest antinomies of modern discourse.

We have finally come to recognize and acknowledge this paradox, but we have not yet solved or moved beyond it. Today the naturalistic classification systems that would reify human variability into moral categories, the Eurocentric teleologies that would excuse if not justify colonialism, and the phallogocentric binaries, which would obscure relations of domination by presenting them as 'separate spheres', have been largely exposed as specious. And the realm of the visible, or what is taken as self-evidently visible (which is how the ideology of racism naturalizes racial designation), is recognized as the product of a specific form of perceptual practice, rather than the natural result of human sight. Thus Foucault claims that:

> the object [of discourse] does not await in limbo the order that will free it and enable it to become embodied in a visible and prolix objectivity; it does not pre-exist itself, held back by some obstacle at the first edges of light. It exists under the positive conditions of a complex group of relations.[4]

His central thesis in *The Birth of the Clinic* is that the gaze, though hailed as pure and preconceptual, can only function successfully when connected to a system of understanding that dictates its use and interprets its results:

> What defines the act of medical knowledge in its concrete form is not . . . the encounter between doctor and patient, nor is it the confrontation between a body of knowledge and a perception; it is the systematic intersection of two series of information . . . whose intersection reveals, in its isolable dependence, the *individual* fact.[5]

On this account, which is largely unique to Foucault, visibility itself cannot serve as the explanatory cause of the development of racial taxonomies. The apparent obviousness of racial difference – the emphasis on hair type, nose shape and skin colour – is a produced obviousness.

The visibility of racial identity is a peculiarly variegated phenomenon, with little acknowledgement of this by dominant discourses. Those of us with hybrid identities surely have a better sense of this, as our public identity is variously interpellated across geographical borders or even just neighbourhoods. When the mythic bloodlines which are thought to determine identity fail to match the visible markers used by identity discourse to signify race, one often encounters these odd responses by acquaintances announcing with arrogant certainty 'But you don't look like . . .' or then retreating to a measured acknowledgement 'Now that you mention it, I can sort of see . . .' To feel one's face studied with great seriousness, not for its (hoped-for) character lines, or its distinctiveness, but for its tell-tale racial trace, can be a peculiarly unsettling experience, fully justifying of all Sartre's horror of the Look.[6]

Anti-essentialisms have corroded the sense of visible difference as the 'sign' of a deeper, more fundamental difference, a difference in behavioural disposition, in moral and rational capacity, or in cultural achievement. Moreover, there is a newly emerging scientific consensus that race is a myth, that the term corresponds to no significant biological category, and that no existing racial classifications correlate in useful ways to gene frequencies, clinical variations or any significant human biological difference. For semantic realists such as Anthony Appiah, the only philosophically respectable position one can take in the face of this evidence is that the concept of race cannot be used correctly, that there is no philosophically defensible way to realign the term 'race' with a referent, even one which would invoke historical experience or culture rather than biology.[7]

So today race has no semantic respectability, biological basis or philosophical legitimacy. However, at the same time, and in a striking parallel to the earlier liberal attitude towards the relevance and irrelevance of race, in the very midst of our contemporary scepticism toward race stands the compelling social reality that race, or racialized identities, have as much political, sociological and economic salience as they ever had. Race tends toward opening up or shutting down job prospects, career possibilities, available places to live, potential friends and lovers, reactions from police, credence from jurors, and presumptions by one's students. Race may not correlate with clinical variations, but it persistently correlates with statistically overwhelming significance in wage levels, unemployment levels, poverty levels, and the likelihood of incarceration. As of 1992, black and Latino men working full-time in the USA earned an average of 68 per cent of what white men earned, while black and Latina women earned 59 per cent. As of 1995, Latino and black unemployment rates were more than double those of whites.

But these sociological facts are not thought to be of philosophical significance. For those still working within a liberal framework, the devastating sociological reality of race is but an artificial overlay on more basic elements whose specificity can be legitimately set aside toward the aim of a general analysis. For postmodernists, race is a contingent construction, the epiphenomenon of essentialist discourses, and thus ultimately without any more explanatory power or epistemological relevance than the liberal view. Thus, for all our critical innovations in understanding the vagaries of racist domination and the conceptual apparatus that yields racism, we remain stuck in the modernist antinomy that race is (fundamentally) irrelevant, even though all is race. It will be my contention that we will not be able to progress beyond this unworkable dilemma until we acknowledge the philosophical salience of racial identity, a project that must begin with understanding what racial identity is.

RACE AS ONTOLOGY

Refusing the reality of racial categories as elements within our current social ontology only exacerbates racism, because it helps conceal the myriad effects that racializing practices have had and continue to have on social life, including philosophy. In claiming that race is an ontological category, I do not mean to say that we should *begin* by treating it as such, but that we must begin acknowledging the fact that race has been 'real' for a long time. And I am not putting this forward as a strategic essentialism: the claim that race is philosophically salient is not merely a strategic claim but a truth claim. There is a visual registry operating in social relations that is socially constructed, historically evolving and culturally variegated, but nonetheless powerfully determinant over individual experiences and choices. And, for that reason, it also powerfully mediates subjectivity. Consider the following passage from Richard Rodriguez:

> I used to stare at the Indian in the mirror. The wide nostrils, the thick lips. Starring Paul Muni as Benito Juarez. Such a long face – such a long nose – sculpted by indifferent, blunt thumbs, and of such common clay. No one in my family had a face as dark or as Indian as mine. My face could not portray the ambition I brought to it.[8]

This mediation through the visible, working on both the inside and the outside, both on the way we read ourselves and the way others read us, is what is unique to racialized identities as against ethnic and cultural identities. The processes by which racial identities are produced work through the shapes and shades of human morphology, and subordinate other markers such as dress, customs and practices. And the visual registry thus produced has been correlated with rational capacity, epistemic reliability, moral condition and, of course, aesthetic status. Yet, as a result of the theoretical critique of race, this visual registry has largely not been brought into theoretical play, in either cultural studies or philosophy.[9]

This visual registry cannot be fully or adequately described except in ontological terms, because the difference that racializing identities has made is an ontologizing difference, that is, a difference at the most basic level concerning knowledge, subjectivity, being and thinking. If we say that race is not an ontological category, and that it is a mere artificial overlay on top of more basic and more real categories, we risk losing sight of how significant the effects of racial identities have been, and how those effects have permeated every philosophical idea. Ontology itself might then be able to avoid a needed self-critique. Metaphysics and epistemology could proceed with their habitual disregard for issues of race, and political philosophy could continue to introduce racial topics only in the stages of applied theory.

Obviously, when I say that race is an ontological category I am using ontology here to refer to basic categories of reality which are within history, at least partly produced by social practices, and which are culturally various. Race itself signifies differently and is lived differently between different discursive and cultural locations. This usage of ontology is controversial, and I cannot take the space here to justify it fully, but I will make one point. The problem with the social constructionist, anti-essentialist view that we should give up the language game of ontology altogether is that we are then left with a reduced ability to offer *deep* descriptions of reality; descriptions which can differentiate between more and less significant and persisting features of reality. The weakness of a strict social constructionist approach is that it tends towards flattening out all descriptive categories as having equal (non-)metaphysical status. Thus, for example, male/female is put on the same plane as masculine/feminine, and the importance of the biological division of reproduction is made analogous to gendered dress codes. In order to avoid this, without lapsing back into essentialism, the traditional ontological project of ascertaining certain basic categories can be reconfigured as the attempt to ascertain those elements of reality which, although mutable, currently intersect and determine a wide variety of discourses and practices, and thus are more fundamental not because of their ahistorical or transcendental status but because of their central intersectional position.

The fact that race has lost its scientific credibility does not entail, then, that it has lost its ontological status, since on this usage ontology does not imply a reference in a transcendental reality. Race does not need to refer to a natural kind or a piece of reality in a metaphysical realist sense if it is to have any ontological meaning. What is race, then? Race is a particular, historically and culturally located form of human categorization involving visual determinants marked on the body through the interplay of perceptual practices and bodily appearance. Race has not had one meaning or a single essential criterion, but its meanings have always been mediated through visual appearance, however complicated.

The criteria determining racial identity have included ancestry, experience, outside perception, internal perception, coded visibility, habits and practices – all these and more are variously invoked for both individuals and groups. The criteria that will be primarily operative vary by culture, neighbourhood, historical moment, so that some people place ancestry as all determining, while others make subjective identification the key.

What is a philosopher to do in the face of this variation? We could take ordinary language, the way in which people speak of race, and use it to sift through these criteria to show which are most consistent with the way we speak. This approach could certainly be useful in pointing out contradictions between the way we speak and what we believe, and in showing the presupposition to which we are implicitly committed by the way we speak, but it cannot show us what the 'truth' of racial identity is. Phenomenological description of the experience of racial designations would also be useful in achieving a better understanding of the lived reality of race, but this again is not decisive in establishing the 'underlying essence' of race. My view is that the meaning of race will shift as one moves through the terrain and interplay of different discourses, where here discourses signify practices and institutions as well as systems of knowledge (a usage well exemplified in Wittgenstein's concept of a language game, which involves linguistic practices connected with and embodied in actions). The 'answer' to the question of what racial identity really is will depend on what language game we are playing, although the relativism of this situation can be mitigated by showing overlaps between language games, and by offering immanent critiques that reveal internal contradictions, such as a language game that claims to be non-racist but actually is racist.

Philosophy is a prime example of the latter. It has committed both crimes of omission – the neglect of race – and crimes of commission – correlating race with epistemic reliability (Kant) and potential for self-government (Mill). But given this, we still have yet to understand either what racial identity is or how we should articulate its relationship to philosophy. In order to answer these questions we must first address several others, not only the scepticism towards race but also the postmodern critique of identity and the visible, and the political debate over identity politics. It is these debates, more than the scientific status of race, which will determine the future of philosophical treatments of racial identity. I will summarize some of the relevant issues in these debates, and then try to address them in the context of race.

The principal argument against identity politics has been that it assumes an essentialist, coherent identity that is efficacious over one's political orientation, epistemological standpoint and justificatory status. And so it might be thought that making racial identity epistemologically salient, for example, could lead to a reductionist form of evaluation that puts identity considerations over argument, that is, holding that that which is pious is so because the gods love it rather than the gods love it because it is pious.

Also relevant is the critique of the tyranny of the visible, as in Rorty's denigration of the visual metaphor for metaphysical realism, to Martin Jay's discussion of the anti-ocularcentric thrust of critical theory, to Jameson's blunt claim that 'the visual is essentially pornographic'.[10] One thing that this view has in its favour is that it would make sense of the non-reciprocal visibility of dominant and non-dominant racial identities: where the invisibility of whiteness renders it an unassailable form, the visibility of non-whiteness marks it as a target and a denigrated particularity.

And the concepts of identity and race are both often charged with assuming a unity and homogeneity that do not in fact obtain. Iris Young, building on Derrida and Adorno, criticizes the idea that identity is a coherent unity which can serve as the origin of thought and practice, and which can be neatly separated from external things such as others or discourses.[11] This description is metaphysically incorrect, for reasons with which we are all familiar, having to do with the fundamental disunity of the self, its lack of complete self-knowledge, and its constitution by and through processes of narrativization which are only partially accessible to the subject herself.[12] On the basis of these arguments, Young would have us make a parallel case against group identity, and reject identity concepts altogether.

Racial identities are increasingly recognized as particularly disunified (since their group status is even more obviously arbitrary or conventional than nation or culture), split within by class, gender, sexuality, etc., and as Danielson and Engle point out in their collection *After Identity*, without clear borders or a unifying internal essence.[13] Moreover, Freud argued that the effort to overcome disunity through collective identification or group solidarity might itself be the sign of a pathological condition caused by 'the inability of the ego to regain autonomy following the loss of an object of desire'.[14] Thus, the conclusion of these critiques is that racial identity is a dangerous illusion.

Now, I take all of these worries about racial identity very seriously. My original entry into this area of work was motivated by a concern to understand and in some sense validate hybrid identity or hybrid positionality against purist, essentialist accounts. And the motivation for this was the felt alienation of having a mestizo identity (normative in Latin America and the Caribbean) but living in a purist culture (the USA), where racial categories are assumed to be mutually exclusive. In my nuclear family, which is anything but nuclear, I have a *cholito* Panamanian father (mixed Spanish, Indian, African), a white Anglo mother, and, through my father's multiple liaisons, a range of siblings from black to brown to tan to freckled, spanning five countries and three continents at the last count. This personal genealogy has not motivated me to try to repair dissonance into a coherent unity, but rather to understand the formation and position of the self precisely within an unresolvable heterogeneity.

If I did not have any sympathy for the anti-essentialist, my concern with the persistent paradox of the relevance of race would not be felt so strongly. It is because the arguments against racial identity have merit that the paradox is a paradox and not simply an error. But in the face of these anti-race arguments, we need a better position than one that merely relies on the withering away of racial categorization. And we need one that can do two things the anti-essentialist position cannot do: (1) take into account the full force of race as a lived experience, understanding this not as mere epiphenomenon but as constitutive of reality; and (2) acknowledge and account for the epistemological and theoretical importance racial perspective has had on, for example, the undermining of modernist teleologies (for example, Du Bois's use of slavery to undermine US supremacist claims, and the Frankfurt School's critique of Western rationality from the perspective of the Holocaust). These facts suggest that we need to understand racial identity as having both metaphysical and epistemological implications.

RACE AS IDENTITY

Racial identifications have been causally associated with classical liberalism and philosophical postmodernism. Given the fact that the practices of racializing identity developed within the greatest period of colonialism and genocide the world has ever known, anti-racists have been understandably sceptical about the possibility of racial identity co-existing alongside equality and justice. Furthermore, the liberal conceptualizations of justice and enlightenment presupposed a decrease if not an end to the social relevance of racial particularity, and this can be traced out in the history of integrationist thought in the USA, as Gary Peller has so usefully shown:

> A commitment to a form of universalism, and an association of universalism with truth and particularism with ignorance, forms the infrastructure of American integrationist consciousness . . . integrationist beliefs are organized around the familiar enlightenment story of progress consisting of the movement from mere belief and superstition to knowledge and reason, from

> the particular and therefore parochial to the universal and therefore enlightened.[15]

Where truth and justice require universalism, racial identity cannot be accorded salience without endangering progress. Racial identity threatens to return us to a feudal hierarchy, a system in which identity determined one's life, which was precisely the system against which liberal enlightenment was organized and developed. As a result, anti-racism is assumed to require an anti-racial identity (at least in so far as race has political or non-trivial salience).

Furthermore, an anti-racism that pursues universalism against particularism also 'confirms our sense of the possibility of true and authentic relations that transcend racial status and other forms of cultural distance and difference'.[16] It thus legitimates our perhaps natural hope for significant human relationships against ones that are necessarily deformed or atrophied by structurally produced separations. For whites and others who benefit in the present from a history of oppression, the appeal of universal racelessness may also lie in its ability to deface their/our race-based connections with that unpleasant past; in other words, it may entitle whites to believe they/we don't need to acknowledge the salience of white identity and thus to avoid the moral discomfort that that identity cannot help but prevent.

But there is an argumentative complicity – whether intentional or not does not matter of course – between the suspicion against the visible, against identity, and certainly against the intersection of these which would occur in a racialized conception of identity, and the continuing inattention to race matters in philosophy and political theory. As many people have pointed out, one of the persistent problems with the discourses in the USA on multiculturalism and cultural studies is that race, racism and racial hierarchies are relatively ignored. Explorations of culture and ethnicity can all too easily avoid any account of white supremacy and focus instead on the recognition of difference, flattening out differences in a way that makes them appear equal. Race, on the other hand, is difficult to focus on for very long without it working to discredit the imagined landscapes of pluralist difference that cultural studies so often presupposes. And mainstream political language in both Britain and the USA codes racial talk as cultural talk, so racist claims can be cloaked as claims about cultural difference.

Increasingly in this context, Lewis Gordon's *Bad Faith and Antiblack Racism* argues that, in an antiblack world, blackness signifies absence, the absence of identity in the full sense of a self, a perspective or a standpoint with its own self-referential point of view.[17] In other words, what is denied black people is the ability to wield the Look, to be a source of value and meaning. The infamous three-fifths formulation from the US Constitution might be explicated as a concept of black personhood as having a consciousness without judgement, or a limited capacity for affective sensibility and cognitive distinctions. Antiblack racism denied visible black people the standpoint of a subject as capable of judging and knowing and reciprocating in an intersubjective relationship between persons.

Charles Mills argues in his essay 'Non-Cartesian Sums: Philosophy and the African-American Experience' that the concept of 'sub-personhood', or *Untermensch*, is a central way to understand 'the defining feature of the African-American experience under conditions of white supremacy (both slavery and its aftermath)'.[18] By this concept, which he develops through a contrast drawn between the Cartesian *sum* and Ralph Ellison's invisible man, Mills elucidates the comprehensive ramifications that white racism had on 'every sphere of black life – juridical standing, moral status, personal/racial identity, epistemic reliability, existential plight, political inclusion, social metaphysics, sexual relations, aesthetic worth'.[19]

To be a sub-person is not to be a non-person, or an object without any moral status whatsoever. Rather, Mills explains:

> the peculiar status of a sub-person is that it is an entity which, because of phenotype, seems (from, of course, the perspective of the categorizer) human in some respects but not in others. It is a human (or, if this seems normatively loaded, a humanoid) who, though adult, is not fully a person . . . [and] whose moral status was tugged in different directions by the dehumanizing requirements of slavery on the one hand and the (grudging and sporadic) white recognition of the objective properties blacks possessed on the other, generating an insidious array of cognitive and moral schizophrenias in both blacks and whites.[20]

On the basis of this, Mills suggests that the racial identity of philosophers affects the 'array of concepts found useful, the set of paradigmatic dilemmas, the range of concerns' with which they must each grapple. He also suggests that the perspective one takes on specific theories and positions will be affected by one's identity, as in the following passage:

> The impatience, or indifference, that I have sometimes detected in black students [taking an ethics course] derives in part, I suggest, from their sense that there is something strange, for example, in spending a whole course describing the logic of different moral ideals without ever talking about how *all of them* were systematically violated for being blacks.[21]

The result is an understanding that black lived experience 'is not subsumed under these philosophical abstractions, despite their putative generality'.[22]

As a further example of Mills's claim, consider the following passage from Hannah Arendt:

> In America, the student movement has been seriously radicalized wherever police and police brutality intervened in essentially non-violent demonstrations: occupation of administration buildings, sit-ins, et cetera. Serious violence entered the scene only with the appearance of the Black Power movement on the campuses. Negro students, the majority of them admitted without academic qualifications, regarded and organized themselves as an interest group, the representatives of the black community. Their interest was to lower academic standards. They were more cautious than the white rebels, but it was clear from the beginning (even before the incidents at Cornell University and City College in New York) that violence with them was not a matter of theory and rhetoric. Moreover, while the student rebelling in Western countries can nowhere count on popular support outside the universities, and as a rule encounters open hostility the moment it uses violent means, there stands a large minority of the Negro community behind the verbal or actual violence of the black students. Black violence in America can indeed be understood in analogy to the labor violence in America a generation ago: and although . . . only Staughton Lynd has drawn the analogy between labor riots and student rebellion explicitly, it seems that the academic establishment, in its curious tendency to yield more to Negro demands, even if they are clearly silly and outrageous, than to the disinterested and usually highly moral claims of the white rebels, also thinks in these terms and feels more comfortable when confronted with interests plus violence than when it is a matter of non-violent 'participatory democracy'.[23]

The ambivalence Mills points to can be discerned in this account. On the one hand, black students are clearly persons, having a self-interested perspective which they pursue through collective action, and capable of greater collective activity across campus and community divisions than white students. On the other hand, this perspective is less intelligent, hence its desire to lower standards; and (probably as a result) it is too self-interested, too particular, and thus unable to achieve the moral approbation of the purportedly disinterested white rebels. Arendt clearly pits morality against self-interestedness, the universal against the particular, once again. But the result is a curious replay of the liberal antinomy between having a racialized self and having a less developed self; between being a person with a perspective and being a non-person precisely because of that perspective: having 'demands' but demands which are silly, outrageous, and pursued through what she clearly considers unnecessary violence.

There is no question but that Arendt's white racial identity affected her ability to assess black student actions, or that her response to the possibility of black-organized violence was affected by her identification with its targets. This is so obvious as to be uninteresting. But does this judgement entail the reductionist evaluations imputed to adherents of identity politics? Are we forced into holding that Arendt's views can be reduced to a consideration of Arendt's race? Or, if we want to avoid such a position, are we forced to conclude that her race was irrelevant to the above account? It seems clear to me that racial identity is a crucial category of analysis to have at our disposal in order to understand Arendt's reactions to and assessment of black students. Yet I believe we can retain this category without essentializing racial identity or reducing philosophical analysis to racial identification. I will develop this case through a reading of Paul Gilroy's *The Black Atlantic: Modernity and Double Consciousness*.[24]

This book has a dual purpose. On the one hand, Gilroy's purpose is to reconfigure and reconceptualize the concept of black identity so important to cultural studies, black studies and Afrocentric theory, in such a way that he can avoid the metaphysical criticisms of prior concepts of identity and develop a more adequate accounting of the cultural formations and political practices created under diaspora conditions than Afrocentric theories can explain. As Gilroy tells the story, there is an identifiable cultural formation organized by the black diaspora and existing in multiple sites that he groups together under the term 'black Atlantic'. Given the internal cultural, linguistic and geographic heterogeneity of this group, to call it a 'culture' would be actually misleading and more evocative of homogenization than 'black'. Moreover, the racial designation more accurately signifies the principal organizing logic of this group, which was and is the historical experience of an institution of slavery that operated through phenotype. This experience has yielded an ongoing process of identity formation that cannot be traced back to an African essence or distilled into its pure type, but that is persistently involved in the proliferation of ever new hybrid identities. Thus, Gilroy's analysis is both centred around identity and insistent on the fundamental hybridity and openness of identity.[25] Against those who emphasize the enduring manifestation of roots in black culture, and against the association of black liberation with a return in some sense to those roots, Gilroy uses the imagery of the diaspora precisely to articulate a mobile and mediated identity, internally heterogeneous, and whose very survival and ability to flourish have been predicated on its character as always open to new mutation.

> In opposition to . . . nationalist or ethnically absolute approaches, I want to develop the suggestion that cultural historians could take the Atlantic as one single, complex unit of analysis in their discussions of the modern world and use it to produce an explicitly transnational and intercultural perspective.[26]

His choice of the word 'produce' rather than 'discover' is clearly intentional.

The second major purpose of Gilroy's book is to show how this perspective has been and can be brought to bear on an account of modernity generally. Along the lines of Mills's argument above, Gilroy claims that a critique of modernity that is entirely immanent is insufficient. That is, a critique which uses the Enlightenment's concepts of reason and liberation to critique its practices in its self-understanding will not go deeply enough. In his readings of Du Bois, Richard Wright and others, Gilroy claims to be able to trace:

> the formation of a vernacular variety of unhappy consciousness which demands that we rethink the meanings of rationality, autonomy, reflection, subjectivity, and power in the light of an extended meditation both on the condition of the slaves and on the suggestion that racial terror is not merely compatible with occidental rationality but cheerfully complicit with it.[27]

Thus, it is through 'the slaves' perspective' that a more thoroughgoing critique of the Enlightenment can advance. This perspective begins from a more sceptical position on 'the democratic potential of modernity' than, for example Jürgen Habermas is said to have. It would insist that Columbus accompany Luther and Copernicus as the standard bearers of modernity, with all the repercussions that must then follow concerning how we assess that standard. Locke's *Second Treatise* could no longer be taught without a mention of his contribution to writing the Carolina slave constitution.[28] Gilroy uses Frederick Douglass's slave memoirs to suggest a revision of Hegel's Lord and Bondsman narrative, wherein it is the slave that 'actively prefers the possibility of death' rather than the master. Douglass's version reveals the prior structure of enslavement that mandates the slave's survival in bondage over the possibility of death, and locates the slave's first moment of agency in his determination to counter violently the violence that has already been inscribed in the social relation. This retelling of the narrative more correctly locates the origin of institutional violence as prior to the slave's enslavement, and thus raises 'queries about the assumption of symmetrical intersubjectivity' which grounds so many modernist accounts of self-formation.

Gilroy's point is not to draw a sharp border between slave and non-slave perspectives, and at one point he even aligns Habermas with 'a good many ex-slaves' in his commitment to 'making bourgeois civil society live up to its political and philosophical promise'.[29] But, although there is much intermixture and overlap between perspectives, they are not all coextensive, and one can shift the horizons of visibility by occupying the centre as opposed to the periphery of a black Atlantic perspective. This understanding of identity in terms of perspective suggests a definition of identity as a social location, a location within a social structure and marked *vis-à-vis* the other locations which gives the identity its specificity rather than deriving this from its internal characteristics.[30]

Gilroy is not arguing here that the perspective engendered by identity has a singularly deterministic effect on thought. He rejects Patricia Hill Collins's 'collapse' of being and thinking 'so that they form a functional unity that can be uncritically celebrated.'[31] And he suggests, rightly, that a determinist view of the impact of identity on thought would inhibit the scope of critical reflection on that thought. Moreover, he argues that such an account of knowledge would 'simply end up substituting the standpoint of black women for its forerunner rooted in the lives of white men', simply replacing white men with black women in the myth of 'stable, ideal subjects'.[32] And as a myth, postulating a convenient but specious concept of self, such an account cannot last very long.

However, despite his hybrid, postmodern-influenced problematized notion of identity, for Gilroy 'identity' – and in *The Black Atlantic* it is racial identity he is exploring – remains the central term of the analysis. He repeatedly criticizes those whose critiques of racial essentialism leave them 'insufficiently alive to the lingering power of specifically racialized forms of power and subordination' or those who have been 'slow in perceiving the centrality of ideas of race and culture' to the investigation of modernity. And he repudiates theories of the self that would, like Marshall Berman's, try to conceptualize it at a more abstract, more putatively universal level, below the effect of racial configurations.[33]

The Black Atlantic does a masterful job arguing against purist, nationalist paradigms by showing how these cannot account for what is essentially an 'intercultural and transnational formation'.[34] It makes the unifying theme not an internal core or original historical moment or homogenous cultural elements, but the 'well-developed sense of the complicity of racialized reason and white supremacist terror' which provides a perspective informing literary, musical and philosophical creativity.[35] In this way, hybridization and identity can coexist, at least as long as global white supremacy continues to structure intersubjective relations through racialized identities.

Gilroy's book also serves as an empirical rejoinder to the metaphysical arguments of postmodernism, which set *a priori* limits on the plasticity of identity concepts.[36] Gilroy's argument comes out of specific analyses of cultural products, rather than accounts of the limits of language, and demonstrates the usefulness of a unifying concept like the black Atlantic to understand and appreciate a wide range of forms.

There are others besides Gilroy who are making similar moves. Kobena Mercer's recent collection of essays exhibits the same reluctance either to embrace nationalist or Afrocentric treatments of black identity or to dispense with identity as irrelevant.[37] And, like Gilroy, Mercer negotiates between these conceptions through a diasporic aesthetic, which relies on analogous positionality and historical experience rather than a deep self or unified politics to establish identity. Roberto Fernandez Retamar's 'Caliban' is another example, proposing Caliban, a figure from English literature, as the symbol of Latin American identity. Fernandez Retamar's account exemplifies what Trinh T. Minh-ha calls the fearless affirmation of the hyphen, as well as a conception of identity primarily in positional terms:

> To assume our condition as Caliban implies rethinking our history from the *other* side, from the viewpoint of the *other* protagonist. [Quoting Marti:] 'We must stand with Guaicuipuro, Paramaconi [heroes of Venezuela, probably of Carib origin], and not with the flames that burned them, nor with the ropes that bound them, nor with the steel that beheaded them, nor with the dogs that devoured them.'[38]

I would argue that the concept of identity found in these works, as in Gilroy, Mills and Gordon, is a concept not organized around sameness, which is what invites much of the criticism of identity concepts. Rather, as in Gordon's diagnosis of racism as positing an absence, what the claim of identity here is organized against is the assumption of lack. In this context identity is put forward not as sameness opposed to difference but as substance opposed to absence. It is also opposed to notions of the self that formulate it primarily as an abstract form without content, a decontextualized ability to reason without any interested positionality. Examples here would be the Cartesian *sum*, a self as a thinking, abstract process or ability, and the early Sartrean model of the self as the ability to negate.

Against such contentless models, works such as Gilroy's could be understood as consistent with a more substantive understanding of the self that can sustain particular identities in a way I have time here to just sketch. From

Bourdieu one might take the concept of the self as a sedimentation of dispositions and practices developed through a personal history, and understand that history in terms of an experience that is always carried forth even if interpreted anew (as in the later Sartre). Racial identifications will affect the particular manifestation of both these elements (practices, experience), but in order to account more fully for race we must also include the element of visibility, as an embodied manifestation that invites and elicits determinate though contextually variable meanings.

On this kind of account, race can be understood to figure in identity formation not as a metaphysical necessity but as a necessity with a given historical context. And from here one might go on to develop a phenomenology of racial identity as, for example, a differentiation or distribution of felt connectedness to others.[39] This will necessarily be a complex issue, undetermined solely by phenotype. The felt connectedness to visibly similar others may produce either flight or empathic identifications or other possible dispositions.

Gilroy's description of the black Atlantic identity has the power to incorporate this openness and constant mixture with the connecting elements of a post-slavery diasporic perspective, such that phenotypic race is never sufficient yet never completely absent. This provides us with a metaphysically more accurate, and politically less problematic, formulation of racial identity, not based on purity or the continuity of original essence, and one not closed to new incarnations.

I began this chapter with the example of a *non sequitur* exchange, where an Inuit questioned the point of map-making and a white man responded with a reassurance of accuracy. The assumption in some of the anti-identity dismissals of race seems to take the form of an inverse of this exchange, such that a denial of the possibility of accuracy is somehow taken to entail a denial of the possibility of maps. My argument would be that this response is no less of a *non sequitur* than the one before.

ACKNOWLEDGEMENT

This essay was first published in *Radical Philosophy*, 75, Jan./Feb. 1996. It is reproduced here with permission.

CHAPTER 2

Fanon, Phenomenology, Race

DAVID MACEY

'The black man is not. Nor the white.'[1] Thus Fanon in the concluding section of *Peau noire, masques blancs* (1952), in my translation; it is quite impossible to work with the existing versions, the most obvious index of that impossibility being the unfortunate decision to translate the title of Chapter 5 as 'The Fact of Blackness' and not as 'The Lived Experience of the Black Man'.[2] Indeed, the point of Fanon's exercise in socio-diagnostics is to demonstrate that there is no 'fact' of blackness (or, by the same criterion, whiteness); both are a form of lived experience (*expérience vécue*; *Erlebnis*). To mistake a lived experience for a fact is to betray Fanon's text to such an extent as to make it almost incomprehensible.

The black man and the white man are not. And yet they are, and the reality of their being is Fanon's starting point: the black man trapped in his blackness, the white man in his whiteness, both trapped into their mutual and aggressive narcissism.[3] What, then, brings them or calls them into being, or sentences them to non-being? Writing of his childhood and emergence from it, Fanon remarks: 'I am a negro [*nègre*], but naturally I don't know that because that is what I am.'[4] I am going to use *nègre* in French because of the ambiguity of its political semantics and because there is no single English equivalent: it is distinct from both *noir* (black) and the more recent *homme de couleur* (man of colour) and covers the whole semantic field from 'negro' to 'nigger', the precise meaning being determined by context, the speaker's position or even the speaker's tone of voice.

Fanon's comment that he had to be told what he was is at one level a fairly banal example of the bracketing out of facticity in favour of simply being: at home, he remarks (meaning, presumably, in Martinique), the black man does need to, experience his being-for-others.[5] Judging by my own it is, for example, perfectly possible to grow up in a uniquely white in the North-East of England without knowing in any real sense e white. There is no need to know that, and it is well known that fish have no sense of wetness. I am not suggesting that there is some equivalence between a white childhood in the North-East of England and a black childhood in Martinique, merely that we may have to be told who and what we are, that we may not know it 'naturally'. Perhaps being-for-others is, in ethnicity as in other domains, a precondition for self-knowledge. Fanon's sense of not knowing *what* he is because *that* is what he is, is to a large degree an effect of his being Martinican, and there is considerable textual evidence to indicate that *Peau noire* could not have been written by anyone but a Martinican.[6] It is deeply rooted in the Martinican experience, in the experience of people who were French citizens and not colonial subjects, and who occupied a curious position within the racial hierarchy. One of the island's more peculiar exports was the French-educated black civil servant and citizen who 'administered' black subjects in the African colonies, and who was in a sense neither black nor white. Fanon found himself in that anomalous position as a young soldier at the end of the Second World War: he was neither *indigène* nor *toubab*, neither 'native' nor 'white man'. Fanon's 'black man' is Martinican, or in other words:

> [a] West Indian who does not think of himself as black; he thinks of himself as West Indian. Subjectively, intellectually, the West Indian behaves as a White. But he is a *nègre*. He will notice that once he is in Europe, and when they talk about *nègres*, he will know that they are talking about him as well as about the Senegalese.[7]

Talking about the *nègre* is one way of calling him into being and of giving him a position akin to that of other marginal groups. One recalls Adorno's lapidary remark in *Minima Moralia*: 'Anti-Semitism is the rumour about the Jews.'[8] And one recalls the advice given to a very young Fanon by his philosophy teacher in Martinique: 'When you hear them talking about the Jews, prick up your ears. They're talking about you.'[9]

One of the agencies that lets Fanon know he is a *nègre* by talking about him is of course that child who, one cold day in Lyons, fixes him with its white gaze, thus reducing him to a state of complete being-for-others. The child does not in fact speak to Fanon or tell him anything. The child turns to its mother and says 'Tiens, un nègre' ('Look, a *nègre*').[10] The form of the utterance is structurally similar to the 'smut' described by Freud in that it requires the copresence of three parties: 'In addition to the one who makes the joke . . . a second who is taken as the object of the hostile or sexual aggression, and a third in whom the joke's aim of producing pleasure is fulfilled'.[11] For the mother, the final yield of this exchange is embarrassment rather than pleasure, but verbal (and perhaps sexual) hostility or aggression is certainly involved.

WHY A NÈGRE?

Before going on to examine Fanon's description of this encounter and to ask why he analyses it in phenomenological terms, it seems appropriate to look more closely at the question of why the child in fact sees a *nègre* and not a man with a scar on his face, or a man with the build of the footballer that Fanon was. How does the child know who and what it is seeing? One might also ask why the child sees a *nègre* and not a *noir* or a *homme de couleur*. What pre-understanding, what stock of knowledge to hand, is in play here? These questions are in a sense posed by Fanon when he administers word association tests – which he wrongly describes as an exercise in free association – to white friends and colleagues and comes up with a rich crop of stereotypes. But while he collates his informants' associations, he does not ask why the child knows he is a *nègre*. Where do racist ideas come from? Part of the answer may come from a geography textbook published in 1903 and cited in a recent study of racial stereotyping in France:

> Paul is usually a very punctual pupil. But one day he is late for school. 'I'm sorry, sir', he says, 'I didn't realize what time it was. I was watching a nègre on the Grand'Place.' 'Was he a real *nègre*?' 'Yes! Yes, sir. A real *nègre* with all black skin and teeth as white as milk. They say he comes from Africa. Are there lots of *nègres* in that country?' 'Yes, my friend.'[12]

The authority of the textbook confirms the *doxa* of 'they say', of the rumour about the *nègre*. It also confirms that Fanon is, in the eyes of white France, precisely what he is not in his own eyes: a *nègre* from the Africa that Martinicans of his generation had been taught to despise because *they* were French. As Fanon remarks in 1953, it was only when Aimé Césaire began to speak of negritude that is became possible for a few Martinicans to learn that 'it is well and good to be a *nègre*'.[13]

Freud's study of jokes anticipates the three-party structure of Fanon's encounter with the child and its mother; a second theorist of humour supplies another element. In 1899, Henri Bergson – not, I think, a philosopher one would usually regard as racist – asks quite straightforwardly, indeed innocently: 'Why do we laugh at a *nègre*?' He then answers his own rhetorical question by recounting the anecdote about the Parisian coachman who turned to his black passenger and called him '*mal lavé*' – not properly washed. We laugh, explains Bergson, because the *nègre* is a white man in disguise, because he has put on a mask: colouration may well be inherent in the skin but we regard it is as something that has been put on artificially, because it surprises us.[14] The *nègre* is a figure of fun, not because his white masks conceal a black skin, but because his black skin is a disguise. *Tiens, un nègre*.

We know nothing of the life history of the child who saw Fanon that cold day. We do know something of that of a girl nine years older than Fanon, Françoise Marrette, who would become Françoise Dolto, psychoanalytic grandmother to the nation. She was eight at the time. And her experience may teach us something about the stock of knowledge that makes a child so familiar with the paradigm: 'Look, a *nègre* . . . Look at the *nègre*, Mum. I'm frightened.'[15] On the beach at Deauville during the First World War, Françoise Marrette saw a black family; her nanny laughed at the sight. Dolto's childish correspondence, preserved and published for God alone knows what reason, is, for a while, full of conflicting images of black people, and they all originate in the meeting on the beach and in an encounter with a wounded *tirailleur sénégalais* (a Black colonial infantryman) who was being cared for by her mother. Perhaps the young Françoise did say, 'Tiens, un nègre.' The soldier kissed the little girl because she reminded him of his own daughter. The nanny's reaction was to wash her vigorously: being *mal lavé* is obviously a contagious condition that might be passed on to a child. There follows an exchange of letters with her uncle, who warns her not to play with the black troops she meets on the beach: they are handsome, but not as good as 'our' mountain troops. From London, her father sends her a comic postcard of 'four little *nègres*' – I assume them to be a group of street minstrels. In a letter, Françoise summarizes the school composition she wrote about a bayonet charge: it features a *tirailleur* called Sid Vava Ben Abdallah: 'Vava' was the child's nickname, and she clearly identifies with her infantryman, whom she describes as having a black face, white teeth, a flat nose and a red turban. Finally, her mother sends her a postcard of a *tirailleur* smoking a cigarette. On the back she has written: 'Here is Bou ji ma's portrait. Are you frightened of him?'[16] After that, there are no more mentions of black people in Dolto's letters. Small wonder that a child in Lyons could move so quickly from surprise to fear. Small wonder that he or she knows she has seen a *nègre*, knows how to recognize one, and knows why she should be afraid of him. To say, 'Tiens, un nègre' is an act of recognition, not of cognition.

To digress for a moment. It is significant that Dolto's experience centred on a *tirailleur sénégalais*. The colonial regiments recruited in Africa were surrounded by a particular aura. On the one hand, they were highly regarded as fighting men; on the other, they had a nasty reputation for rape and pillage – and were, apparently, encouraged in those practices by their white officers. When they were stationed in the French-occupied Rhineland after the First World War, their unenviable reputation spread to England. The *Daily Herald*, of all papers, ran headlines like 'Black Peril on the Rhine', 'Sexual Horrors Let Loose by France', 'Black Menace of 40,000 Troops' and 'Appeal to the Women of Europe'.[17] During the First World War, the image of the *tirailleur sénégalais* became still more ambiguous when it was used to sell Banania, a breakfast drink made from banana flour, cocoa and sugar.[18] All over France, posters showed a grinning soldier dressed in his exotic uniform, and spooning Banania into his mouth. The image of fear merges with one of cosy domesticity, as in the image of the wolf-granny in Little Red Riding Hood. Anyone with a taste for racist kitsch might like to know that shops in Paris now sell whole breakfast sets in bright yellow porcelain that reproduce the original Banania poster. I don't know if Banania was part of Fanon's childhood, or even if it was sold in Martinique, but he certainly knew about the *tirailleurs*. When a *sénégalais* unit stopped in Martinique in transit from French Guiana, his father brought them home. The family was 'delighted with them'.[19] The Fanon family behaved in much the same way as the Marrette family: they were hospitable to their 'colonial boys', recognized them as *nègres* and misrecognized themselves. Residence in France would put Fanon right on that score.

LIVED EXPERIENCE

To turn from the seer to the seen. Fanon is not a terribly sophisticated phenomenologist, and he is a very selective one, not least because he had little philosophical training and was self-taught. He makes little use of the concept of situation, of the founding moment of the cogito, or of themes like being-with-others, and concentrates almost exclusively on his being-for-others. Fanon's account of his lived experience, his *Erlebnis*, his 'act of consciousness', in Merleau-Ponty's phrase,[20] obviously draws heavily on the well-known passage in Part III of *L'Etre et le néant* (1943) in which Sartre describes the intersubjective structure of the gaze and the shame it induces. Sartre writes:

> Shame is a non-positional consciousness of the self as shame and, as such, it is an example of what the Germans call '*Erlebnis*'. What is more, its structure is intentional; it is a shameful apprehension *of* something and that something in *me*. I am ashamed of what I *am*.[21]

Sartre's shame is occasioned because he had been seen making a clumsy or vulgar gesture. That is not the case with Fanon, who has done nothing, said nothing. Unlike Jean Genet, he has not been caught or seen in the act of stealing.[22] He is simply *there* as an object of the gaze. Nausea floods in as Fanon apprehends what he is for the other: he is *that*, the grinning *tirailleur* advertising Banania, and a close relative of Bamboulette, the housemaid from Martinique who advertised shoe polish (and yes, it was black polish).[23] The same effect can be achieved through language: to speak to the black man in *petit nègre*, which is the singularly demeaning French equivalent to pidgin English, and to expect him to reply in kind, is 'to attach him to his image, to lime him, to imprison him, to make him the eternal victim of an essence, of an appearance (*apparaître*) for which he is not responsible'.[24] That appearance is the creation of others, the creation of school textbooks, philosophers and all those who teach children to know a *nègre* when they see one.

Had Fanon been a psychoanalyst – and he was not, whatever he may say – he might have described his *Erlebnis*, his negative epiphany, in terms of the infliction of a narcissistic wound or a symbolic castration. Borrowing from Merleau-Ponty, he actually describes it in terms of the destruction of his corporeal schema, described by the philosopher as 'a résumé of our bodily experience' and as 'a way of expressing the fact that my body is in the world'.[25] It is a kind of dialectic between the body and the world. Fanon in fact does more than borrow from Merleau-Ponty; he goes back to the philosopher's sources, quoting at some length from Jean L'hermitte's somewhat obscure *L'Image de notre corps*, in which the corporeal schema is described as an idea of the spatio-temporal existence of the body, and as a necessary precondition for any action in or on the world.[26] A clearer image of what Fanon himself understands by a corporeal schema emerges from his description of the Algerian women who, during the war of independence, took off their traditional veils, adopted European dress and planted bombs: 'The absence of the veil alters the Algerian woman's corporeal schema. She has to rapidly invent new dimensions for her body, new means of muscular control. She has to create a woman-outside-without-a veil way of walking.'[27] What is at stake is a very physical, fleshy – as the later Merleau-Ponty would put it – mode of being in the world. In the encounter with the child, it is the personal schema that Fanon has built up, the schema of an ego that exists in the spatio-temporal world that is under attack, together with the historico-racial schema he has constructed. It gives way to an epidermal-racial schema, as Fanon – Fanon's body – is taken over by a host of stereotypes.[28] Fanon experiences not only alienation, but obliteration and even incineration: 'All this whiteness burns me to ashes.'[29] I will return to the possible significance of the image of burning.

Just why Fanon chooses to analyse his *Erlebnis* in Sartrean and Merleau-

Pontyean terms is a surprisingly difficult question to answer. After all, neither *La Phénoménologie de la perception* nor *L'Etre et le néant* is a treatise on racism and anti-racism. And Fanon did not read them as such; he quite rightly reads *L'Etre et le néant* as 'an analysis of bad faith and inauthenticity'.[30] The whole of *Peau noire* might be described as an attempt to answer the question: is black authenticity possible in a white world? Bad faith and inauthenticity are the main themes he discovers in his readings of a group of books dealing with the woman of colour and the white man, and the woman of colour and the black man: Mayotte Capécia's *Je suis Martiniquaise* (1948) and *La Négresse blanche* (1950), Réné Maran's *Un Homme pareil aux autres* (1947), and Abdoulaye Sadji's *Nini, mulâtresse du Sénégal* (1951). The contrast between how the Senegalese novelist and the Martinican psychiatrist deal with the mulatto woman is telling. For Sadji, the life of Nini, like that of all mulattoes, is a lie, but it is a lie forced upon her by her destiny and even by her name (Virginie, abbreviated to 'Nini': *ni . . . ni*, 'neither, nor');[31] for Fanon, Mayotte Capécia's problems (and Nini's) stem from her inability to assume her facticity, from the bad faith of her repeated 'I know, but . . .':

> I wanted to get married, but I wanted to marry a white man. The trouble is that a woman of colour is never quite respectable in the eyes of a white man. Even if he loves her, and I knew that . . . I knew that white men do not marry black women.[32]

'I know, but . . .' is the classic structure of bad faith. While Fanon is certainly a masculinist writer, I suggest that the harshness of his condemnation of Capécia is not, as has been suggested,[33] evidence of misogyny, but of a condemnation (and perhaps fear) of situational bad faith.

The question 'why phenomenology?' is hard to answer, mainly because we do not have any documentary evidence: there are no preparatory materials or drafts, no correspondence, and no helpfully revealing diaries or notebooks. We know relatively little of what Fanon had read, or of when he read it. We have only the evidence of the text itself. And the text suggests that Fanon turns to phenomenology after a process of elimination. Of the theoretical discourses available to him, it is, apparently, the most suitable for his purposes. Part of the appeal is obviously phenomenology's concentration on experience and immediacy. As written by Merleau-Ponty ('I reach for the ashtray') and Sartre ('I see my friend Pierre'), it is also philosophy in the first person; no other philosophy would have allowed Fanon to say 'I' with quite such vehemence. What were the alternatives? The Marxism of the day, and particularly that of the Parti Communiste Français, would have had little to offer except banalities about the colonial question, and probably a brusque reminder that Martinique was not a colony but an integral part of the universalist French Republic. Hegel's dialectic of master and slave ignores the reality of the cane fields; the plantation-owner wants work from his slave, not recognition, and when Fanon comments that 'struggle' is the only answer to the plantation workers of Martinique, he does not mean the struggle for pure prestige.[34]

THE REAL IN SIGHT

The psychiatry Fanon had studied had taught him about the 'primitive mentality' of blacks and North Africans, and his writing career begins and ends with its critique.[35] Adler's individual psychology might be able to explain the inferiority complex of an individual Martinican, but not the inferiorization of an entire population. Mannoni's 'dependency complex' seeks to prove that colonialism is impossible unless it is desired by the colonized, and fails signally to see that, when 100,000 people have been shot dead after the Madagascan insurrection of 1947, the Lebel rifle in the hands of a soldier that appears in a dream is unlikely to be a symbolic penis, or phallus (as you will). Whatever the properties of the symbolic phallus may be, it is not normally a weapon of mass destruction. Jung has nothing to say to black youth. As Fanon remarks, 'Neither Freud, nor Adler, nor even the cosmic Jung were thinking about blacks in the course of their research.'[36] Without going into any great detail or any extended discussion of the claim that there are no Oedipal neurotics (and no homosexuals . . . only there are) in Martinique, it has to be said that Fanon's relationship with psychoanalysis is fraught.[37] He does state that an analysis of the black man's *Erlebnis* requires a psychoanalytic input, but he also argues that Lacanian psychoanalysis in particular is culture-bound and has nothing to say about *his* experience.

Virtually every mention of psychoanalysis is hedged with the reservation 'Yes, but . . .' Discussing Mannoni's book on Madagascar,[38] he comments with deceptive mildness: 'We must not lose sight of the real.'[39] Fanon is not concerned with symbolic wounds, but with the absolute wound of colonialism.[40] 'Alongside phylogenesis and ontogenesis, there is sociogenesis.'[41] The insistence that psychoanalysis loses sight of the real, and the stress on the need to keep it in sight, may explain Fanon's quite extraordinary misreading of Freud. He rarely quotes Freud, and when he does so he claims that Freud proves that neuroses originate in a determinate *Erlebnis*. He takes his supporting evidence from the 'Five Lectures on Psychoanalysis' of 1909. Unfortunately for Fanon's argument, Freud is in fact describing how he came to reject the so-called seduction theory which did trace the aetiology of neurosis to an actual sexual trauma.[42] The misreading is the result of keeping the real in sight, the 'real' being the absolute wound.

Hegel and Freud do not think about blacks, and nor was Sartre thinking about blacks when he wrote *L'Etre et le néant*, but Fanon was not the only black writer of his generation to conclude that Sartrean phenomenology could be an aid to his analysis of his lived experience. In his paper on 'The Negro Writer and his World', presented in 1956 to *Présence Africaine*'s First Congress of Black Writers and Artists, George Lamming remarks that 'the Negro is not simply *there*. He is there in a certain way . . . The Negro is a man whom the Other (meaning the non-Negro) regards as a Negro.'[43] Although Lamming gives no reference, this is an obvious allusion to Sartre's *Réflexions sur la question juive*: 'The Jew is a man whom other men regard as a Jew . . . It is the antisemite who *makes* the Jew.'[44] Fanon cites this text too, but immediately spells out its limitations: he is not the victim of someone else's 'idea' of him. He is the victim of his own appearance (*apparaître*), of the black skin on to which white fantasies and fears are projected.[45] Sartrean phenomenology can help Fanon analyse the mode of his being-for-others, but it too lets him down. Sartre lets him down in his preface to Senghor's anthology of the poetry of negritude, where he assumes that negritude is a temporary phenomenon that will disappear when it is subsumed into some quasi-Hegelian universalist synthesis.[46] Fanon was dubious about negritude – that 'great black mirage'[47] – but he could also invoke it to finesse Sartre by remarking 'It is the white man who creates the *nègre*. But it is the *nègre* who created negritude.'[48] At other times, Fanon does assume the stance of negritude, does exploit Spivak's moment of strategic essentialism – and negritude is certainly an essentialism. This is how the encounter in Lyons ends: The mother: '"Look, he's handsome, this *nègre*"' . . . Fanon: '"The handsome negro says bugger you, madame." Shame flooded across her face. Two birds with one stone. I identified my enemies and I created a scene.'[49] The same defiance reappears later: 'You come to terms with me, I'm not coming to terms with anyone.'[50] Although Fanon does not flag it as such, this is a quotation from the great poem of negritude, Césaire's *Cahier d'un retour au pays natal*.[51] It may be a mirage, but negritude has its strategic uses.

The irony is that, when he 'abolishes' negritude with his vision of a future world without class, without race, Sartre falls into the very trap that he denounces in *Réflexions sur la question juive*, where he mocks the 'Democrat' who can recognize the Jew as Man, but not as the creator and bearer of Jewishness, just as the 'humanists' of *La Nausée* love an abstract universal man so much that they have no interest in concrete individuals. Sartre's little problem may go some way to explaining why so much of the French Left was lukewarm about supporting the Algerian cause and, ultimately, to explaining why certain French intellectuals appear to be convinced that the presence in a French classroom of a girl in an Islamic headscarf (*hijab*) puts the entire Republic in danger. But I will leave that, and the question of why some erstwhile Third Worldists appear to be mutating into Islamophobes, for another occasion.

THE GAZE THAT BURNS

The theme of the threatening white gaze and the trope of visibility/invisibility are, of course, not uncommon in black writing. Almost at random, one thinks of Du Bois's veil of invisibility, of Ellison's invisible man, or, more recently, of bell hooks in *Wounds of Passion*: 'The gaze of white folks disturbs me. It is always for me the would-be colonizing look.'[52] One of the reasons why Fanon is so critical of psychoanalysis is that, 'As the racial drama unfolds in the open air, the black man does not have time to "unconsciousnessize" it' (*inconscienciser*).[53] I suggest that there might be something very specific to Fanon's experience of the gaze and use of figures of visibility, and that it might pertain to Martinique. In Aimé Césaire's reworking of *The Tempest*, it is Prospero's gaze that forces Caliban to see himself as he is seen: 'You have finally imposed upon me an image of myself. An underdeveloped man, as you put it, an undercapable man. That is how you have made me see myself.'[54] *Tiens, un nègre.* And there is a Martinican saying: 'Zié Békés brilé zié Nèg' ('the eyes of the *béké* burned the eyes of the black man').[55] The *béké* is not just any white man; he is the white creole, the descendent of locally born plantation owners. The *béké* is Martinique's answer to The Man, Mr Charlie. It is through the internalization of his gaze that the *Nèg* (this is the Creole for *nègre*) has been blinded. And it is the white gaze that burns Fanon to ashes. To speculate, which is all we can really do here: when Fanon is gazed at by that child, he is experiencing anew a traumatic moment in Martinican history and in the Martinican imaginary: he is being looked at by the *béké* and his eyes are burning. Is this why the schema of the gaze is not reversible, as it is for Sartre? Is this why Fanon can put up no ontological resistance, cannot look back? Speaking of Madagascar, Fanon described colonization as an absolute wound. In the case of Martinique, the wound was more absolute still, so absolute that it cannot be staunched. In a strange way, it was a settler colony, or rather a settled colony. The aboriginal population having been exterminated, it was repopulated with slaves whose eyes were burned by the *béké*'s gaze. Martinique has no pre-colonial history: it all began with the absolute wound and the eyes that were burned.

ACKNOWLEDGEMENT

This essay was first published in *Radical Philosophy*, 95, May/June 1999. It is reproduced here (with minor amendments) with permission.

CHAPTER 3

Primordial Being:
Enlightenment and the Indian Subject of Postcolonial Theory

CHETAN BHATT

Postcolonial theory, especially in the writings of Gayatri Spivak, has undertaken intricate critiques of specifically Western Enlightenment humanism and foundationalism and by extension the broad European philosophical tradition. While postcolonial theory in its deconstructive mode can face many ways at once in its claims about the West, Europe and (post)colonial India, it contains some consistent themes that can sharply demarcate European Enlightenment, conceived as science, truth, rationality and humanism, from its truly abject, the colonized or the genuinely subaltern that can only be 'impossibly', if ever, articulated by or heard within humanist, rationalist paradigms. Spivak, for example, draws a very clear distinction between a universalizing German philosophical tradition and the world of the non-European, the former representing untainted and irreducibly Eurocentric philosophy that did not have a concern with 'comparative' discipline:

> Cultural and intellectual 'Germany', the place of self-styled difference from the rest of what is still understood as 'continental' Europe and Britain, was the main source of the meticulous scholarship that established the vocabulary of proto-archetypal ('comparative' in the disciplinary sense) identity, or kinship, without direct involvement in the utilization of that other difference, between the colonizer and the colonized; in the nascent discourses of comparative philology, comparative religion, even comparative literature . . . The field of philosophy as such, whose model was the merging of science and truth, *remained untouched by the comparative impulse*. In this area, Germany produced authoritative 'universal' narratives where the subject remained unmistakably European.[1]

This main claim of postcolonial theory forms the uneasy background for an essay that is primarily focused on how some eighteenth- and nineteenth-century Enlightenment philosophers – others could have been chosen – considered the place of 'India' and some of its religions and philosophies in their grand civilizational, cultural and philosophical chronographies. This is a difficult area whose complexities can be elided by the easier claim that there was no comparative philosophical project. Can the claims of postcolonial theory be unified with statements such as the following made by Arthur Schopenhauer, the main focus of this article?

> Kant's philosophy is therefore the only one with which a thorough acquaintance is positively assumed in what is to be here discussed. But if in addition to this the reader has dwelt for a while in the school of the divine Plato, he will be the better prepared to hear me, and the more susceptible to what I say. But if he has shared in the benefits of the *Vedas*, access to which [was] opened to us by the *Upanishads* . . . if, I say, the reader has also already received and assimilated the divine inspiration of ancient Indian wisdom, then he is best of all prepared to hear what I have to say to him.[2]

The function of 'the subaltern' artifice is another aspect of postcolonial theory that is implicitly criticized below. In postcolonial theory, the genuinely subaltern cannot be figured as the subject of humanism and cannot be brought into any kind of representation-in-itself within the universal discourses of humanism or reason. The word of the Indian subaltern can seem like an ever-delayed moment of revelation that functions to provide the theoretical integrity of postcolonial theory. However, this unrepresentability is also applied rather widely by Spivak to a range of evidently non-subaltern phenomena, including the livedness of 'everyday Hinduism' as well as Vedantic 'theological' debates which, it is claimed, can at best only be inauthentically simulated in Western humanist discourse. There is a third theme emergent in recent postcolonial theory, relating to the distinction between elite and subaltern in the (post)colonial world in which the elite, another agile concept, is conceivable only in so far as it is a subject of knowledge (or ethics) within Western humanism and against which the genuinely subaltern lives on in some kind of dense, unrepresentable, unheard world with its own eco-logic that can be only impossibly narrated within the discourses of the Indian humanist elite. If these postcolonial arguments are new, it is also worth examining the possibility that they have entirely European historical or philosophical precedents.

THE CRADLE OF REASON AND THE HEARTH OF CULTURE

After the mid-eighteenth century, Voltaire made several pronouncements about the primordial antiquity of Indian civilization and the superiority and rationality of ancient Indian culture in comparison with that of Europe. 'Almost every people, but particularly those of Asia, reckon a succession of ages which terrifies us.' For Voltaire, like several Enlightenment thinkers, India received the first revelation and was the cultural hearth for world civilization. Indians were those 'whom we look upon as the first nations', 'the men who were the most anciently united into a body of people'.[3] India, for Voltaire, was also the primordial homeland of European peoples. Fundamentally, the example of ancient Indian culture, apprehended through some of the texts that were available in Europe in the mid-eighteenth century, demonstrated for Voltaire and others a *rational* civilization that could be compared favourably with the superstitious, irrational and barbaric forms of institutional clerical authority that dominated Catholic Europe. It is well known that, in an extremely influential dispute, Voltaire mobilized the fact of the antiquity of Indian culture sharply against the chronologos of humankind that was presented in the Old Testament. Indian antiquity was marshalled on the side of reason against the Abrahamic,[4] Noachian and Mosaic chronography within Judeo-Christendom. Voltaire's understanding of Indian texts was initially based on a fabrication, claming to be 'Vedic', that contained an invented dialogue between two Indian sages.[5] The 'rationalist' arguments of one sage were contrasted with the idolatrous beliefs of the other, and provided Voltaire with his own justifications for 'rational religion' against medieval superstition and arbitrary clerical power. Later, Voltaire had access to renderings of Hindu texts, often translated from Persian, but these did not alter his beliefs about Indian primordiality, nor that India was the cradle of reason or of world civilization.

To be sure, Voltaire's enthusiasm for India was not shared by many of the *philosophes*, who saw in India only barbaric or enlightened 'despotism' overseen by the religion of the Brachmanes that privileged both an internal turn towards metaphysical dissolution and 'nothingness' – a state often described as opium-induced – and an obsession with caste purity which was forbiddingly intolerant and oppressive, and certainly not conducive to ideas of liberty or freedom of will. China was initially, though not exclusively, the favoured ancient source of inspiration for rationalist Enlightenment thinkers. However, the example of Voltaire's fascination with the rationality of India highlights a number of densely complicated themes about the imagination and judgement of India in Europe during the eighteenth and nineteenth centuries, as well as the way this has been articulated in more recent postcolonial theory.

What is now called 'the universal humanist subject of Enlightenment' can be said to have arisen as a product of the 'comparative' philosophical world histories, histories of humankind and philosophical anthropologies whose writing preoccupied so many Enlightenment and Romantic thinkers. Where did the history of humanity begin? If 'the first abode of man was a garden', Herder asked, 'Where then lay the garden where the creator placed his gentle, defenceless creature?' For him the traditions of Genesis and the mythologies and traditions of the Chinese, Tibetans, Arabs, Persians and Indians pointed to one place:

> there can be no doubt . . . that this primal seat should be a region between the Indian mountains. The land [described in tradition as] abounding in gold and precious stones, can hardly be any other than India, which has been known from the days of yore for these treasures. The river that flows round is the twisting, sacred Ganges; all of India recognizes it as the stream of paradise.[6]

Herder, like many of his contemporaries, was familiar with some of the work of early British and European Orientalists, including Dow, Holwell, Halhed, Wilkins, Anquetil-Duperron as well as William Jones's pioneering *Asiatic Researches*.[7] However, it has been argued that his main image of India was based on the translation of Kalidasa's classical Sanskrit play, *Sakuntala*, from which Herder derived his view of the Indian as 'child-like'.[8] It is conventional, especially after the dominant interpretation of Hegel (though it was stated most clearly by Friedrich Schlegel), to read the representation of the primordiality of India within many such texts as one of the infancy ('cradling') of humanity which was superseded by the mature civilizations of Greece and then Europe. However, while such sentiments are clearly apparent in Herder, especially in his view of different countries contributing in a decisive way to the process of world history, there is a far more complex comparative judgement at work, certainly one which allows a space for contemporary Europe to be contrasted unfavourably with both ancient and contemporary India.[9] We might call Herder's work a founding statement of 'unity-in-diversity multiculturalism' with all the problems that it entails:

> [The] history of humankind also needs to be observed and treated with humanity. In other words, we must examine even erring nations without prejudice, anger, hatred, envy, or slander; we must view them as brothers or as children [of a common God]. For are they not all brothers of human reason and of every error of reason?[10]

For Herder, a founding reason, justice and language defined the essence of what it meant to be human (*Humanität*). It has been argued that the concept of *Humanität* was influenced by and gained stature for Herder because of 'the discovered relevance to it . . . of values from the Indian world' that he found in his readings:[11] if this is the case, then does the metaphor of what were conceived as 'Indian values' already reside inside Herder's conception of universal humanity?

Against Rousseau, Herder argued that it was not inarticulate sounds that formed the basis of language. Some kind of fully formed, especially poetic language was natural to all humanity. Religion, for Herder, was also both its oldest and highest expression – and here Herder alluded to the possibility of primal philosophy. Furthermore, 'all mankind are only the one and the same species'.[12] If the founding unity of humanity was in reason and justice, the diversity arose through the precision of the relation between what he called the 'genetic force' of nature and the environment ('climate') in which it was manifest:

> No people of Europe, let alone all of Greece, has ever been more savage than the people of New Zealand or of Tierra del Fuego. This can be expected if one takes the analogy of climate into consideration. These inhumane peoples nevertheless possess humanity, reason, and language. No cannibals devour their own children or brothers; their inhumane practice is in their eyes a ruthless custom of war that preserves their courage and terrifies their enemies. It is, therefore, nothing more or less than the work of a crude form of political reasoning, which repressed the humanity of these peoples in the face of these few sacrifices to their country.[13]

The original cultural differences of humanity were described by Herder through the conceptions of *Völker* and *Volk*. From this cultural carapace – though in one important sense the term 'cultural' is being used here to describe the moment of its modern creation – Herder strongly criticized Kant's preoccupation with 'race'. Kant was later to castigate Herder, and indeed Kant's authority was important for the unequivocal acceptance of the concept of 'race' and a warning against the admixture of 'races'.[14]

However, Herder's conception of the genetic force of nature, with which 'climate' acted 'merely as an auxiliary or antagonist', provided for a wider epistemic field that could encapsulate powerful conceptions of cultural identity and cultural becoming based on an invocation of eco-logical, filial, naturalist, organicist and in some indeterminate way 'hereditarian' ideas that did not need to rely on the resources of biology proper. The dense ecological relation between a specific branch of humanity and the particular environment in which it thrived resulted in its unique epistemological difference. Herder may have identified all such variations as inhabited by a primal reason, but we should note the contemporary resonance of the kinship established here between primal ecological harmony and epistemological rupture. If 'there is one race, the human race, the differences are of culture', then the 'culture' of today's cultural studies and postcolonial theory owes its foundation to this manoeuvre of Herder's. In particular we also note the oscillation between the universal *Humanität* of reason and justice to which one must appeal, and the particular and primeval ecological determination of *Volk* which one must be compelled to respect. Herder's conception of national culture was a *strong* one. For example, the cultural integrity of the Indian people under Brahmin hegemony, the latter seen by Herder as both oppressive and, through its education, enlightening, was one which rampant European colonialism, 'like the Mongol yoke before it', was unable to annihilate. In the face of Brahmin 'dominion over the soul' of the Indian, 'which will endure, as far as I can see, as long as an Indian shall exist, all European institutions touch only the surface'.[15]

Herder's philosophy of the history of humankind is therefore based on a comparative and differential judgement of national cultures in which the ancient Indians were the *Urvolk* and the mountainous regions of India were not simply the primal *Urheimat*, but the cradle of human reason, emotion, poesis and aesthetic. However, while Herder was extremely important for making available a non-necessary association between early Romanticism and nascent German Indophilia, and indeed legitimizing India as a central resource for the projects of contra-Classical German Romanticism that followed, a judgement of the place of India in his work is at once complex and definitive. India alternates as a place of spirited, primordial and indeed inexhaustible infant reason and of mature sophistication of idea and aesthetic that could be contrasted favourably with early modern Europe. In Herder's case, this is less an ambivalence than an optimistic celebration that was denigrated by other Enlightenment thinkers.

PREHISTORIC BEING-IN-ITSELF

Kant had famously stated of India that:

> This is the highest country. No doubt it was inhabited before any other and could even have been the site of all creation and all science. The culture of

> the Indians, as is known, almost certainly came from Tibet, just as all our arts, like agriculture, numbers, the game of chess etc., seem to have come from India.[16]

Kant had said this in the context of a disagreement about the primordial homeland of humanity and against the view, derived from the speculative astronomy of Bailly (which Hegel was also to disparage), of an Arctic[17] *Urheimat*. Kant was engaging with the speculations about primordiality that were to intensify considerably over the coming century around the *Urvolk*, the *Ursprache*, the *Urheimat* and the '*Ur-Mythus*'. Kant also believed that an original and pure religion had been manifest in India and survived in some contemporary religious forms.[18] However, he had little sympathy with the celebration of all things Indian. For Kant, India was fundamentally an *erosion*, even if it had possessed an original state of primordial purity. Here Kant was echoing an established orientation towards India that was to find its theoretical-materialist fulfilment in the nineteenth century, via Hegel, in Marx's statement about the 'Asiatic mode of production' and his theory of ideology and religion. It was, however, in the aftermath and as a consequence of Kantian transcendental idealism that Indian metaphysics acquired a different resonance.

Hegel, in attacking the Romantic conception of history, had said in one of his lectures on world history:

> [I]t has been argued . . . that a primitive nation [India] once existed, and that all our knowledge and art has simply been handed down to us from it. This original nation, it is contended, existed before mankind proper had come into being, and is immortalized in ancient legends under the image of the gods; distorted fragments of its highly developed culture are allegedly also to be found in the myths of the earliest nations. And the condition of the earliest nations, as described in history, is represented as a gradual decline from the high level of culture that preceded it. All this is put forward with the claim that philosophy required it to be so, and that it is also supported by historical evidence . . . We certainly owe very much that is valuable to the interest which has fired such historical research, but this research can also be indicted on its own testimony. For it sets out to prove by historical methods that whose historical existence it has already presupposed.[19] . . . *This notion of perfect primeval condition does, however, contain a philosophical element – namely the realisation that man cannot have originally existed in a state of animal sensibility*.[20]

Hegel was here sternly dismissing both Schelling's and Friedrich Schlegel's philosophies of history and the foundational place of India within them.

Schlegel claimed the primordiality of the Indians, and that Indians were the first to see the face of God.[21] This was the first Revelation, which Schlegel saw as the original and purest form of the Christian religion. For Schlegel, however, Indians had committed the primordial wrong, the fall from grace. This was the start of degeneration and deterioration, 'the slow and gradual declension' of India that signalled the fall of all humankind. In an instructive move, Schlegel inverted the temporality of natural Romanticism: a 'degeneration' from 'low' state of cultural development into 'high' modern culture became instead a degeneration from a 'high' state of ancient cultural development into a 'low' modern culture.[22]

Hegel's critique of Schelling and Schlegel could not, of course, recuperate the meaning Rousseau attributed to his own temporality. Hegel's and Schlegel's chronographies can be seen as travelling in opposite directions along a line that plots a desirable state of civilization against a judgement of civilizational worth in time; Rousseau's crosses this line obliquely. However, Hegel had to provide the location on a chronographic tabula for the existence of an early Indian philosophical tradition, a tradition with which he was very well acquainted.[23] This had to be a coordinate in relation to *philosophical* history. The empirical 'science of events' required metabolizing into 'that radical mode of being that prescribes their destiny to all empirical beings'.[24] There is another, important factor which pressed Hegel: the 'great historical discovery' elaborated in Hegel's time of the connections between the Sanskrit language and Europe, including its 'insight into the historical links between the Germanic nations and those of India'.[25] The chronographic and taxonomic organization of the system of kinship between languages was the opening created by the 'archaic cries'[26] that had been discovered in Sanskrit. Hegel argued that:

> *Externally*, India sustains manifold relations to the History of the World. In recent times the discovery has been made, that Sanscrit lies at the foundation of all those further developments which form the languages of Europe; e.g. the Greek, Latin, German. India, moreover was the centre of emigration for all the western world; but this *external* historical relation is to be regarded rather as a merely physical diffusion of peoples from this point. . . . The spread of Indian culture is prehistorical, for History is limited to that which makes an essential epoch in the development of Spirit.[27]

This much is known about Hegel's views of India's place in mere 'general history', or as 'pre-history', and therefore its exteriority to philosophical history.[28] However, Viyagappa and Halbfass have presented more nuanced readings of Hegel that are advantageous for the arguments advanced below.

For Hegel, India possessed a 'true philosophy' based on a conception of an absolute, the indivisible substance of the universe from which Indians created a philosophy of pure, abstract Being-in-itself. Indian philosophy was for Hegel a highly developed but singular focus on substantiality. It was practically manifested in the other-worldly, dreamy, opiate state[29] of the Brahmin apprehending the absolute. We can read this as an attribution of a kind of pure objectivity to Indian philosophy. However, for Hegel, it was content-less, regressively ineffable, an almost wilful and decided apprehension of pure substance that did not have subjectivity, form, particularity or determination. (Though, for Hegel, reason is also this infinite substance of the universe.)[30] Indian philosophy was founded on an abstract negation of the subjective element, of the finite, the practical or the determinate. Hence, the elemental lack in Indian philosophy was both of the concreteness of the world, and of every subjective or multiple conception that lay beyond abstract unity. For Hegel, this lack was filled with imagination, fantasy, sensual abandon, and a representational excess of the illusion (*maya*) that was the phenomenal world.

Consequently, Indian philosophy had no true ground for subjecthood, individuality, freedom and humanism. The Brahmin cared more for animals and nature than other humans, the latter unconstitutable as subjects of humanism or freedom. The negation of subjectivity, particularity, determination, the concrete-in-the-world also meant that Indian philosophy could not have a conception of dialectical mediation: no dialectic and thus no history. However, Halbfass has argued that in the movement of Spirit in history, the pure Being-in-itself of Indian philosophy is already contained in and available to the unfolding of Spirit in the European present. The ancient philosophies of India can stand guard against the egoistic excess that arises from pure subjectivity. Hegel paradoxically identified egoism with the German Romantics, who were obsessed with India for their own motives and had consequently misunderstood its philosophical warning.[31] For Hegel, the fundamental deficiency in the Indian world-view is that of its foundational incapacity to individuate Indians and bring them into a subjecthood of the kind enjoyed in European Enlightenment reason and humanism; its fundamental gift was to destabilize the excesses of European subjectivity. Hegel can be said to have instituted a paradigm in which the possibility of rational, humanist subjecthood – and consequently freedom – for the Indian subaltern is perpetually theoretically inconceivable. There is also a hauntology[32] here in which 'India' travels across the sciences-disciplines of rationalists and Romantics alike. Conversely, that Spirit might have come and gone from ancient India leaves it now only as decaying *corpus*,[33] an omnibus of archaic texts, a barely living body that finds fulfilment in the grotesque excess of somatic functions and pleasures, and a glimpse, through an opium haze, of 'substance', but otherwise in a state of putrefying slumber. The spectre that haunted both Hegel and Schlegel was that of the stagnation and decay of modern civilization, for which the archaic corpus of India was variously poison, drug, remedy and recipe.[34]

THE IRRATIONAL MOSAIC

It was perhaps Arthur Schopenhauer who brought this into sharpest relief and ultimately forbidding resolution. For Schopenhauer the Indian corpus was a canon. If Hegel denigrated the lack of mediation of abstract Being by the concrete within Indian metaphysics, Schopenhauer was to privilege 'the Indian' conception of Being while his ontology displaced entirely the dialectic. Schopenhauer had already rejected the foundational basis of Hegel's claim through his dismissal of both Fichtean subjectivism (which Hegel indeed identified as an example of 'egoistic' philosophy for which Indian metaphysics might act as a rebuke) and materialist objectivism, and indeed of the limitations of sufficient reason that derived from any reflective philosophy of subject and object. If Hegel placed India outside of philosophical history because of its undialectical preoccupation with pure content-less Being-in-itself, Schopenhauer valorized precisely this aspect of Indian philosophy through his belief that it spoke to his completion of the project of post-Kantian Western philosophy. If, for Hegel, Indian philosophy was solely one of abstract unity, for Schopenhauer, unity and the plurality were phenomenal objectifications that were sidestepped by the 'real determination' of the noumenal 'will' which India had uniquely apprehended in other ways. Hegel's belief that Spirit was progress and history had direction was precisely the illusion (*maya*) that both Schopenhauer and ancient Indian philosophers had discovered. Similarly, if history was rationality, for Schopenhauer this claim was a subterfuge that masked blind directionless movement. Frivolously, Schopenhauer used the Upanishads to turn Hegel both sideways and on his head.

While Schopenhauer was initially close to intellectuals and writers influenced by the interest in India, and lived in a period where German 'Indomania' was coming to fruition, there was an important practical link between Herder and Schopenhauer in the figure of the enthusiastic German Indologist, Frederich Maier, a student and close friend of Herder, who was to introduce Schopenhauer in 1813 to 'Hindu' texts.[35] Another key influence was Karl Christian Frederich Krause, a philosopher and Sanskritist,[36] who both translated texts for Schopenhauer and apparently taught him how to meditate.[37] Schopenhauer had already written his dissertation on the basis for sufficient reason prior to his revelatory encounter with Anquetil-Duperron's anachronistic Oupnekhat, his rendering into Latin from Persian of a translation from

Sanskrit into Persian of some of the Upanishads, the Hindu texts that creatively followed, commented on and elaborated Vedic ideas and introduced new ones. There is little question of the profound importance for Schopenhauer of the Upanishads, other Hindu texts, and early translations of (mainly Burmese) Buddhist texts that had become available in Europe. He was to say of the Oupnekhat that 'it has been the consolation of my life and will be that of my death'.[38]

Schopenhauer claimed a relation between Indian and European thought not because of philological or mythological similarities, but because of their philosophical affinities.[39] The question about the relationship between his philosophy of 'will' and 'denial of the will-to-live' and Upanishadic and Buddhist thinking is particularly interesting. Schopenhauer later said of his philosophy of will that it arose when 'the Upanishads, Plato and Kant were able simultaneously to cast their rays into one man's mind'. He was to say of Kant that 'The "maya" of the Vedas [and] the "phenomenon" of Kant are one and the same',[40] the phenomenal world being the necessary illusion or delusion that we live. However, he also said of the relation between his philosophy of will and Buddhism 'inasmuch as in my own philosophizing I have certainly not been under its influence',[41] though the strong influence of Buddhism came later in his work. Schopenhauer had probably read the Oupnekhat in late 1813 or early 1814[42] and had met Krause around 1815.[43] In the first (1818) and second (1844) editions of *The World as Will and Representation* and in both volumes of *Parerga and Paralipomena* (1851), he repeatedly refers to the Upanishads and the Oupnekhat, the Vedas, the Puranas and the Bhagavad Gita, as well as the translations and writings of Colebrooke, Jones's *Asiatic Researches*, Julius Heinrich Klaproth's *Asiatische Magazin*, the *Transactions of the Royal Asiatic Society*, the writings of the eighth-century Indian philosopher Shankara and numerous other Hindu and Buddhist sources. Magee has argued that the core elements of Schopenhauer's philosophy were fully formed at the time that '*he then almost immediately discovered*' their similarities to Hindu or Buddhist doctrines.[44] Certainly, his critique of the Kantian division of phenomena and noumena, and of the principle of sufficient reason were prior to his encounter with Hindu thinking. There is less clarity about the *authority*, rather than interpellative function, of Hindu and, later, Buddhist concepts that he often used in his development of the philosophy of 'will'. However, in *The World as Will and Representation* and in his later work there is a definitive engagement with Hindu and Buddhist ideas. While he often made associations between his and Hindu or Buddhist concepts, these were not uncomplicated identifications (for example, 'phenomenon' is '*maya*', 'will' is '*Brahman*', the aporetic state of the 'denial of the will-to-live' is 'nirvana') but a more complex and fruitful expansion and negotiation with Hinduism and Buddhism through his own philosophy.[45]

Accepting with Kant that the mind imposes space, time and causality to create the phenomenal world available to its intuition or reflection, Schopenhauer famously began the first book of *The World as Will and Representation*: 'The world is my representation: this is a truth valid with reference to every living and knowing being, although man alone can bring it into reflective, abstract consciousness.'[46]

For Kant, the distinction between appearances and things-in-themselves is conclusive, but, for Schopenhauer, not concluded. The thing-in-itself, for Kant, is unavailable to us in-itself. It was the resolution of these distinctions between phenomenon and noumenon, and adjacently subject and object, appearance and essence, empirical reality and transcendental ideality that was Schopenhauer's objective. Schopenhauer rejected philosophical systems that started from either the subject or the object: these could at best only provide explanations based on the limit of sufficient reason, and were valid only for the phenomenal world. If representation was the primary form of the division into subject and object,[47] what remained after we eliminated the form of representation and all forms subordinate to it that were explained by the principle of sufficient reason?

Schopenhauer started his discussion on the relation between subject and object by focusing on *the body*, and in this sense displaced the Cartesian privilege of mind over body that was arguably foundational to what later became sufficient reason. As my body acts, it objectifies my 'will' in an immediate way that is indivisible from that 'will'. Hence, my body may be my representation, but it is also, and otherwise, my 'will'. This is the excessive, unavailable to sufficient reason, to the relation of subject and object or causality that I also have with my body.[48] The body (and indeed sexual plenitude) was thus the privileged site of the objectification of the thing-in-itself.

Schopenhauer extended this conception of 'will' outward: the 'will' is the thing-in-itself of all things. Schopenhauer used several different conceptions of 'will', but in this grand conception of 'will' Schopenhauer was referring to the in-itself of the universe beyond the phenomenal world, though this cannot be a simple identification with 'the real'. 'Will' is foreign to the phenomenal forms in which 'will' appears or passes; nor can 'will' be identified as object or concept. The conditions of space and time and the plurality and differentiality of objects are examples of what Schopenhauer called the *principium individuationis* ('principle of individuation') that is coextensive with and the condition for subjecthood and knowledge. It is the essential differentiability of phenomena that 'separates' them from groundless and unconceptualized 'will'. 'Will' also has no direction or purpose, no telos or history. For Schopenhauer, 'will' is 'blind impulse, an obscure, dull urge', a 'striving devoid of all knowledge'.[49] Schopenhauer also identified 'will' as the 'will-to-live' since 'everything in nature presses and pushes towards *existence*, if possible towards *organic existence*, i.e., *life*, and then to the highest possible degree thereof'.[50]

One of Schopenhauer's conceptions of 'will' is the idea of one's own will in self consciousness that is the basis for judging 'the illusion of plurality (Maya)', the form of objective apprehension in which the world of objects 'always meet with this one being'. The 'will' might be recognized as a 'unity' that lies beyond the phenomenal world, and we may have 'isolated glances' of this unity in the relation of things in nature.[51] We may, he said, understand 'will' through a kind of aesthetic contemplation. In the aesthetic method, and hence beyond the principle of sufficient reason, we can know objects as (different grades of Platonic) Ideas.

We can also apprehend the consciousness of the knower 'not as an individual, but as pure, will-less subject'.[52] This 'will-less' subject is necessary for Schopenhauer because for him the world is a miserable, purposeless place, 'the battle-ground for tormented and agonized beings who continue to exist only by each devouring the other'.[53] Conversely, the 'will-less' subject of knowing is one of pure contemplation, 'lost in the object', forgetting all individuality, 'abolishing the kind of knowledge which follows the principle of sufficient reason', exemplifying a denial of the will-to-live, delivered from the miserable self, and which has become entirely one with objects.[54]

For Schopenhauer this was the start of what could be found in the soaring metaphysics of his beloved Indian wisdom. Hindu and Buddhist philosophy had recognized the world as a place of suffering and (*because*) of the blind, purposeless 'will-to-live'. We cannot 'escape' this 'will-to-live' since it is the true nature of all things. We might, however, apprehend it in a way that temporarily 'halts' it. This apprehension cannot be willed, nor can one desire it: instead, it comes to one, from the outside. Crudely put, this is through the practices of the philosophies of what Schopenhauer called 'the denial of the will-to-live'. Such practices may include renunciation, mystical apprehension or aesthetic contemplation (especially of music) that in some way 'cease the world': the wheel of Ixion stands still. It is precisely in this 'recognition' or 'apprehension' that one does not capitulate to the illusion of subject and object (a necessity of representation) or a futile optimism about a purposeless and miserable world. In the state of the 'shaking off of the world', 'seeing through the *principium individuationis*', there is an apprehension of a kind of pure, 'will-less', subject-less Being-in-itself of the kind that Hegel criticized Indian philosophy for. This state of Being is complex and the site of a theoretical aporia in

Schopenhauer. It cannot be a knowledge of 'the real': instead, at the moment where one is at one with objects, purely in the world of representation, the 'phenomenon comes into contradiction with itself' and the in-itself of its true nature 'ultimately abolishes itself'. In some important way, Indian consciousness had the capacity to first escape subjecthood, ego-hood and individuality, and then slip away altogether from the possibility of representation.

Schopenhauer contrasted this Hindu or Buddhist 'refusal' with the odious and false optimism of 'the will-to-live' he saw in the Judeo-Christian-Islamic traditions. Those traditions contained founding errors: the belief in the creation of humankind out of nothing by a Creator or Deity in whom one must forever have monotheistic faith; a false conviction that humankind is free to will what it does in life; a belief in death as an ending; and a rejection of metempsychosis and the transmigration of 'souls'. This led to an optimistic, cheery, ego-dominated and individuated orientation to life, a celebration of the 'will-to-live' and hence to a disastrous misrecognition of what the world actually is. For the Western religious tradition, death is 'the great reprimand' for the 'will-to-live' in a way that it cannot be for the Hindu or Buddhist.

In Schopenhauer's discussion of the Hindu and (some) Buddhist ideas of metempsychosis and palingenesis, we get a sense of how his post-Kantian ontology and an atheism both dominate and negotiate with Hindu and Buddhist philosophies. For Schopenhauer, the subject and the object were essential to each other as a consequence of the form of representation; both resided in the realm of phenomena 'excessive' to which is the 'will' as noumenon. The extent to which one lived in ego was the extent to which one had not apprehended the connection and unity of all things: hence, death was regarded as annihilation.

The egoistic fear of death was contrasted with Hindu and Buddhist philosophies. The latter emphasized existence as an original necessity, rather than an accidental creation, in which the fact of one's individual existence necessarily implied accepting the infinite time and infinity of changes that preceded it. 'Every possible state has already exhausted itself without eliminating' the possibility of one's individual's existence. Similarly, this 'immanent proof of the imperishableness of our real inner nature' (the 'will') must show that if we were to live in a happy state this would have already occurred in the infinity of time that has elapsed. Conversely, we should have ceased to exist if we could have.[55] '"I perish, but the world endures," and "The world perishes, but I endure," are not really different at bottom.'[56] Schopenhauer compared this idea with the Buddhist conception of nirvana as 'nothingness'; he also frequently used the famous Upanishadic declaration *tat tvam asi* ('Thou art that!') to show the imperishable identification with the universe that existed ('will') and which, in the same way, was also 'void'. For the Indian, dissolution is preferable to humanist subjecthood and its fears of suffering, death, annihilation, which, for the Indian, have been transcended.

Schopenhauer's discussion of 'metempsychosis after the critique of Kant' contained at its core an endogenous dimension to Schopenhauer's strong attachment to Hinduism and Buddhism that is often glossed (together with his misogyny) in the English Schopenhauer literature. It is stated clearly in his laudatory discussion of Anquetil's Oupnekhat. Schopenhauer was very much aware that suspicions had been raised about the veracity of Anquetil's translation, especially since direct translations from Sanskrit sources of the Upanishads and parts of the Vedas were available in Europe. Schopenhauer rejected these in preference for Anquetil's translation:

> how thoroughly redolent of the holy spirit of the Vedas is the Oupnekhat! . . . From every page we come across profound, original and sublime thoughts, whilst a lofty and sacred earnestness pervades the whole. Here everything breathes the air of India and radiates an existence that is original and akin to nature.[57]

Schopenhauer, however, immediately followed it thus: 'And oh, how the mind is here cleansed and purified of all Jewish superstition that was early implanted in it, and of all philosophy that slavishly serves this!' For Schopenhauer, Judaism was culpable for the philosophy of the blind 'affirmation of the will-to-live' that he detested and that he found in Christianity and in the philosophies that existed in his day (such as Hegel's). Schopenhauer contrasted 'the Sublime' Oupnekhat with other translations of Indian texts he had read. With some exceptions, such as August Wilhelm von Schlegel's translation of the Bhagavad Gita, and Colebrooke's translations of sections of the Vedas, most 'had the opposite effect on me'. Schopenhauer complained about the 'padding' to the original texts, 'wherein I notice something foreign'. The texts were Europeanized, Anglicized, 'Frenchified'. 'Only too often is there in them also a trace of the *foetor Judaicus*.'[58]

The phrase '*foetor Judaicus*' (and 'the Jew's pitch') occurs many times in Schopenhauer's work. It is a potent, heavily overdetermined symbol of medieval anti-Semitism in which the 'foul stench' of Jews was 'punishment' for their 'crimes' against Jesus and against Christianity. It evokes both the host desecration libel and the blood libel in which, respectively, Jews were alleged to have desecrated Christian churches to recrucify Christ, and Jews were alleged to kill and drink the blood of Christians in the belief that it would eliminate the fetid odour. The *foetor Judaicus* was contrasted with 'the odour of sanctity' emanating from the Christian body. *Foetor Judaicus* is also at the core of the anti-Semitic symbolization of the Jew as disease, parasite, filth and the source of death. *Foetor Judaicus* represented for Schopenhauer a contingent, historical and foreign contamination by 'Jewish metaphysics' of an authentic, pristine and primal wisdom that arose in India. Schopenhauer indeed bemoaned 'the great misfortune that the people whose former culture was to serve mainly as the basis of our own were not, say, the Indians or the Greeks, or even the Romans, but just these Jews';[59] one of his many such expressions.

If Voltaire can be said to have legitimized (though not initiated) an Enlightenment polarization between the civilizational arche-histories of the Hindu-Buddhist and the Judeo-Christian, *within which* modern European civilization must be compelled to find for itself a place in history, Schopenhauer refined this polarization with a second hauntology of the death and putrefaction of Western civilization that leaves Judaism isolated in the history of the world. This was because Christianity, according to Schopenhauer, also had 'Hindu blood in its veins' and was 'Indian in spirit'. In the figure of Adam, Christianity symbolized nature. In the original sin, it symbolized 'the affirmation of the will-to-live'. However, Christian teaching also symbolized 'freedom as the kingdom of grace' and of grace or salvation coming, unwilled, from outside to one's apprehension or intuition. This for Schopenhauer was that very 'denial of the will-to-live' of which Christ was the personification, and which was abundant in the *philosophia perennis* of Hinduism and Buddhism. Those who rejected this view of Christianity were clinging to a 'Jewish doctrine of faith' that was an accidental accretion to its original teachings and of which they must be purified. Schopenhauer made frequent and unambiguous contrasts between Hinduism and Buddhism (and those aspects of Christianity that he thought accorded with them) and Judaism (and Islam); the Brahmins and Buddhists against the Jews. Schopenhauer did indeed believe that Jesus must have been Indian.

Schopenhauer provided a philosophical grounding for an anti-Semitic mythology of 'the worldliness of the Jew' and the 'Jewish' denial of life after death, the latter contrasted with the *other* worldly, 'immortalizing' philosophies of the East. He thus revitalized a polarization that was even, though just, in his lifetime to find aesthetic fulfilment in Wagner's appropriation of Schopenhauer's philosophy, and that was to find its way into Dietrich Eckhart's metaphysics of the 'Jewishness *in* and around us' that had to be identified, replaced with a different conception of Being-in-itself, identified ultimately with Being-in-nature. Schopenhauer's conception of Being as prior to sufficient reason, and hence Being as pre-ontic and having the capacity to be in some way pre-ontological through its displacement of the 'will-to-live', was to have different resonances in the later German Idealist project that was to elaborate a relation between *Dasein* and ancestral *Volk*.

THE 'NOUMENAL HINDU' IN POSTCOLONIAL THEORY

The path elaborated above from Voltaire and Herder through Hegel and into Schopenhauer is an attempt at a strategically provocative rewriting of the accepted place of what was conceived as 'Indian' or 'Hindu' civilization in Europe during Enlightenment. The narrative can also be read as a scurry through the philosophy of a primordial cultural hearth, of ancestral blood communities, of the authority of 'race', of the philosophy of lost unity, the inevitability of history, and the metaphysics of will and of dissolution that results in an identification of one's primordial being with a community of others or with cosmic nature. Some of these philosophical tendencies were a prelude to (were they necessary for?) National Socialism.

The article concludes with a strategic interpretation of a few claims of postcolonial theory in Gayatri Spivak's writings.[60] The focus of the discussion below is about some of the claims that postcolonial theory has advanced about humanism, subjecthood, and the 'ineffability' within humanist discourse of non-European or non-Western or genuinely subaltern 'livedness'. Postcolonial theory can make the explicit or metonymic assertion that it is the most sophisticated and indeed theoretically the only immanent and sustainable critique of Western imperialism and colonialism that can also maintain a persistent critical vigilance against collusion with either Western, claimed 'nativist' or diasporic identitarian epistemologies, the latter two bearing a catachrestic relation to the nineteenth-century nationalist, colonial or humanist episteme of their European adversary. The methodological manoeuvre in deconstruction which can rigorously interrogate the excessive to meaning in rationalist, humanist, or logocentric discourse is characteristically utilized by Spivak to create a theoretical space to argue for the excessive nature of the 'genuinely subaltern', the 'Third World', or 'Hindu polytheism' or the gendered not-yet-subject for any Eurocentric or Western humanism that cannot recuperate these into discourse, certainly not into any kind of stable 'positivity' within humanism, within which they are always in-themselves unspoken or unheard.

Spivak's condensation of 'the Enlightenment' into a project of 'science and truth'[61] and her theoretical investment in claiming that there was no (German or European) comparative philosophical project is a *stratagem* which needs to be sustained in order to make certain foundational arguments about Orientalism, colonial discourse, postcolonialism and 'decolonized space'. However, the association of primordial 'India' or Indian philosophy with reason cannot be conceived as liminal, let alone a foundational difference, nor is there a completed and concluded, irreducibly European (undifferentiated) subject of reason and humanism that can be contrasted with its obstinate antipode, (the not-yet-subject of) India or Hinduism. Something like a project of 'comparative philosophy' was also important in the eighteenth and nineteenth centuries. Not only did a form of 'comparative philosophy' exist in its own right, as well as through its sometime adjacent ventures (such as philosophical anthropology), but it can be difficult indeed to comprehend the better-known eighteenth- and nineteenth-century 'comparative sciences' of philology and mythology without recourse to the resources of the former. For Voltaire, and in different ways for Herder and Schopenhauer, the subject of humanism or reason was not essentially European. For Schopenhauer, indeed, the subject of reason was not 'the Jew' ('Reason does not belong to Judaism'), but the Indian, who had both comprehended and surpassed reason. Even Hegel, in conceding an abstract philosophy of Being to the primordial Indian, seems to imply within the terms of his own philosophy its coming into reason.

The reduction of Enlightenment to a project of science and truth is also problematic. Voltaire's *œuvre* cannot be placed in solely rationalist, scientific or Romantic camps. It would be as difficult to situate Schopenhauer's 'completion' of the Kantian and Humean project, and his philosophy of the natural sciences, through a different idea of lost unity derivable from the Upanishads or the elite Buddhist canon. To affix the label 'Romantic' or 'anti-rationalist' to Schopenhauer's philosophy would be seriously misleading – and there are tendencies that would make this association *only* because of Schopenhauer's interest in the East, such that the philosophies of the East can only be prefigured as 'Romantic'.

If the perceived antagonism in the relation between Enlightenment and Romanticism is muddied, a range of other analytical directions become possible and allow for a consideration of the differentiated places of non-Europeans in the European idea of founding civilization and cultural hearth. The question, then, becomes one about the inadvertent complicity with European *and non-European* discourses of civilization, culture and elite. There are parallels between eighteenth-century Enlightenment and 'Romantic' discourse and the contemporary critiques of the latter that share an investment in what is essentially the possibility of a modified recovery of Indian civilization. Its cost is the effacing of the 'people without cultures' and the 'cultures without civilization'. If one wants to put it in those terms, 'the figure' of the complex and differentiated 'Indian' other is kept intact for the academic gaze precisely because its study elides the 'cannibals' of Tierra del Fuego and New Zealand, the 'Aborigine' of Australia or the Andaman Islands, or the German colonial subjects in 'Tanganikya', Namibia or Togo. A subjected marginality is required for an authoritative discourse of the *other civilizations* that can be framed within a critique of Europe but can also sanction the idea of civilizational timetables.

With very few exceptions, the exteriority of 'the sub-Saharan African' or 'the Aborigine' sustained the tabula of the scale and reach of civilizations and the philosophies of civilizational time they entailed, and which were virtually universally written about in the world histories, philosophical anthropologies and philosophies of history that were fashionable in the eighteenth and nineteenth centuries. The condition of demarcation as an elite civilization was the basis of appropriation into the timetables of historical development, genius or stagnation.

It can also be a small step from stating that the Hindu texts encountered in the West were so grossly distorted as to be meaningless to claiming that they were *tabula rasa*. This is an innocence that continues to be maintained by the memory of the suffering of colonial victimhood and now neo-imperialism. The substantive content of the Hindu text becomes irrelevant in the face of its Western appropriation or distortion. The Hindu text is unwritten at the moment of its colonial appropriation. Alternatively, there is a founding incommensurability from a European hermeneutic gaze, and hence Hindu writing is always invisible. Perhaps the text has been so radically misapprehended that it is nothing more than a new creation that is in its entirety European.

However, the actual texts that informed eighteenth- and nineteenth-century Europe were primarily renderings of the foundational, mainly northern Indian, Sanskrit, Vedic and Vedantic elite Brahminism (but could also include the texts of northern Indian Vaishnavaite sectarian traditions). The representation in the seventeenth, eighteenth or nineteenth centuries of the actual Brahmin of India, rather than the philosophies of 'his' primordial ancestors, is more complicated, ranging from complete revulsion to a sometimes highly qualified respect to almost adoration. The aspects of Hinduism that were usually monstrous to the European imagination were, in the main, aspects of *bhakti*, *tantra*, *shudra*, *dalit*, *adivasi* and various southern Indian texts, beliefs and practices (but could also include elite and non-elite sectarian, primarily Shakta and Shaivite, traditions). With some Dionysian exceptions, the European preference was for Sanskritic, Brahminic world-views of which the others were seen as, and were genuinely though differentially, subordinate. Caste, hierarchy, ideas of nobility and purity, and varieties of Rig Vedic and Manusmriti xenology and ethnology were read by Europeans both into and out of the Hindu corpus. Many of these ideas were archaic but foundational legitimations for existing caste and gender domination. It can be accepted that Brahminic, but by no means only Brahminic, texts contained very important philosophies. It can also be accepted that there existed processes of European distortion that might have been unauthorized in every sense by the texts. However, while an antagonistic corrective to the fabrication and denigration of elite Indian texts within European discourse may be a necessity, as would a critique of the persistent charisma of Christianity in Western philosophy, these critiques can only be sustained on the basis of a complicity with elite cultural and civilizational claims within Hinduism. Do archaic, nineteenth-century or contemporary Hindu conceptions of *dasyus*, *dasas*, *mleccha*, *varnashramadharma*, *jati*, *dharma* and *adharma*, *stri-dharma*, *sati*, ethical systems founded on ideas of 'nobility', 'purity' or 'the will to action', or the social and political systems authorized by the Manudharmashastra or the Arthashastra become innocent at the moment that it is established that they were subject to Western humanist recuperation, distortion or invention? Does *arya* become harmless at the point at which it is demonstrated that its racial inflexions were fabricated in nineteenth-century Britain or Germany?

Postcolonial theory can paradoxically magnify this elite comparative civilizational quest even while it can claim to undertake a critique of Indian elites. Spivak has certainly come very close indeed to confirming the unique and special nature of elite Hinduism which cannot be brought into a ('maximally tracing', presumably universal-humanist) discourse that is claimed to be based on Semitic conceptions of the religious.[62] In criticizing the Christian or monotheistic frame from which Jean-Luc Nancy elaborates the relationship (or lack of) between philosophy and the body after 'the death of God', Spivak counterposes what she calls the 'everyday polytheism' of Hinduism, as well as the irrecuperability in Western humanist or Eurocentric discourse of the livedness of 'everyday Hinduism', and of what she claims is otherwise mistakenly called in Western discourse the distinction between *dvaitin* as 'dualist' and *advaitin* as 'non-dualist'. There is no theoretical or polemical system or vocabulary, she claims, within which the dense livedness of 'everyday Hindu polytheism' or of *dvaita-advaita* (dualism/non-dualism) can be made available. 'Everyday polytheism' is only capable of being brought meaningfully into Western discourse as the anecdote of a 'native informant' constituted in Western humanism, though this manoeuvre only confirms its ineffability. Academics in India are (rather startlingly) also criticized for being unwilling or unable to take on such tasks.

Spivak also contrasts the 'expansiveness' of Nancy's conception of 'corpus' with a Derridean 'concentration', a dense focus at the limit of contradiction, which she applies to what she says were articulated reductively in Western humanist discourse as the abject victims of the devastating cyclone that hit Bangladesh in 1991. In the ecological, spatial world-view of the inhabitants of the coastal areas of Bangladesh, subject to the patterns and cycles of the forces of nature, living what seems to be articulated by Spivak as a happy existence congruent with nature, the conceptual humanist schemes of disaster relief or the necessity of migration, refuge, property and aid are ineffable. Their lives can be articulated in humanist discourse only at the risk of not hitting the contradiction with that discourse which is their everyday, lived 'eco-logic'. It is striking here that Spivak institutes a naturalized ecology of the subaltern as the basis for its epistemological incommensurability with Western humanism.

There may not be much to disagree with in a critique of the Christian frame of and metaphors within Nancy's discussion. However, there are complex ethical commitments when it is done in the name of some (whatever) kind of Hinduism. Christianity and Christian or, for that matter, Islamic monotheism are not foreign to India (and were not so prior to the colonial period); to institute that division in the 1990s between a grounded Hinduism and an imperializing (Christian or Islamic) monotheism is troubling, even though Spivak makes the declaration of her opposition to what she calls Hindu communalist 'identity politics'.

Spivak also utilizes that old bifurcation between Hinduism and the Judeo-Christian-Islamic traditions to sustain a critique of the subject of Enlightenment rationality and humanism which, for some philosophers of Enlightenment, was formed precisely through the same division, but with India marshalled on the side of reason. It may be accepted that this was an entirely Western project. However, what is to be made of the similarities between the Hegelian and the postcolonial theoretical vision of the Indian as only impossibly articulated within a European humanist or rational subjecthood?

Spivak's claim about the necessary academic unfulfilling of aspects of Hinduism, such as the 'livedness' of *dvaitin* and *advaitin*, also requires sweeping away the historic indigenous and wide-ranging elite caste discussions in India which have come down to us as *dvaita–advaita* commensurabilities and distinctions, and which have preoccupied various strands of Indian Vedantic philosophy since at least the early medieval period. Similarly, the use of the term 'everyday' cannot elide the circumstance that discussions of the ethical systems of the Upanishads and the Gita were 'everyday' discussions primarily for elite Brahmins.

Postcolonial theory has become an important pedagogic source, often and disastrously the main source for Western academics and students for their knowledges about historical and contemporary India. While postcolonial theory often performs critical gestures about elites in the Third World or the diaspora, their status is not clear, because the disciplinary focus and indeed most of its material tend to focus on either highly elite mainly Brahminic, Sanskritized, Vedic, Vedantic and already comprehensively Hinduized Indian traditions. The erasure of the 'Indian Muslim' in this work might even be viewed as a gesture.

Today, the phrase 'Hindu *dharma*' is a deadly one, inseparable from the civilizational claims in which it is manifestly embedded. The claim that one can attempt to use Hindu *dharma* as the basis for a different, non-Western ethical project, untainted by the Semiticized Hinduism of the nineteenth century, unmarked by communalist claims, still has unique conditions of possibility unmistakably indebted to northern Indian Vedic or Vedantic Brahmin traditions in their attempts to create a singular *dharma*. That claim has also been an explicit component of the elitist projects of northern Indian Brahminism (since at least the mid-nineteenth century), as well as of varieties of caste-Hindu and *sampraday* devotion that have already prefigured the place within or outside Hindu *dharma* of women, *sudras* and *dalits*. One can certainly argue against these conceptions of *dharma* for a progressive ethical *dharma*, but at the cost of the erasure of irreducibly secular possibilities, the latter in an important sense inconceivable in posthumanist postcolonial theory. This is aside from that other hard rock: Hindutva neo-fascists have been making this same proposal about Hindu *dharma* in relation to Western ethical systems since at least the 1920s in a totalitarian project that also conceives Hindu ontologies to be exceptional, hermeneutically irrecuperable and for which there can be no full understanding in a Western discourse from which they will persistently slip away.[63]

The idea that there is a primal ineffability of (what is now known as) Hinduism or the world-view of the Hindu in the face of Western philosophical or Judeo-Christian traditions is also a comprehensively European, Enlightenment claim. It is positively articulated in Hegel's conception of the Indian philosophy of pure Being-in-itself that cannot be fully conceived in the terms of subjecthood or practical determinateness available to Western philosophy. It is stated differently in the 'will-lessness' and 'extinction' that were imperative for Schopenhauer's philosophy. It is a Schopenhauerian claim that Hindu and Buddhist philosophical systems are precisely unsignified or incommensurable in those Western philosophies based on the Judeo-Christian or reflective philosophical tradition for which the subject is unmistakably European. The Hindu desires to slip away from the world of subject, object and representation. Spivak's valorization of the incommensurable and hard contradiction of the ecological, nature-driven world-views of the ordinary populations living in flood areas against the Bangladeshi doctors and relief workers who can only articulate them in terms of humanist subjecthood also has systematically Western conditions of philosophical and cultural possibility. For these coastal populations, there is no 'death' of the kind conceived in humanism, despite the horrors nature inflicts on them. They live with(in) nature, indifferent or unreceptive to a humanism that is forcibly attempting to compel them to subjecthood. This is the other side of Herder's unresolved eco-logic of nature, that exhalation of nature in culture that demarcates a people as epistemologically distinctive, even as the *Humanität* imposes its understanding on their lives and actions. It is also there in Schopenhauer's 'denial of the will-to-live' that identifies an aporetic cosmology and a different relation to death and nature. Here the distinction between posthumanism and anti-humanity dissolves, for Schopenhauer's Hindu or Buddhist, as much as for the victims of cyclones.

ACKNOWLEDGEMENT

This essay was first published in *Radical Philosophy*, 100, March/April 2000. It is reproduced here (with minor amendments) with permission. I would like to thank John Solomos, Kirsten Campbell, Parita Mukta and Jane Hindley for their comments.

CHAPTER 4

Race and Language in the Two Saussures

ROBERT J. C. YOUNG

Literary theorists are accustomed to talking about the two Saussures – in the sense of the author of the *Course in General Linguistics* (1916; given 1907–11) and the altogether stranger author of *Words upon Words*.[1] In *Words upon Words*, Saussure attempted to prove that the acronyms of individual authors were concealed in the letters of the lines of Latin poetry. He never, however, solved the problem that the effects he was analysing could have been simply random – a mirror image, curiously, of the argument with respect to the arbitrariness of the signifier in the *Course*. In the latter he attempts to create a concept of language detached from individual determination, as well as biological or psychological origins in race and nation; in the former he attempts to turn the language of poetry into an acronymic instantiation, unconscious or intentional, of its authorial origins. There is also a third, almost forgotten Saussure, the professional academic Sanskritist whose major work in this area consisted of the analysis of vowel and case variations in Sanskrit texts.[2] While general claims have been made that some of the major ideas of Saussure's *Course* were derived from the Sanskrit grammarians, Ananya Vajpeyi's detailed demonstration of their relation has shown that the issue cannot be separated from the larger and more complex question of the role of Sanskrit in enabling the formation of Historical Linguistics and Comparative Grammar as a discipline in the first place.[3] These internal differences within Saussure's work are themselves repeated externally as the differences between two actual Saussures, the well-known linguist Ferdinand de Saussure, and his rather lesser known brother, Léopold.

FERDINAND (1857–1913)

Of all Saussure's ideas, that of difference has perhaps been the most influential beyond his own realm of linguistics, and remains central to many current notions of ethnic and gender identities. What is remarkable is that Saussure, in the context of the late nineteenth and early twentieth centuries, should have formulated a notion of difference as performative – difference without positive terms, as he put it – when the context in which he was writing was so replete with notions of difference as a positive term, that is, difference as the basis of the gap between core material identities. This is what he says:

> Everything that has been said up to this point boils down to this: in language there are only differences. Even more important: a difference generally implies positive terms between which the difference is set up; but in language there are only differences *without positive terms*.[4]

However, at the same time, Saussure also suggests that when the two negative differences of signifier and signified are put together in the sign, 'their combination is a positive fact'. Signs are 'positive terms' composed of two negative differentials: 'When we compare signs – positive terms – with each other, we can no longer speak of difference . . . two signs, each having a signified and a signifier, are not different but only distinct. Between them is only *opposition*.'[5] Signs are, then, distinct rather than different. Though the sign, one might say, gives the appearance of substantive difference, in practice it is only constituted, by a double negative, as opposition. This corollary to Saussure's theory, which leads us back to what Jindrich Toman characterizes as 'the stiff Saussurean world of antinomies', has been neglected in contemporary theorizations of difference for which Saussure remains an ultimate reference point.[6] In simple terms, it means that identity, for example, would be oppositional rather than differential, which would challenge some of the thinking associated with contemporary identity politics. Moreover, difference itself is predicated on an idea of a system that is impersonal and not amenable to individual choice, which refuses any assumption that it can form the basis for a personalized model of individual identity. Nevertheless, it does remain a non-essentialist account.

Saussure's emphasis on the value and meaning of language resulting from its form not its substance was made in the context of a highly political agenda among his contemporaries. One of the main objects of the *Course* was in fact to remove the study of language from its politicized role in cultural analysis.

Saussure was the founder of linguistics as an autonomous discipline precisely because he ruthlessly excluded all considerations other than linguistic ones. In particular, he detached the study of language from any identification with or considerations of race, in a context in which philology was still being used for a variety of cultural-political purposes. Since William Jones had first suggested, and Franz Bopp elaborated, the idea of an Indo-European language family, as a result of their encounter with a Sanskrit previously unknown in the West (as has already been mentioned, Saussure himself was a Sanskrit scholar, like many nineteenth-century historical philologists, for example, Nietzsche) the idea of the Indo-Europeans as a superior civilizing race, derived in part from the irresistible implications of the metaphor of the family and tree, had been promoted by linguists such as Ernst Renan in France, and the German Max Müller in Britain.[7] Max Müller was particularly influential in the middle of the century in promoting a general notion of an Anglophone Aryan culture founded, ultimately, on linguistic evidence. His extreme position in this respect was represented by his defence of the British occupation of India on the grounds that it represented a second Aryan invasion.

However, the rise of a corporeal ethnology, racial science, increasingly made the simple identification of language and race more problematic. In the face of the growing German nationalism evident in the Franco-Prussian war of 1870, in later life both Renan and Max Müller began to backtrack on one – perhaps the most powerful – version of the language and race equation, that is the absolute identification of language and nation. Saussure describes the correlation of nationality with language as one of the fundamental mistakes of the earliest Indo-European scholars.[8] Given that he was himself Swiss, a citizen of a country which, as he put it, allowed 'the coexistence of several [linguistic] idioms', it is easy to see that Saussure might have reasons for being out of sympathy with this notion so dear to cultures such as the French and the German that have striven for linguistic unity. Saussure, however, went much further than criticism of any intrinsic link to the nation. It is equally a mistake, he insists, to go so far 'as to see language as an attribute, not of the nation, but of the race, in the same way as the color of the skin or the shape of the head'.[9] In a remarkable section on 'Language and Race', he insists that any identification between the two is 'largely an illusion':

> It would be wrong to assume that a common language implies consanguinity, that a family of languages matches an anthropological family. The facts are not so simple. There is, for instance, a Germanic race with distinct anthropological characteristics: blond hair, elongated cranium, high stature, etc.; the Scandinavian is its most perfect example. Still, not all populations

> who speak Germanic languages fit this description . . . Consanguinity and linguistic community apparently have no necessary connection and we cannot draw conclusions from one and apply them to another.[10]

In one simple assertion, Saussure dismisses almost a whole century of philological assumptions, including those of his own teacher and mentor, Adolphe Pictet, who had sought to affiliate language and race. However, notice that his objection is focused on using evidence of the one in relation to the other, not against the notion of race as such, a concept to which he evidently fully subscribes, but on exclusively scientific physiological grounds. (I do not use the term 'pseudo-scientific' because it makes us too complacent about our own science. Commentators who use the term, moreover, seem to be unaware that certain forms of racial science still constitute an element in contemporary medicine and human physiology.) In the same vein, Saussure also denies that linguistic changes have any relation to other historical events, such as political upheavals, though he allows that the effects of discontinuity produced by historical acts such as colonization can play a role in accounting for linguistic differences.[11] Saussure's emphasis on arbitrariness, so famous in his account of the sign, which he himself derived from Whitney and which in fact can be found as far back as Locke, works right through his account of linguistic change, and demonstrates the influences of a Darwinist evolutionary perspective: language is a self-enclosed institution, whose processes involve arbitrary, not organic, changes and in which characteristics endure by 'sheer luck' ('*un effet du hasard*'). '*Change itself* . . . in short, the instability of language', Saussure argues, 'stems from time alone'.[12]

More striking still than this detachment of language from race is Saussure's argument, in an apparently modern form, that while race is not necessary for a linguistic community, language does possess another kind of unity, 'constituted by the social bond: *ethnisme*', a word variously translated as 'ethnic unity' and 'ethnicity'. This word was in fact invented by Saussure himself, and seems to have been a nonce word, in that the only French dictionary that includes it, the *Trésor de la langue français*, cites Saussure's definition as its only example.[13] The dictionary defines it, alongside Saussure's definition, as an 'ensemble of bonds which unites groups of individuals sharing a common socio-cultural inheritance, particularly language'. The closest current term '*ethnie*', which first appeared in *Larousse* in 1930, is defined as 'a group of human beings who possess, more or less for the most part, a common socio-cultural heritage, particularly language', with an example from 1956 making the distinction between race and ethnicity. *Robert* defines '*ethnie*' as a 'mass of individuals who share a certain number of traits of civilization, notably the community of language and culture', illustrating it with an example which distinguishes between race, nation, and '*ethnie*'.[14] As Engler's edition of the original student lecture notes from which Saussure's *Course* was reconstituted by its editors makes very clear, Saussure himself made no such distinction, but rather identified the two:

> Another observation. If it is immediately assumed that language is something geographically diverse, should one not regard it as ethnically diverse? This question is very complex. The idea of race is mixed up with this difference noted in speech. Undoubtedly one could go beyond geographical diversity, but the relations between language and *ethnisme* is more complex.[15]

Language only operates as a characteristic of race, Saussure continues, when it persists through time. It is this condition of variation or non-variation through time that Saussure identifies with an 'ethnic' identity. In the published text of the *Course*, where Saussure's identifications between race and language have been carefully edited out, '*ethnisme*' is defined as the unity constituted by a social-political bond that makes the linguistic group. Saussure defines it as follows: 'Let us understand by this a unity based on the multiple relations of religion, civilization, common defence, etc., which spring up even among nations of different races and in the absence of any political bond.'[16] Even here, however, Saussure's definition is strikingly ambiguous and contradictory. The linguistic community first of all can be multi-racial, and can occur in the absence of any political bond: what is significant is that it should have a common civilization and religion. However, the word 'civilization' begs a lot of questions – what defines a civilization has never been easy to specify. The requirement of a common religion also seems problematic – does this exclude the French Protestants from the French linguistic community? And if '*ethnisme*' requires a common defence, this sounds like a version of a nation, but the possibility of the absence of any political bond also makes this equation unlikely. Saussure seems rather to be describing relatively small-scale local communities, somewhat on the model of a geographical region: communities who will share a common language and local culture. From his emphasis towards the end of the *Course* on the ways in which a language, such as French, is not uniform across a nation, but rather a mosaic of changing dialects whose characteristics overlap, this common language would involve a regional dialect with local accent, vocabulary and particular syntactic forms. Unless it describes this notion of a common dialect or language (Saussure argues that the difference between the two is hard to specify) Saussure's '*ethnisme*' remains something of a chimera, since he defines it in terms of a group constituted by a social bond which creates a language community, which then in turn, 'in a certain measure', creates ethnic unity.[17] Saussure's circular argument is thus that a social bond creates a linguistic bond, which creates an ethnic bond, which guarantees the relatively permeable boundaries of a language that then does not have to be defined in other than linguistic terms.

In making this argument for a social concept of ethnicity, rather than a biological concept of race, Saussure seems in certain respects strikingly modern, given that the term 'ethnic', in French as in English, was commonly used at that time as the adjectival form of race (and Saussure himself sometimes uses it in this sense); the term 'ethnicity' was not invented in English until 1953. Even today, the boundaries between race and ethnicity are still very fluid. However, Saussure is not using a notion of ethnicity as a more acceptable substitute for a discredited notion of race, as in the modern Western formulation, but as a concurrent alternative to it. In his invention of '*ethnisme*', Saussure is essentially following Whitney's argument that linguistics forms a part of the social rather than the natural sciences: the point was to find a social rather than a biological concept such as race in which to anchor language. Beyond that, his strategy is focused absolutely on his aim of removing the study of language from any other social and cultural considerations, in his promotion of language as a phenomenon worth studying in its own right and exclusively in its own terms. From Saussure's point of view, his significant argument is less in the detail of his theory of the sign, or in his account of the relation of language to ethnicity, than the 'fundamental argument' of his course in relation to his own discipline that '*the true and unique object of linguistics is language studied in and for itself*'.[18] His deliberately vague definition of '*ethnisme*' betrays the moment in which his account of language has to encounter the 'social bond' that gives it the unity to make up a *langue*. At this point, the purely formal analysis of 'abstract objectivism' has to encounter what, after Saussure, we might call 'the positive fact'.

Having accepted that linguistic unity predicates a social community of some sort, Saussure does his best to keep the two separate and to minimize any defining determining relation between the two. He suggests that language only rarely reveals minimal details regarding the nature of this 'common ethnic unity', and effectively rejects the whole project of 'linguistic palaeontology', associated with the work of the arch-Aryanists Adolphe Pictet, in his book *Origines indo-européenes. Essai de paléontologie linguistique* (1859–63), and Max Müller, who used language to reconstruct a whole racial history. In the 'Linguistic Type and Mind of the Social Group', Saussure similarly dismisses notions of the application of a race psychology to language, rejecting the idea that phonetic changes are caused by 'racial predispositions'.[19] He then reverses the perspective, to ask:

> Does language, even if it fails to supply much precise and authentic information about the customs [*mœurs*] and institutions of speakers, serve at least to characterize the mental type of the social group that speaks it? A popular notion is that a language reflects the psychological character of a nation. But one serious objection opposes this viewpoint: linguistic procedures are not necessarily determined by psychological causes.[20]

Saussure produces a series of examples to demonstrate his thesis that:

> the psychological character of a linguistic group is unimportant by comparison with the elimination of a vowel, a change of accent, or many other similar things that may at any moment revolutionize the relation between the sign and the idea in any language form whatsoever.

The determinations of languages and the classification of languages according to the 'procedures that they use for expressing thought', he contends, allow the linguist to 'draw no certain conclusions outside the domain of linguistics proper'.[21] Saussure concludes that:

> We now realize that Schleicher was wrong in looking upon language as an organic thing with its own law of evolution, but we continue, without suspecting it, to try to make language organic in another sense by assuming that the 'genius' of a race or ethnic group tends constantly to lead language along certain determined routes.[22]

These theses of arbitrariness and a negative account of difference thus all work in the service of an argument that is resolutely anti-biological, anti-historical and anti-psychological – as far as language is concerned at any rate.

LÉOPOLD (1866–1925)

What is notable about this whole argument is that it stands in direct contradiction to the fundamental basis of a book, published eight years earlier by Saussure's younger brother, Léopold de Saussure's *Psychologie de la colonisation française dans ses rapports avec les sociétés indigènes* (1899).[23] Léopold's book was an attack on the French colonial doctrine of assimilation that was derived, via the Revolution, from an Enlightenment belief in a common liberty, equality and fraternity for humankind. Despite the prevarications of French colonial politics, from Napoleon to Jules Ferry, this had remained the effective basis of

French colonial policy throughout the nineteenth century, and the foundation of the *mission civilisatrice* whose avowed aim was to bring the benefits of French culture, religion and language to the unenlightened races of the earth. There were many individual exceptions to this rule in actual practice, particularly in Indo-China, but it remained not only the general principle but also the generally agreed rule in French discussions of colonial policy.

There was a paradox contained within this policy: on the one hand, it was the most progressive, to the extent that it assumed the fundamental equality of all human beings, their common humanity as part of a single species, and assumed that however 'natural' or 'backward' their state, all native peoples could immediately benefit from the uniform imposition of French culture in its most advanced contemporary manifestation. On the other hand, such an assumption meant that this model had the least respect and sympathy for the culture, language and institutions of the people being colonized – it saw difference, and sought to make it the same – what we might call the paradox of ethnocentric egalitarianism. Increasingly, however, in the course of the nineteenth century, successive writers – to name only those writing in French – Joseph Arthur comte de Gobineau, in his *Essai sur l'inegalité des races humaines*, (1853–55), and Gustave Le Bon in his *Les Lois psychologiques de l'évolution des peuples* (1894), proposed the scientifically legitimated differentiation of the races into different types or species, whereby their differences were portrayed as absolute, so that education and other civilizing influences were useless or of limited value because of the intellectual and cultural differences, that is, incapacities of primitive peoples.[24] It was not to be until the very end of the century, however, that these arguments were developed as an attack on the whole basis of French colonial policy predicated on the Republican doctrine of assimilation and the transformation of natives into *evolués*. The person who made the strategic and significant move that effectively shifted French colonial policy in a different, racialized direction was none other than Léopold de Saussure, an officer in the French navy who by then had taken on French nationality. After the publication of his work on the psychology of French colonization, he spent the rest of his life devoting himself to research into Chinese astronomy, for which he was later praised by Jacques Lacan ('geniuses tend to pop up from time to time in that family') who himself characteristically then translated the Chinese astronomical system as defined by Saussure into an illustration of the 'affinity between the enigmas of sexuality and the play of the signifier'.[25] The links between astrology and Lacanian psychoanalysis were thus firmly established.

Léopold de Saussure himself found a different set of signifiers in the realm of national psychology by means of scientific racialism and its elucidation, as he put it, of 'the anatomical structures that distinguish the various races of men'.[26] This provided a basis for Saussure and others to attack the egalitarianism of a system of assimilation based on the philosophy of the rights of man. Léopold attacks the assumption of human equality and the fundamental moral and intellectual identity of humans everywhere; at the same time, he dismisses the *philosophes*' belief that all humans are derived from a single species. Léopold de Saussure broadly follows Le Bon's characterization of the differences of races according to a hierarchy of innate intellectual competence and achievement. He invokes the standard arguments for superior and inferior races as separate species.[27] As a corollary of this innate difference, he suggests that the assumption of the assimilation doctrine that that difference can be bridged through the imposition of the colonizer's culture constitutes its fundamental misconception, one which it has derived from the Christian missionaries:

> This commonality of origin throws light on the illusions of the assimilative school and on the transforming power it attributes to its program of action. It seeks to impose language and institutions absolutely in the same way missionaries seek to impose religious faith; that is to say, without opportunistic motives and with the conviction that this 'conversion' will suppress that sole cause of the inferiority of the native races, that it will regenerate and re-establish the equality they possess in themselves, in a latent state, as members of 'mankind'.[28]

Léopold goes on to suggest that because France's subject races are fundamentally different, then the imposition of French institutions, political and religious beliefs, and even the French language, will only cause them to degenerate in the colonial environment. Instead of translating the natives into Frenchmen, the natives' incapacity will translate French culture into more primitive forms. He illustrates this with a discussion of the effects of the colonial imposition of French education, institutions and the French language. Here his work overlaps directly that of his brother, but operates in the very mode that Ferdinand is trying to remove. Léopold argues that language 'is tied to the mentality of the race'. Specifically, the different linguistic forms of agglutination and inflexion correspond to a hierarchy that reflects the increasing mental powers and subtlety of reasoning of the people whose language it is. The imposition of French on a native people whose own language, and therefore mental capacity, has not developed further than, say, analogy will cause French to degenerate and regress into a bastardized creole, rather than develop the mental capacities of the natives to the level of the Aryan French.[29] Whereas assimilation theory sees differences between races as historical and cultural products resolvable through education, association theory sees them as innate, and unchangeable, constituting 'profound mental divergences which separate the races',[30] products of the different evolved physical capacities of the brain. At this point, Léopold moves into the realm of colonial psychiatry, with its theories of inherent native inferiority, against which Fanon reacted so strongly.

Although much of the book is concerned to demonstrate the futility of the assimilative project, the main basis of Léopold's argument is not to establish the absolute cultural difference of other races, which he regards as the established scientific fact of an evolutionary anthropology, but rather to conduct a psychological analysis of the French theory of colonization in order to explain why the French persist with the doctrine of assimilation in the face of its evident unsuitability and failure. In this perception, Saussure was right to the extent that assimilation as a policy, in Algeria, for example, was sometimes completely unworkable, given that the colonial state in fact operated, as Fanon pointed out, according to an apartheid structure. According to Léopold, the particular method of colonization adopted by individual European nations is 'imposed by the national character, by national sentiments and dogmas'. The real problem, he suggests, is not the dogmas as such but the hereditary psychological roots in the French people of a tendency to 'excessive centralization which necessarily results in uniformity',[31] a problem that he calls *classical latinism*. He explains this as follows:

> It is a tendency towards uniformity, simplicity, and symmetry. An antipathy for all that is disparate, complex, unsymmetrical. Born of certain Roman and Judaic traditions, cultivated by the monarchy, it became a mental habit in France, a hereditary ideal, and one of the principal characteristics of the race. It begat the genius of the French language, as it did later the metric system. By contrast, in creating an exaggerated need for simple and single formulas, it substituted principles for experience, theory for practice, fiction for a sense of reality. It has engendered the extreme centralization of the administration.[32]

By contrast, Saussure emphasizes the advantages of what he calls the system of 'association', the empiricist colonial method of the British and Dutch (he also, more improbably, includes the Romans). Here there are no illusions of equality, but a hard pragmatic calculation, which follows 'natural law', that the best way to deal with colonized nations is to leave as much of their native culture intact as possible, which the colonial rulers then control by proxy for the advantage of commerce and their own economic profit. The British, Saussure comments, keep themselves aloof from their colonized peoples, emphasizing their racial difference, a method fundamentally suitable for a situation not of colonization, in the sense of settler colonies such as Australia, but of exploitation colonies such as India and West Africa, where the colonial rulers, not out of cultural respect but out of a pragmatic sense of the cultural inferiority of the colonized, leave their culture well alone and make little attempt to impose European cultural values – merely introducing useful infrastructural material projects such as roads and railways. With the British and Dutch system we find the opposite paradox to that of the French assimilation policy, namely that the colonial method which according to modern perspectives seems more sympathetic, leaving indigenous cultures and peoples more or less as they found them, and not superimposing a colonial culture upon them, is ironically founded on the assumption that these people are so different from Europeans, so inferior, that there is really no point in trying to impose institutions or a language which is far too sophisticated and complex for the child-like native. 'The conquerors who have sensed the meaning of race', Léopold observes, have known perfectly how they should govern. At the same time, he expresses sympathy for and interest in the preservation of indigenous languages and cultures, a form of racialist cultural relativism that was in fact characteristic of such attitudes in the nineteenth century.[33]

Saussure's arguments were actively taken up at the International Colonial Congress of the following year (1900), and his views became widely and rapidly accepted in the France of the Dreyfus affair.[34] This facilitated a change of French policy whereby at best assimilation was seen as a long-term project of considerable duration. French colonialism remained a system in organizational terms, but was increasingly split in two between French and native subjects. Administratively, the cohesive uniform attitude continued: what was jettisoned was any residual sense of human commonality.[35] The doctrine that Léopold helped to initiate was unusual in the explicitness of its view of the foundation of colonialism on an always-continuing form of force and violence, and on a strict basis of racial hierarchy. This is Jules Harmand, in the classic work of twentieth-century French colonialism, *Domination et colonisation* (1910):

> The Right to True Empire Founded on Moral Superiority
>
> It is necessary, then, to accept as a principle and point of departure the fact that there is a hierarchy of races and civilizations, and that we belong to the superior race and civilization, still recognizing that, while superiority confers rights, it imposes strict obligations in return.
>
> The basic legitimation of conquest over native peoples is the conviction of our superiority, not merely our mechanical, economic, and military superiority, but our moral superiority. Our dignity rests on that quality, and it underlies our right to direct the rest of humanity.[36]

FERDINAND VS. LÉOPOLD

In the context of his brother's arguments, and those of his fellow-travellers such as Harmand (Léopold cites Harmand's earlier Preface to the translation of Sir John Strachey's *India* (trans. 1892) with approval), let us look again at Ferdinand de Saussure's notion of the linguistic community, as an '*ethnisme*' which was defined against any identification of language and race. Saussure, as I suggested, did not quarrel with the notion of race as such, and there is elsewhere evidence of racialism in Saussure's work: he makes the usual sorts of comments about savages and civilization common to most writers of his period,[37] there is evidence outside the *Course* to indicate anti-Semitism (such as his reading of the anti-Semitic journal *Libre Parole*);[38] and, as we have seen, he certainly accepts the findings of physiognomy with respect to corporeal differences. He also dismisses the attempt by Bopp, Bunsen and Max Müller to prove that the family of languages show the common universality of the human – Saussure argues that they in fact demonstrate 'absolute diversity' ('the universal kinship of languages is not probable')[39] – an argument which was certainly used by others in support of polygenetic theories of race. On the other hand, it is noticeable that Saussure's basic denial of the connection between language and race flatly contradicts Léopold's fundamental thesis of the effects of race psychology. He also contradicts Léopold's common racialist argument that the physical construction of the throat and larynx of the different races determined their ability to speak in certain ways.[40] Moreover, Ferdinand makes no suggestion of the different mental capacities of different races for different levels of linguistic development. In almost every respect, in fact, Ferdinand's definition of a linguistic community directly follows the non-racialist French colonial assimilation model. The stress on cultural and religious uniformity also corresponds to assimilation theory – in Algeria, the indigenous Algerians had to renounce Islam for Christianity in order to enjoy access to French legal rights (only a handful did). At one point, Saussure even seems to accept the fiction that assimilation is a peaceful process, not one of colonial violence as Harmand stressed. Discussing the case of territories that display multilingualism, Saussure comments that the phenomenon is usually the result of one language being superimposed on another, normally by invasion 'but', he adds, 'it may also come through peaceful penetration in the form of colonization'.[41] The homogeneity of a linguistic community, according to Saussure, is not the product of racial uniformity – indeed, a linguistic community can be racially diverse – but of its civilization, its religion, and (normally) its 'political bond'. Nor is it even the product of a geographical cohesion, as one might have expected Saussure to argue given the implicit homogeneity of his concept of *la langue*. A language, Saussure takes pains to argue, has no natural geographical boundary.

This raises the significant question of the relation of Saussure's linguistics to those of his brother Léopold. In his ground-breaking analysis of Léopold's 'colonial linguistics', John Joseph has argued that Saussure's notion of *langue*, as well as his account of 'ethnicity', can be interpreted as having affinities to certain of Léopold's and Le Bon's notions of race as a historical and psychological construction.[42] Saussure nevertheless ends the *Course* by denying the idea that the 'genius' of race or ethnic group can determine the development of language in certain directions. As Joseph points out, Saussure also firmly refuses the idea of language being the product of history in any direct way. Moreover, the emphasis on 'multiple relations' implies that it is not necessary for the system to be absolutely homogenous and bounded; it is open rather than closed and can clearly be made up of a variety of different elements in different degrees. The system is one that includes diversity: even unilingual countries, like France, he argues, display a diversity of dialects that is the product of temporal change and geographical diversity. France and Italy are geographically a gradual succession of dialects, differences that are only arbitrarily divided by national boundaries.[43] It is ethnic unity (*ethnisme*) which creates the cultural bonds that join linguistic communities, while conversely linguistic community 'is to some extent responsible for ethnic unity ('*unité ethnique*').[44] Whatever Saussure really means by '*ethnisme*', it is clearly supposed to represent a social category differentiated from the contemporary discourses of the biologism, psychologism and historicism of 'race', and thus an antithetical argument to that of his brother Léopold. It is also the point, as the problems interpreting what he means by '*ethnisme*' indicate, where Ferdinand has to touch upon the problematic realm of materiality and the social foundation of language which otherwise he wishes to deny.

So the two Saussures, though commonly steeped in, and accepting, the developments of contemporary anthropology, what is sometimes referred to as scientific racialism, and the evolutionary thesis of human difference, in fact stand on opposite sides with respect to colonial models. They have two different notions of difference, one based on organic substantive assumptions about racial (and hence linguistic) identity, and innate racial characteristics, the other based on an attempt to separate human languages, and indeed implicitly their cultures, from non-linguistic historical and psychological categories through a notion of difference that is one of form, not substance. What is striking about the positions of the two brothers is that, as I have suggested, they illustrate how the competing colonial models each stand on both sides of the moral equation – the first denying difference in the name of equality, and the second affirming difference in the name of inequality. I want now in conclusion to spell out some of the contemporary implications of this.

The French colonial theory of assimilation was essentially an extension of a model that was simultaneously applied internally to the state – the drive for centralization, as Saussure observes, has a long history in France. Either the King was trying to control the nobles, or the revolutionary government was trying to control the conservative provinces. The tight uniformity of a centralized administration was also part and parcel of the general Enlightenment assumption that a rational system could and should be uniformly imposed. French colonial policy was simply an extension of this (just as contemporary poststructuralism represents a challenge to its centrism in various forms). In the nineteenth century, for example, there was no colonial office because all the territories were constitutionally part of France – the colonies were simply France *d'outre-mer*. The assumption was that any people becoming part of France would be assimilated, and would wish to assimilate themselves, to this cultural uniformity. This colonial system was thus a logical extension of the system that had been set up internally for the state so as to achieve both equality and control within it. Assimilation constitutes one model of internal colonialism. Léopold de Saussure comments that this French doctrine also infiltrated the American Anglo-Saxon. Indeed it was practised very effectively by that colony which had itself become a state, and which looked to Enlightenment France for its political framework. What is now rather loosely called, and dismissed as, the ideology of the melting-pot, according to which all immigrants, wherever they come from and whatever their language, reconstruct their identities according to the American way of life in pursuit of the American dream, is nothing other than a home-spun version of the same assimilation model. Needless to say, this inclusiveness typically excluded those who were considered culturally too different, particularly native, African and Chinese Americans. US Immigration laws, until Bobby Kennedy's revolutionary change of quota criteria in 1965, followed the same presuppositions.

This model of American identity is highly contested today by minority groups who wish to assert their ethnic and racial cultural difference from the dominant culture, while at the same time arguing, in a sense paradoxically, that assimilation's promise of equality has not been made accessible to them. We want to be different where we are supposed to be the same, but we want to be the same where we feel we are different. It is often argued in postcolonial cultural writing, particularly emanating from India, that American postcolonialism has nothing really to do with the postcolonial, or the colonial, as such, and is really just about an identity politics which is of interest only to Western audiences. However, what the two Saussurean models show is that US postcolonial cultural writing, far from being caught up in the seductions of postmodern Western culture, doing its own thing in indifference to the very different conditions of the Third World, is in fact not really even postcolonial, but caught up in contesting the basis of a state which operates according to a colonial theory of assimilation. This is why the issue of English as the language of instruction in state education remains so significant.

This is true of the UK also. As Léopold de Saussure and others pointed out, the British had no interest in the idea of colonial assimilation (this was a position reinforced by the experience of the loss of the American colonies). However, although it was never practised as a theory – nothing in Britain ever gets as dangerous as that – assimilation was practised in fact. Faced with the contiguous territories of Ireland, Wales and Scotland, the British state performed a succession of acts of Union, most notably in 1707 and in 1800, whereby the trio of Celtic nations were all translated constitutionally into parts of the same British state and integrated within it. The paradoxes that resulted, with the Scots, for example, as Linda Colley has shown, being assimilated so fast in the eighteenth century that they began to run major portions of the British state, the army and increasingly the colonies, make for interesting complexities in the history of colonialism.[45] What we are seeing today at the political level of devolution, with a corresponding devolution back to individual nations regarded as relatively autonomous states overseen by the UK Parliament, is in fact a reversion, paradoxically, to the fundamental precepts of British colonial policy, where colonies were run effectively as separate and fairly autonomous states, overseen by the Colonial or India Office in London. It was on this basis that the claim for 'Home Rule' was first made in Ireland and in India. The final irony of this historical process is manifest in the slogan that has started appearing on walls and motorway bridges: 'Home Rule for England'.

Even though assimilation was never set up as a policy in Britain in the way it was in France, it remains the case that it is still assumed as the norm by much of the population. Objections to immigrants, for example, often centre on their apparent refusal to assimilate to the dominant culture. The colonial assimilation model remains dominant, but in contesting it with difference there is also a constant need to reassert its political values of sameness against the alternative German organic model of intrinsic, hierarchical difference – invoked typically by those who do not want assimilation at all, just to send immigrants 'home', which by implication is anywhere but here. This means that ethnic and other minorities in Britain who contest the uniformity of the state are in fact in the same position as those in the USA who are grappling with the internal version of the colonial assimilation model. As too are all those in postcolonial states who are struggling against the results of the assumption that a nation can only develop successfully through the processes of assimilation and the erasure of the differences of all minority cultures and their languages within it. To that degree there is much more of a correspondence between contemporary politics of activists in the North and the South, the West and the East, than is often claimed, and more of a rationale in bringing it all under the umbrella of a common term such as 'postcolonialism'. The paradox is that in challenging the model of assimilation for the nation, as a form of internal colonialism, minorities find themselves necessarily invoking a revised version of the same challenge issued by Léopold de Saussure, a hundred years ago, the object of which was the very opposite of their own political goals. To achieve that, it has been necessary to make a revision that extends Ferdinand's arguments about the nature of language into the realm of difference more generally, so that ethnicity can now be as ungrounded as language after Saussure. Saussure's arguments about language and ethnicity, however, are equally based on an assumption of ethnic and cultural uniformity that leads them back to the 'positive fact' of the communal bonds of the social – on which Saussure's logic ultimately depends even though his fundamental argument consists of the attempt to exclude it.

ACKNOWLEDGEMENT

I am grateful to the British Academy for providing me with research leave which enabled me to write this article. I also thank John E. Joseph for his advice and information about Ferdinand and Léopold de Saussure.

PART II

CHAPTER 5

Unspeakable Histories:
Diasporic Lives in Old England

BILL SCHWARZ

Becoming postcolonial – if that is, indeed, what has occurred – has required, and been triggered by, explicit and systematic encounters with prevailing philosophies of race and ethnicity. These encounters possess their own internal intellectual conditions of existence. Other chapters in this volume chart the complex cartographies of these internal intellectual movements. My own contribution is less concerned with the formal properties of particular propositions and more with some of the external or historical conditions which have underwritten recent attempts to rethink race and ethnicity. My concern is not to critique or deconstruct this or that theory, but rather to locate particular modes of thought within specific histories. It is to remind us of the not very startling proposition that abstractions, even the most abstract abstractions, have a life outside their own intellectual horizons, in a larger history.

More particularly, I focus on the idea – about which we have heard much in recent times – of the diasporic subject. Or more properly, I focus on one, late aspect of the idea; not on its strictly Judaic associations, but the later, black and deconstructive articulations of the contemporary moment.[1] The idea of the 'diasporic', in company with the cognate term 'hybridity', have entered the critical vocabulary of our age, so much so that a discernible reaction against them has gathered pace. The formal critiques can be followed elsewhere.[2] My purpose is to indicate how these ideas acquired new meanings and why – formal critiques notwithstanding – they proved serviceable. 'Serviceable' may suggest an insufficient intellectual rigour, smacking of the contingent and the provisional. But in so far as my survey carries with it an implicit defence of the idea of a diasporic subject, it does so in terms of a reasoning which is historical rather than formal. In the intellectual *disorder* of decolonization entire systems of thought were breached. The vocabularies which emerged from this turbulence remain in contention: in need, no doubt, of conceptual refinement. But there is a virtue in recalling the degree to which, even in the metropolises of the old colonial bastions, the 'disordering' of the colonial heritage was an intellectual as well as a political process, and that this represented an intellectual history which was not narrowly philosophical, in its restricted meanings, but organic and vernacular as well.

What follows can be seen as a kind of one-act dramatization of this larger, global and epochal history. I focus on England during the years of decolonization and their immediate aftermath. The story, as I see it, begins with Enoch Powell and his attempts – explicitly – to rethink race and nation in a postcolonial manner.[3] As I've suggested elsewhere, I believe Powell can be seen as Britain's first authentically postcolonial politician, albeit a postcolonial of the racist right.[4] As a response to the prevailing Powellite ordering of the public cultures of postcolonial England there arose – out of a seemingly repetitious, infernal history – a new set of historic possibilities created from precisely that indigenous black culture which felt itself to be most cornered. As one might expect, this had disparate manifestations: joyful, retrograde, creative, violent, confused. But in sum, an energetic movement gathered momentum through the 1970s and 1980s in which blacks in Britain confronted the structures of their exclusion. A powerful cultural renaissance occurred, specifically attuned to the peculiarities of English life, which only tangentially touched the formal institutions of political society. From the specificities of this historical experience, and from the social experience of immigration which preceded it historically, there emerged new means for conceptualizing the workings of ethnicity. Though these theories had been formed from a specific historical experience, they could also serve more general purposes – not only for the first-generation sons and daughters of black immigrants to Britain, but for the white inhabitants too. In a word, abstracting from the immigrant experience provided a way of imagining what England decolonized might look like. Different memories could come to life and interrupt historical patterns of repetition.

FOREVER ENGLAND?

Enoch Powell's speeches in the late 1960s and early 1970s (and, in a more vernacular idiom, the views of those who adhered to his cause) were organized by the conviction that an increasing number of non-white immigrants was bringing about the downfall of the nation. In part, this was an argument based on a perception that particular neighbourhoods were 'becoming black', and thereby ceasing to be English. In part, also, such views registered the anxiety that miscegenation, by more surreptitious means, was compromising the purity of England 'from within', defiling English womanhood and producing children who were 'neither one thing nor the other'. To many of those who complained about the presence of non-whites in the territorial space of the nation, loss of the capacity to imagine the nation was experienced as loss of self. What previously had been recognized as the *heimlich* transmuted into the *unheimlich*: 'the *unheimlich* is what was once *heimlich*'.[5] Everything which was once familiar seemed now to collude with the unfamiliar and with the unsettling. A zealous follower of Powell's put it like this, with admirable insight:

> Concepts once entirely and unthinkingly trustworthy – 'we', 'ours' and 'us', 'nation', 'history', 'heritage', 'destiny', 'character', 'culture', 'country', 'British' (for instance) and 'un-British', 'English' and 'un-English' – such concepts, and innumerable others, become opaque, or retain their meaning only by conscious (and often distorting) emphasis.[6]

Nothing remained in place, as a matter of trust. The single most prominent refrain in Powellite discourse was framed in terms of nation: the nation was 'losing its identity' or becoming a 'no man's land', even ceasing to be. Essentially, identity was experienced pre-eminently as national identity. In such circumstances it did not seem that, consequent upon the perceived loss or defeat of the nation, there existed the subjective means to re-negotiate an alternative individual identity. On the contrary, loss of nationhood appeared to represent the termination of subjective life itself: the end of the self.[7]

From such logics emerge authentically fundamentalist modes of thought. And such reasoning still provides apologists for Powell with the chance to mount a defence. His biographers are exemplary in this regard. First, Patrick Cosgrave:

> I record the view that Powell was right on immigration, and that the extraordinary reaction to the Birmingham speech had almost nothing to do with its simple statement about numbers. While he was accused of being racist, he was merely talking about identity; and it was for identity that people feared. He was attacked by people who wanted to be polyglot, people who would pretend (and often believe) that there was no serious difference of race, nor culture, nor creed, between the inhabitants of these islands and those leaving the Empire's successor nations to their own devices, and moving across the world to England.

> . . . Powell was stating the right to a British identity, one exclusive to the native inhabitants of these islands – exclusive both historically and geographically.[8]

And Simon Heffer, on Powell's April 1968 speech, remembered as his 'rivers of blood' address: 'it is a speech as much about Powell's sense of history and nation as about anything else. Sadly for him, it would be interpreted, by supporters and opponents alike, as being racial in motive'.[9]

These are curious readings indeed, readings which assume that 'merely talking about identity' or thinking about a nation's history precludes the possibility of racism. In such readings, identity and nation exist as transcendent categories, immune from the profanity of anything as vulgar as racism. But in the debates of these times, identity was not an attribute owned equally by black and white, or immigrant and host. White England, supremely, was centred: it possessed history, tradition, civilization in abundance. For its inhabitants, confirmation of belonging was so richly encoded in an infinity of banal rituals that to draw attention to the privilege of having such an identity could in many situations be regarded excessive, even vulgar. The black immigrant, on the contrary, had no history, or at least had none in the sense of having *made* it. His or her entitlement to possess an identity was commensurately precarious. In the popular imagination memories of the plantation intervened: from slaves everything had been taken, even their sense of self. Now – or so it seemed – history was being turned around. The black man was to have 'the whip hand', while the white man was to lose what history had bestowed upon him – not only his prowess, but his very being.[10]

This way of imagining the contemporary white predicament in the England of the 1960s and 1970s operated both by a complex conjunction of memory and forgetting, and by a series of displacements. From the late nineteenth to the early twentieth century, ideas of race, nation and empire increasingly became fused together. By the time of Powell and decolonization, race (especially) was spoken most fluently, by default, through memories of nation and empire. To talk of the loss of the nation was also therefore to speak the loss of whiteness. Everything turned on the apparently abstract notion of identity, in which belief in the absolute power of national provenance predominated.

We can see this being acted out in many different situations. One example is particularly instructive. In the summer of 1965 BBC television screened a discussion about sex and race. Approaching such a contentious topic directly confirmed that this public debate would be viewed as courageous and *frank*. Colin MacInnes, who was not shy about proclaiming the pleasures of sex between black and white, spoke as a white man. James Baldwin provided topicality, gravitas and a black voice. The discussion was chaired by James Mossman – a smart, well-informed BBC journalist, admirably liberal and free-thinking, the last person in the world to give credence to atavistic notions of racial superiority. Even so, this enlightened quest for truth soon turned to the enigma of black identity. Mossman was puzzled. He pressed Baldwin. 'But . . .', he persisted in his questioning, 'I still ask: who are you? You're clearly not an American in the ordinary sense of a White American, are you? You're not an American Negro; that's not an identity really.' To this Baldwin – always sceptical of what would later be termed identity-politics – replied in the only way left open to him: 'Then I can't answer it. I'm part of a totally incoherent people at the moment, of African origin, with Indian, Spanish and European blood in my veins. I'm part of a country which has yet to discover who and what it is.'[11]

Both Mossman and Baldwin were clear. For Mossman, there was the unquestioned authority of self-evidently 'ordinary' identity, informed by whiteness, by nation or by the combination of the two; anything other represented some kind of non-identity, of such unknowable provenance it could barely be put into words. For Baldwin, on the other hand, there was incoherence, plurality and possibility. Baldwin could *think* of the past, and hence the future; Mossman could only act it out. Baldwin's own words in *The Fire Next Time* must have seemed to him all the more urgent. Writing about whites in the USA he had said: 'They are, in effect, still trapped in a history which they do not understand . . . the danger . . . is the loss of their identity.'[12]

CONFRONTING UNREALITY

In these years there was, I believe, a deep symmetry between the fabrication of a particular historical memory (whose central component was organized around the agency of the white man) and a particular conception of identity (in which entitlement to identity was weighted ethnically, as well as by gender). Part of the dynamic of the postcolonial situation is the unravelling of these memories and of the consequent prescriptions about who possessed the capacities to be deemed a sovereign individual. This may be an abstract phenomenon, but it has a determinate history and, as we know to our cost, determinate effects. The indication of this in the English context may be illuminated by reflecting on some issues arising from a proposition suggested by Stuart Hall. This conceptual review may, in turn, alert us to a historical conclusion. If Powellism can be said to represent the moment when native Britons were first forced to confront the domestic consequences of Britain 'after empire', then there came, in reaction to the Powellite initiatives, a second postcolonial moment. This second moment turned, not on a reaffirmation of inherited histories, but on an idea of the future in which white Britons could imagine themselves to be at home in a nation which no longer colluded with ancient memories of a white man's country.

In 1987, in a talk at London's Institute of Contemporary Arts, Hall proposed that 'Identity is formed at the unstable point where the "unspeakable" stories of a subjectivity meet the narratives of history, of a culture.'[13] It might appear, if viewed sceptically, that this is intended to be read metaphorically or at least poetically. But I am not convinced that this is right. Hall's description of the issue is a potentially productive formulation open to empirical exemplification. There is a case to be made for taking Hall's conceptualization of identity literally – at least up to a point – and showing that it derives from a specific historical experience.

One ('postmodern') strand within contemporary cultural theory would like to see subjective identity as infinitely plastic, always open to re-invention from within, and – inhabiting a virtual world free from material, institutional constraint – given to endless mobility. In an attempt to explain the properties of this figure the image of the nomad has often been invoked, 'the nomadic' encapsulating the idea of postmodern itinerancy.[14] Although conceptions such as these have on occasion been attributed to Hall, he in fact sees things rather differently:

> the way . . . I'm trying to think questions of identity is slightly different from a postmodern 'nomadic'. I think cultural identity is not fixed, it's always hybrid. But this is precisely because it comes out of very specific historical formations, out of very specific histories.[15]

The 'very specific historical formations' are principally what concerns me here.

Hall made this claim in the course of an interview in which he considered his own formation as a 'diasporic' subject. A powerful theme emerging from these reflections is the necessary inter-connectedness of 'the public and the private self'. 'I could never understand', he says, thinking of the overarching issues of colonialism and postcolonialism,

> why people thought these structural questions were not connected with the psychic – with emotions and identifications and feelings because, for me, those structures are things you live. I don't just mean they are personal, they are, but they are also institutional, they have real structural properties, they break you, they destroy you.

He describes his own background as classically 'colonial', but demonstrates at the same time that his own intellectual and political world in Kingston in the

1940s, and that of his friends, prefigured the formalities of postcolonialism. He reconstructs the traumas and collapses which occurred inside his family life, demonstrating the degree to which 'classic colonial tensions were lived as part of my personal history': 'I was suddenly aware of the contradiction of a colonial culture, of how one lives out the colour-class-colonial dependency experience and of how it could destroy you subjectively.' He remembers the humiliations inflicted on his father, in the first moments of his entering the institutions of the white social world; and the reveries of his mother – thinking 'she was practically "English"' – based on the cultures of the old plantation world, 'with its roots in slavery, but which my mother spoke of as a "golden age"'. Hall rejected both these positions. As much as it would in any such situation, repudiation extracted emotional costs; but the pains involved were overdetermined by the colonial setting. 'You can see that this formation – learning the whole destructive colonized experience – prepared me for England.'[16]

These are, in part, memories of empire. They are centred on the idea of trauma and subjective collapse. They indicate their own 'unspeakabilities': the protracted effort to cast a public language of anti-colonialism; the interior costs of attempting to translate this public language into the private language of family and subjective life; the impossibilities of speaking race. Here indeed 'the "unspeakable" stories of a subjectivity' met the narratives of a larger history, that of colonialism. But these reflections are instructive historically as well as conceptually. In some of the memories of the *Windrush* generation, it can seem as if West Indians arrived in the United Kingdom bearing only loyalty to the crown and fascination for all the flummery of imperial England, a regard for the mother country which weakened as the realities of actually existing England impinged.[17] But this was only ever one dimension of the West Indian experience. As we can see from Hall's reminiscences – and from the writings of George Lamming as well as myriad others – the West Indian immigrant to Britain in the 1940s and 1950s came from societies which were already well advanced in the formal and informal prerequisites of breaking with colonialism.

Hall's was a particular experience, but not unique. Unspeakable experiences of colonialism could take many forms, in the colony and (for the immigrant) in the metropolis. Hall suggests that the full intensity of living a life of colonial subjection, in all its contradictory forms, broke into his imagination and into his consciousness as he was growing up in Kingston. He recognized – with 'sudden awareness' – that there was a problem which needed to be named, or spoken, and that he had to discover a means 'to be somebody else'. For other West Indians of his generation the sharpness of this recognition occurred not in the Caribbean, but in Britain, where they eked out a life less as colonial subjects than black immigrants. This transformation into black immigrant –

fixed from the moment the first steps down the gangplank at Tilbury or Southampton had been taken – also carried with it its unspeakable dimensions.

Hall's recollection about his own transformation into an immigrant is emphatic. The 'destructive colonized experience' *prepared him for England*. For his mother, the journey marked an affirmation of all that was properly inclusive and homely:

> My mother brought me, in my felt hat, in my overcoat, with my steamer trunk. She brought me, as she thought, 'home', on the banana boat, and delivered me to Oxford. She gave me to the astonished college scout and said, 'There is my son, his trunks, his belongings. Look after him.' She delivered me, signed and sealed, to where she thought a son of hers had always belonged – Oxford.

This sense of homely familiarity was not absent from Hall's own response, but his was, in contrast to his mother's, riven with ambivalence:

> Arriving on a steamer in Bristol with my mother, getting on to the train to come to Paddington, I'm driving through this West Country landscape; I've never seen it, but I know it. I read Shakespeare, Hardy, the Romantic poets. Though I didn't occupy the space, it was like finding again, in one's dream, an already familiar idealized landscape. In spite of my anti-colonial politics, it had always been my aspiration to study in England. I always wanted to study there. It took me quite a while to come to terms with Britain, especially with Oxford, because Oxford is the pinnacle of Englishness, it's the hub, the motor, that creates Englishness.[18]

The England imagined by means of literature, by those who did not know the country, worked as a common trope in colonial recollections, confirming the power exercised by the institutionalization of a *national* literature. Most of all, though, Hall's memories confront us with England as dream, a familiar imaginative world co-existing with a discrepant observable reality. This interior dislocation, in which England was both familiar and unfamiliar, homely and unhomely, perhaps even colonial and postcolonial, functioned as a kind of double consciousness. But from this position, as C.L.R. James had always maintained, there emerged the possibilities for a privileged viewpoint into the imaginative workings of England itself. As James said of West Indian immigrants in Britain:

> They will be intimately related to the British people, but they cannot be fully part of the English environment because they are black. Now that is

> not a negative statement . . . Those people who are in western civilization, who have grown up in it, but made to feel and themselves feeling that they are outside, have a unique insight into their society.[19]

As observers of this history we are most commonly asked to witness an unreality contrasted to prior imaginings based (in many instances) on no first-hand knowledge of the country at all. Yet it is, strangely, England itself that remains unreal, not the fantasized expectations of it. Derek Walcott explains this phenomenon in his own experience:

> I knew, from childhood, that I wanted to become a poet, and like any colonial child I was taught English literature as my natural inheritance. Forget the snow and the daffodils. They were real, more real than the heat and the oleander, perhaps, because they lived on the page, in imagination, and therefore in memory. There is a memory of imagination in literature which has nothing to do with actual experience, which is, in fact, another life, and that experience of the imagination will continue to make actual the quest of a medieval knight or the bulk of a white whale, because of the power of a shared imagination.[20]

LEARNING TO BE AN IMMIGRANT

The collective response of black West Indians in the 1940s and 1950s was particular. The proximity of the formal culture of the British Caribbean – in language, religion, schooling, sport, literature – to that of the metropolis was profound, registering not only in the official discourses of the various Caribbean islands, but also (in part) in authentic popular life. This is what C.L.R. James's *Beyond a Boundary* (published in 1963) is about: the cultural proximity and dissonance of colony and metropolis. Yet, as James well knew, the West Indian colonial culture also coexisted with a distinctively hybrid, vernacular indigenous culture, differing from island to island but containing many common elements.[21] Hybridity, these days, has come in for much censure, the sign (it seems) of critical chic at its most predictable; but in the context of the Caribbean nothing could be less contentious: for many years it has done little more than describe a known reality. Indeed, one of the sources for the inventiveness of vernacular West Indian culture has been its fusion of different histories (American, African, European) and different ethnic legacies, not least in James's native Trinidad. In this respect the Caribbean has signified hybridity and racial mixing. And it was *race* and racial impurity which distinguished the Caribbean from those other 'other Englands' transplanted in the self-declared white colonies. This intense combination of cultural proximity and racial dislocation ensured that the final moments of the relations between centre and colony were peculiarly overdetermined, not least in Britain itself.

The tellings and re-tellings of the story of West Indians arriving in post-war Britain have now established their own pattern of repetition as if, whatever the personal details of each individual story, the essentials of the collective experience still need to be told. The transition from colonial subject, legally indistinguishable from white Britons resident in Britain, to black immigrant proved so fierce an experience, and for long one largely unheard in the public sphere, that it required an insistent repetition.

Yet for the West Indian immigrant the affective power of empire still exerted a singular interior power. Only by appreciating this can we understand the depth of the consequences of the confrontation with actually existing Britain, especially when (by the end of the 1950s) it had become increasingly clear that official Britain, even at its most benign, had neither the desire nor the will to surrender the inherited truth that, at the end of the day, the country was still to be managed as if it belonged solely to its white population. Even so, ideas of home had many resonances, and (as Hall made clear in relating his own experiences) these were generally far from unambivalent. The most well-known expressions of this phenomenon at the time are still the most telling. One of the defining images of the *Windrush* moment comes from the Pathe newsreel in which a white reporter, still wearing his Macintosh despite the summer weather, interviews the Trinidadian calypso singer, Lord Kitchener (a.k.a. Aldwyn Roberts) – an image which still circulates in the popular media. Lord Kitchener not only presented British cinema audiences with a bizarrely puzzling reincarnation of a truly memorable, unimpeachably white, imperial figure. He – the colonized, not the colonizing, Kitchener – was also invited by the journalist to sing. The microphone came his way. He looked a bit puzzled, as did those West Indians around him. After all, it was an early Monday morning. In Tilbury. A black man sings.

> London is the place for me, London that lovely city.
> You can go to France or America, India, Asia, or Australia.
> But you must come back to London city.
> I said, London is the place for me. London, that lovely city.
> You can go to France or America, India, Asia or Australia.
> But you must come back, to London city.
>
> London is the place for me. London this lovely city.
> You can go to France or America, India, Asia or Australia.
> But you must come back to London city.

> London, this lovely city.
> You can go to France or America, India, Asia or Australia.
> But you must come back to London city.[22]

The final beat of the calypso runs into, and is overridden by, the rhythms of the more familiarly patriotic tune of the closing Pathe jingle. These words, uttered at precisely that moment in which the colonial subject was becoming an immigrant, were among the very first that the white inhabitants of the metropolis heard spoken from '*Windrush*' Britain. Who knows, more than half a century on, what white cinema audiences would have made of this?

As the genre required, the newsreel revealed no history. It was of its moment, no more. So far as viewers could ascertain Lord Kitchener was 'just another' immigrant, though one (as his interviewer had been reliably informed) with a reputation for singing. There was no way of knowing, sitting in the cinema and waiting for the feature, that the colonial state had banned his early songs, or that (a nice irony) he had performed some of his more ribald numbers for President Harry Truman. His new-found status as immigrant precluded other stories from intervening. He was a man who brought with him (it could seem) no past. He was just an immigrant.

Lord Kitchener, as it happened, had been working for a couple of months in the Shoehead Club in Kingston, Jamaica, when, after a while, he 'started getting a kind of homesick'. But this was a homesickness which drove him, not back to his home town of Arima in Trinidad, but to England. He secured a passage on the *Empire Windrush*.

> But entering England, when the boat had about four days to land in England, I get this kind of wonderful feeling that I'm going to land on the mother country, the soil of the mother country. And I started composing this song, *London is the Place for Me*.
>
> And I composed that song. And it had to be a famous song. Eventually it came up as a famous song. *London is the Place for Me*. And that is when I composed that song. The feeling I had to know that I'm going to touch the soil of the mother country, that was the feeling I had. How can I describe? It's just a wonderful feeling. You know how it is when a child, you hear about your mother country, and you know you're going to touch the soil of the mother country, you know what feeling is that? And I can't describe it. That's why I compose the song. Imagine how I felt.[23]

This is a version of the colonial sublime and it's hard to discount the psychic presence in these memories of child and mother, such that arrival in England signifies a deeper emotional *return* to something indescribably primordial. Yet this ode to London – and to the compulsive need to return to London – was written before Lord Kitchener had ever set eyes on it. It represented an exclusively imaginary identification. And there is, too, something unreal about it: the strange geographical contrasts invoked, and the jarring, not-quite-colloquial refrain of 'London city'.

In what is perhaps the best known fictional account of this same experience – Sam Selvon's *The Lonely Londoners*, published in 1956 – similar structures of narration occur. In the opening sentence, the principal protagonist, Moses, while hopping on the 'number 46 bus at the corner of Chepstow Road and Westbourne Grove', nonetheless existed in an England marked by 'a kind of unrealness', as if it were 'some strange place on another planet'. Unreality, dreary and uniform, possessed as well a magic – from which emerged, less a magical realism, than a diasporic realism. For Moses's friend Galahad particular aspects of London, though never experienced before, carried a delighted, emotional charge, abundant with memories – Charing Cross, Waterloo Bridge. Simply to be there was to be part of a world of promise and excitement.[24]

In fact, it is significant that both Lord Kitchener and Sam Selvon were moved as much by London as by England. They each formed part of a larger migration – from small-town or rural to the metropolitan city, from south to north – which constituted in these years the dynamic of modernity. The memories of London inscribed in the minds of Moses and Galahad derived from the institutions of the mass media – from the movies and popular song, not from official manifestations of patriotic ritual. What might appear on the surface to mark the conventions of regard for the mother country could in fact signify multiple points of identification, some of which were far removed from the rhetorics sanctioned by the institutions of official society.

Becoming a West Indian immigrant in Britain in the 1940s and 1950s required many transformations. It meant learning the difference between immigrant and citizen. It meant learning to adopt a new West Indian identity, as opposed to one defined by the specificities of colonial nationalism (Guyanese, Trinidadian, and so on). 'I became a West Indian in London,' observes Stuart Hall. 'Before that I was Jamaican.'[25] And it meant learning to be black. Just as C.L.R. James didn't recognize himself 'as a black man' until he went to the United States in the late 1930s, so England in the 1950s became the arena in which black identity became both a necessity and a possibility. 'I never knew I was a negro until I came to England', declared one Caribbean woman in a public meeting with James Baldwin in London in 1969.[26] Or Stuart Hall again: 'I became black in London, not Kingston.'[27] Learning to be an immigrant necessitated a certain intellectual agility. But there were palpable costs too.

In a recent study Mary Chamberlain has explored the experiences of

Barbadian emigrants coming to Britain between 1955 and 1962. These were emigrants, she reminds us, whose family histories for two or three generations had been dominated by migration. The journey to Britain therefore repeated patterns of migration which had had a long history, but also turned on new specificities. In reconstructing the lived realities of the 1950s Chamberlain identifies a collective, social experience of subjective crisis. There occurred, she discovered, a silence in which the truths of immigrant life could barely be spoken. Letters home, for example, were systematic in concealing the pains involved, and opted for 'a bland and universal endorsement' of migration. There were many reasons for this, correspondents – especially – not wishing to cause relations back home undue distress when there was precious little they could do to rectify things. But Chamberlain also suggests that a shared 'cognitive dissonance' characterized this moment, in which inherited systems of thought could no longer map the new realities with which they were confronted. (Hence the common experience of declaring these realities to be unreal.) Not the least of these new realities were the actual forms of urban England as opposed to the myths of the mother country. In the early years personal news received by families in Barbados concealed much; but it may also be the case that Barbadians in London exercised a degree of restraint in the belief that those back home either could not or would not heed the stories which the letters told. Chamberlain interviewed Roy, asking him about the stories relayed back to the Caribbean from the emigrants:

> Whether people was up there and didn't want to say what they were going through, or there wasn't sufficient people to speak enough about it, or people, even if they hear it down here, say they wrote their family and tell them things, they probably won't believe it, they probably don't tell it to anybody else. But I can assure you that up to when I left [for] England in 1956, I had nothing but a hundred per cent good picture of England and everybody else that is in England. I felt I was going to a place which would be second to heaven, and that is true . . . they gave us a lot of advice. We weren't short of advice at all. What to expect about the weather. They were very honest about that . . .

Byron put it like this, referring to the riots in Notting Hill in 1958:

> People had written home about it, but you couldn't understand it. You couldn't believe that Britain who you were taught so much of, were going to, was not going to represent you . . . you heard of these things, but you couldn't really imagine it. You couldn't believe it.

In this social experience of immigration the unspeakable, and what Mary Chamberlain calls a 'collective, pervasive muteness', were literal – not poetic – truths.[28]

SYMBOLIC THINKING: WORKING THROUGH

This determinate history, in its many complexities, is the 'very specific historical formation' which lies behind Hall's theorizations of identity. Hall abstracted from that collective history, his own included, in order to think the contemporary dispositions of identity. He arrived at a notion which emphasized precisely what this history had taught, or promised: an idea of identity which was decentred, hybrid, and in which strangeness itself might be embraced without fear.

> So you have what Simmel talked about: the experience of being inside and outside, the 'familiar stranger'. We used to call that 'alienation', or deracination. But nowadays it's come to be the archetypal late-modern condition. Increasingly, it's what everybody's life is like. So that's how I think about the articulation of the postmodern and the postcolonial. Postcoloniality, in a curious way, prepared one to live in a 'postmodern' or diasporic relationship to identity. Paradigmatically, it's a diasporic experience. Since migration has turned out to be *the* world-historical event of late modernity, the classic postmodern experience turns out to be diasporic experience.[29]

To think of identity as diasporic clearly derives, in Hall's discussion, from an interpretation of the black experience in the era of colonialism. As his own autobiographical comments suggest, Hall has drawn from this particular history in order to arrive at a more general conclusion about the structures of contemporary identity. This movement from the particular to the general is always a problematic moment in any social theory; it is also, always, inevitable. He claims only (we need to note) that the diasporic experience is homologous to the late-modern condition or, more specifically, that those who lived a diasporic life are peculiarly prepared for the 'familiar strangeness' of late modernity. Even so, this raises a predictable but difficult question. What of non-diasporic peoples? Of colonizers rather than colonized, of white rather than black? How does a diasporic reading of identity work for those who have no claim to a diasporic history?

Ethnic identifications are pre-eminently a matter of the imagination. The figure of the white man is an imaginative fabrication, and only becomes a given, collective sociological reality (a social fact) through the workings of history. We can think of diasporic identities in the same way. Diaspora, in this sense, denotes a way of imagining oneself, a way of positioning oneself or being positioned as a social being in the modern world. It highlights not the necessary existence of a given diasporic past, but rather what Hall calls here 'a diasporic relationship to identity'. These may seem fine distinctions, in an argument which (it might be thought) is already far enough removed from the requirements of empirically observable histories. Yet these abstract issues are decisive, for they go to the heart of the historical questions posed so far. Simply put, to think in terms of 'diasporic relationships to identity' can serve as an imaginative and intellectual counter, or antidote, to those conceptions in which the figurative ideal of the white man governs what is (and what is not) deemed to be real identity. Diasporic becomes a metaphor which condenses all that the white man *is not*. It suggests a way of thinking which vindicates Baldwin's incapacity to find an appropriate answer to Mossman's questions about identity, just as it deepens the incomprehension of latter-day Mossmanites when confronted by identities which are not of the proper historical pedigree, fixed and authenticated. Or again, it serves to question the authority of the genial Englishman in his Macintosh on Tilbury docks in June 1948. Seeing a new future for England unfolding in front of his very eyes he remained certain of one thing only: that the black man can sing.

As Hall employs the concept, diasporic is both prescriptive and descriptive. It is prescriptive in that it anticipates a politics of identity which is plural in its range of potential identifications, not singular and exclusive; which recognizes the imaginative foundations of identity, as opposed to a politics driven by the search for destinies ordained by birth; and which can live with – rather than repudiate – difference. But the term is also descriptive, in that it carries too the implication that this is how modern identities actually work, in real historical time: they are not fashioned by blood and birth, but are organized through the unpredictable contingencies of the human imagination.

Such an approach also offers the prospect, perhaps, of making speakable the displacements which can occur inside white subjectivities. If there is no adequate way of conceiving of whiteness, then there is no way of conceiving of these historical moments of ethnic disorientation. The only alternative is unconsciously to act out or to repeat prior forms. Arguably, to think in these terms represents the first steps in working through, and in this respect it is to be distinguished from the vertiginous fear that the loss of white authority spells the extinction of the self. What happens thereafter remains, however, an open matter; a matter of contingency, of politics.

To understand these ethnic transformations as diasporic, or more accurately as involving a diasporic relationship to identity, is to think symbolically. It provides a way of subverting the categories of identity bequeathed by the normative imperatives of the figure of the white man. Conversely, however, it implies no equivalence between the inherited histories of black and white. To see the possibilities of a diasporic relationship to white identities does nothing to diminish the historical differences between black and white, nor to diminish the differences between their respective collective memories.

But it does serve to counter those theorizations in which whiteness represents *nothing*, or in which it becomes merely bad faith, and in which blackness represents all that is human and true. The conceptual counter to the figure of the white man is thus not just 'black', in either of its gendered forms, but a contrary conception of what identity is and how it works. The paradox – which gradually became clear for all to see in the black insurgence of the early 1980s in Britain, and in the philosophies it created – is that while in origins a particularist movement, affirming the black presence and announcing the refusal of blacks in Britain to go away, it *also* promised a politics in which race and all the appurtenances of racial thinking might eventually be jettisoned. Or as Thomas Holt puts this in a different context, a new generation needed 'to claim their "blackness" yet lived beyond it'.[30] To think from this vantage undermines a black essentialism as much as it does a white essentialism, bringing ethnicity properly within history. The metaphorical power of a diasporic perspective works to demonstrate the impossibility of an identity – black or white – predicated on the prospect of effecting a return to some imagined point of origin. This, as we have seen, has been a prevalent way of imagining identity in the colonial epoch. When the Trinidadian Kitchener was first approaching Tilbury, he explicitly identified England as a mother about to receive her child, thus believing he was returning to the home he had never known. These are patterns of thought which traverse the divides between black and white. Ethnic identifications, condensing affective relations around home, location and the memories of childhood, are peculiarly poised to invite the desire to 'return': the power of ethnic memories derives from this positioning deep in the self. But the only possible return is a return to ourselves. Diaspora provides one way of thinking of these contingencies, not by erasing the past (hence Hall's strictures on nomadism) but by relocating these memories from a racial logic, in which blood determines, to all the many unknowns of history itself.

CHAPTER 6

Race, Colonialism and History: China at the Turn of the Twentieth Century

REBECCA E. KARL

Historically, philosophical reflections on 'race' in China are linked to the beginnings of nationalism as an articulated albeit highly contested theoretical and political topos at the turn of the twentieth century, during the late-Qing period (1895–1911). This was the time at which China's participation in global systems of signification and power relations – including 'race' and 'nation,' among others – came to be consciously recognized by Chinese intellectuals as at least incipient totalities.[1] As I elucidate below, these systems of signification and power were integrally incorporated into new understandings of history, through which China was constitutively linked to a modern world of flux and instability. This chapter thus argues, contrary to much that has been written recently on 'race' in China,[2] that a philosophy of race was initially elaborated not primarily to define 'others' as non-Chinese – that is, not merely as a permutation of previous systems of Sinocentric civilizational or blood-lineage significations – nor as a wholesale adoption of Spencerian Darwinism,[3] but rather as a politico-philosophical attempt by Chinese intellectuals to mark out an autonomous relationship to a violently invasive modernity, while simultaneously incorporating China into a new sense of globality. As such, despite clear and long-standing Chinese systems for signifying 'others' – for example, as those who stood outside the pale of a Confucian civilizational norm (*huawai*) expressed either in terms of 'raw' (*sheng*) and 'cooked' (*shu*) peoples,[4] or in the less culinary terms of 'barbarian' (*yi*) and 'civilized' (*wen*) – my contention is that these older signifying practices cannot be considered philosophies of 'race', if we take 'race' to be, at the very least, a system of signification that is, in Ato Sekyi-Otu's words, 'an order . . . made manifest in *space*'.[5]

On such a view, exclusive historiographical or ethnological attention to the temporally continuous contemptuous attitudes of (mostly Han) Chinese towards 'others', and the linking of these attitudes to putatively unchanging assumptions of centrality, must be modified by an account of how 'race' came to be elaborated in the late nineteenth and early twentieth centuries in explicitly global spatialized terms. These terms, as I understand them, referred to at least two spatialities simultaneously: to modernity, understood as a global space of transformation; and a newly conceptualized national space that was to be constituted through the reinvention of hierarchies of politics, economy, and culture – hierarchies that were at once demanded and yet also disallowed by the very nation project itself.[6] Dwelling on the second (internalist) aspect without elucidating the former (globalist) one, as much recent commentary does, is to miss the historical complexity of 'race' philosophy in China, and thereby to assimilate the concept too easily either into an unchanging (Han) Chinese culturalist–ethnic normativity or into a simple Western (or Japanese) derivativeness that strips the concept of its contradictions and political potentials.

To grasp the nature of these overlapping global and domestic spatialities and their inherent contradictions and potentials, it is helpful to think the problem of late-Qing race philosophies in terms of what Gilles Deleuze and Félix Guattari have called the process of social subjection.[7] According to Deleuze and Guattari, social subjection is the dominant mode of social coding in modernity, as that coding is pursued through the nation–state, which seeks to order social integration both through a national-level politics/economy and via the articulation of that configuration to the capitalist world.[8] Social subjection is thus a congeries of national and global processes; it is also simultaneously productive and reactive. As such, the process of social subjection is not merely repressive, but also opens onto a productive plane of immanence, through which it poses political (and other) possibilities not immediately derivable from the structure of its superficial logics.[9] Yet, as is clear for a globally subordinated place such as China, both the conditions for national integration as well as the possibilities for global equality through the non-isomorphic processes of social subjection are always illusory. They are illusory, not only because of suppressed strands in the narrative of nation (that is, not because 'nation' in the narrowest sense is an imposed statist narrative ideology or teleology) but at the very least because states – those seemingly bounded spaces – into which global capitalism makes inroads must, on the one hand, resist equality in internal socio-political-economic integration by reconfiguring older inequalities into new unequal formations able to cope with those inroads, while at the same time being forced to succumb to spatially articulated inequality enforced by differential power relations globally.

As a new philosophy in turn-of-the-century China, the multiple strands of 'race' figured and reflected this consciously grasped historical contradiction and modern condition of social subjection, without, however, necessarily resonating very well with existing popularly articulated systems of differentiation. The latter were perhaps more beholden to local regionalisms, language groups, and so on, and only later became racialized. As such, 'race' in late-Qing China reflected upon the intersections between global and national spaces, and many Chinese intellectuals – who themselves were increasingly able to negotiate those spaces both epistemologically and in experiential practice – appropriated the concept to name both national and global desires.[10] In the process of the constitution of the national desire, race and ethnos – with the latter understood initially as a people defined not by common lineage/culture, but by a putatively common commitment to the political project of overthrowing the Manchu Qing rulers[11] – quickly came to be socio-political synonyms; at the same time, however, as a form of immanentism, 'race' also named a desire for the revolutionary transformation of a newly-glimpsed global regime of temporal unity marked by constantly produced and reproduced global division and uneveness: that regime that can be named modernity.[12] This latter version, too, was linked to an imputed common political project: that of non-Western anti-colonial revolutions. In this mutuality, 'race' can be seen as the name of a History[13] that in part repudiated the modernist packaging indicated by nineteenth-century Western imperialist epistemologies – which attempted to codify differences among peoples across the globe in an essentialist way – and attempted to reposition modernity as an enabling political topos, not merely as a prison-house of language and form.[14]

In the sense I explore below, then, 'race' was not primarily a philosophy forged by those directly in the service of power although it was that, too; nor is it to be understood primarily as a lived experience.[15] Rather, I explore the philosophy of 'race,' borrowing Ann Laura Stoler's words, as it was 'embraced . . . by those unmasking the fiction of natural and legitimate rule'.[16] In the specific historical context of turn-of-the-century Chinese intellectual circles, the primary fictions unmasked were, on the one hand, the claims on 'China' made by the Manchu Qing dynasty, whose deposing of the Ming dynasty in the mid-seventeenth century was re-examined at the beginning of the twentieth century in the dual light of newly available discourses of 'race/ethnicity' and the newly grasped import of colonialism as a modern global historical trajectory of dominance and power; and, on the other, the incipient normalization of a modernist teleology derived from would-be hegemonic notions of modernization learned and observed from Western political philosophies and recent Western and Japanese historical experiences.[17]

That said, I should note that the provisional historical outcome of the contradictions introduced and reflected upon through a 'race' philosophy at the turn of the century was the victory of a culturalist philosophy of an essentially racialized ethnos embodied by the Han Chinese (projected as the political essence of the national people) over the more utopian global transformative philosophy. This ethno-nationalist understanding restricted 'race' (and 'nation') to an ethnic normativity delimited by Han Chinese-ness. It was politically motivated by that version of the national project that sought to overthrow the Manchu Qing dynasty in order to restore the Han to their 'rightful' place as rulers of China. This over-determined outcome – over-determined both by changing configurations of political and economic power within China and between Chinese and non-Chinese, and by the posing of the modern question of 'nation' itself in terms of political divisions among 'national peoples' globally – was temporarily solidified by the successful deposing of the Qing dynasty in 1911 and the subsequent inscription of new Republican statist–culturalist discourses of race/ethnos (*minzu*) upon definitions of the Chinese people and of the Chinese nation(–state).[18] The following discussion is less concerned with this historical outcome – which I have treated at length elsewhere[19] – than with the conceptual relationship between 'race', 'colonialism' and 'history' at the turn of the twentieth century in those texts that produced this nexus as a cornerstone of analysis.

ERASING BOUNDARIES AND A GLOBAL UTOPIA

As a point of departure, it is useful to examine one of the most explicitly global and utopian expositions of 'race' in China: that included in Kang Youwei's *Datong shu* [One World Philosophy].[20] Around the turn of the century, Kang (1858–1927) was best known for his reinterpretation of Confucianism in his 1897 volume *Kongzi gaizhi kao* [On Confucius as a Reformer], which was essentially a reworking of the premises of the Song neo-Confucian imperial tradition – or, that version of Confucianism encoded by the civil service examinations that all would-be state officials were required to pass. Kang's Confucianism was thus an activist doctrine of practical statesmanship rather than a conservative doctrine of the status quo.[21] Indeed, Kang's radical (for the time) critique of imperial Confucianism, in addition to his strict focus on the needs of the global present and future, rather than on the glories of the Chinese past, earned him a reputation: those who admired his boldness sought to become his students; those who deplored his challenge set out to destroy him.[22]

Through his reinterpretation of Confucianism, which was heavily informed by his studies in Buddhism, Kang explicitly mobilized his 'sage-Bodhisattva's sense of mission', in Hao Chang's words,[23] to explore how, what he saw as the historically evolved 'boundaries' (*jie*) of the world could be eliminated so as to prepare the way for one-worldism. On Kang's reading of the contemporary global situation, it was precisely boundaries – of space and kind – that prevented the world (or, life in its broadest sense) from achieving its full potential. According to Kang, there were nine such primary boundaries: those of states, classes, race, sex, family, occupation (or property), disorder (or unjust laws), kind (or, species), and suffering (or, perpetuation of suffering). The goal of his quest to define and eliminate these boundaries was to arrive at a just and humane 'one world' (*datong*:unity) which would provide the condition of possibility for the overcoming of suffering (*ku*) and the achievement of happiness (*le*). Without going into the complex sources for Kang's particular utopian vision, it is important to note, as does Hao Chang, that Kang's transcendental utopianism was firmly a this-world affair and had little to do with a dualism between this- and other-worldliness.[24] It is also important to point out that 'culture' was not a boundary for Kang: that is, 'culture' neither defined division nor did cultures need to be abolished, or seemingly even addressed as such.

In his discussion of Kang's philosophy, Hao Chang emphasizes Kang's reliance upon the Confucian realm of *ren* (humane-ness) as an inner-world orientation that described and reflected Kang's desire to achieve a philosophically plausible moral unity between Heaven and the human world. It is with reference to this inner world of moral perfection that Chang places Kang's desire for one-world unity. However, in his concern to trace how indigenous patterns of thought were unsettled by and through China's modern crisis, where he carefully notes the selective incorporations of Western political and social philosophies (most notably, Social Darwinism and the startling turn to a unilinear progressive temporality), Chang under-emphasizes the crucial spatial turn that underpins Kang's philosophy, and, in consequence, the unstable relationship between space and globality assumed therein.[25]

Kang's specification of his current era was placed in the context of what he saw as a strong historical trend leading from 'division to unity'. This trend he elaborated through a whirlwind narrative of China's imperial unification; the unifications of India, Greece, and Rome; all the way to the more recent unifications of Germany and Italy in the mid-nineteenth century. Making clear that his concept of 'unity' was not limited to any necessary sense of contiguous territoriality but was spatially universalist, Kang further noted, for example, that more recently, France's taking of Annam (Vietnam) and Morocco; England's conquest of Egypt, India, and Burma; and the continental swallowing of whole swathes of North America by the United States (which, he surmised, was leading to a full unification of the Americas – North and South

– under the USA), were all evidence of 'parts becoming joined', a trend that, Kang averred in the Social Darwinistic language of the time, was due to 'natural selection, the swallowing up by the strong and large and the extermination of the weak and small'. This trend, he noted, 'may be considered to presage One World'.[26]

It is clear that Kang fundamentally ignored the production of uneveness – internally and globally – in his understanding of the trend towards 'unity'. It thus appears that he was unconcerned with any historically specific explanation for dominance, or for modern colonialism/imperialism as the production of uneven global space. In this regard, what by the early 1900s many were despairingly calling 'imperialism' (*diguo zhuyi*), 'national expansionism' (*guojia pengzhang zhuyi*), or 'colonialism' (*zhimin zhuyi*) was for Kang not only a natural but a desirable move towards boundary elimination. By the same token, it is also clear that a sense of global space is crucial to Kang's utopian formulation. Yet, that space was, for Kang, a continuous and purely immanent affair, marked and shaped by human activity, to be sure, but essentially blank. That is, for him, space was abstract, not particularistically performative,[27] and thus, globality was not one topos of an historically specific lifeworld enacted and actualized as a relationship, but an historically given condition of being. Kang's view therefore posits an abstract and decentred global condition and in this narrow sense, his utopian vision is fully of his time. It could not have been articulated much earlier in China. It is also in this sense that Kang's view is basically ahistorical. For, as we shall see below, it was precisely with the recognition of 'space' and globality as a material and thus historical productivity *and* only in consequence of that productivity an immanence, and with the incorporation of this recognition into new modes of historical analysis, that the question of 'boundaries' and their relationship to 'race' was turned into something else altogether: explicitly spatialized systems of difference and signification that, in the global arena, were potentially politically unifying because of a shared anti-colonialism; and simultaneously in the domestic arena, an exclusionary culturalist ethnic system that rendered differences between Manchu and Han (among others) a cornerstone of nationalist praxis.

For the moment, suffice it to note that Kang's interpretive premise rests upon two primary units of socio-political analysis, neither of which is particularly problematized: *the world*, which stands as an abstract given space and a utopian desire; and *the state*, whose territoriality was the concrete and historical form through which all other boundaries were instantiated and hence whose loosening from territoriality was the process through which all other boundaries could be dissolved.[28] In this regard, democracy – by which Kang mostly meant rule by law – was understood as the governing form that permitted contemporary interstate federations (the 'joinings') as well as the form of government that presented itself as the politically neutral substance of One Worldism.

In Kang's view, then, the current situation yielded two contradictory but potentially complementary movements: the union of divisive states into ever-larger territories, not necessarily understood 'nationally' or contiguously; and the continuing divisions produced within territorial states that spawned conflict among people, where conflict was understood as a temporal, or even temporary, condition, rather than as an historical spatial productivity. That is, for Kang, unity was constructed as a spatial aspiration devoid of conflict (and thus of historicity), and conflict a temporal problem shorn of productive spatiality. In consequence, the absolute conquest of time by space – which I take to be the core of Kang's utopian vision – would spell not only the end to strife but, indeed, the end of history.[29] This quasi-modernist view of the potential utopian reconciliation between space and time – or, the transcendence of time by space – can be likened to a type of *posthistoire*, as Lutz Niethammer has called such a vision, that presents itself as an 'overcoming of chaotic historicity', or, as an end of materiality itself.[30]

It is in this context of a globally spatially construed *posthistoire* magically shorn of any specific cultural meaning or centre that Kang's exposition on 'abolishing racial boundaries and amalgamating the races' can be placed. Many commentators treat this chapter of Kang's *Datong shu* with extreme scepticism – in large part because his solution to racial division is to 'smelt' the races into what he considers to be the only really neutral 'race' (white) through the encouragement of large-scale miscegenation and immigration.[31] Yet, despite Kang's jejune and patently crude equations of skin colour with a slightly modified environmental and biological determinism in his designations of racial essences, and despite his elevation of 'white' and 'yellow' above other colours, Kang's combination of a utopian spatial universalism with a racialized particularism that is *not* tied to culture (understood as a productive spatiality) and that is thus transcendable offers insights into how 'race' became one pillar of a very different organizational philosophy of globality at the turn of the century.

In the 'race' chapter of *Datong shu* – the third section, after 'states' and 'classes' – Kang notes:

> inequality of creatures is a fact. Whenever we speak of equality, it is necessary that creatures have the capacity to be equal in abilities, knowledge, appearance and bodily characteristics before equality can be effected. If not, then even though it be enforced by state laws, constrained by a ruler's power, and led by universal principles, it still cannot be effected.[32]

Because 'difference' in appearance, in and of itself, leads to injustice and the irrational exercise of social and political power, in Kang's estimation, the racial boundary was perhaps the most pernicious as well as the most difficult of all to abolish.[33] As such, 'race' was specifiable as a particularity – an appearance – with consequences in the concreteness of all history, including in the period that would emerge as the threshold to one-worldism (after states had joined completely into spatio-political unity), and the residues of race could continue to structure inimically the achievement of one-worldism. Because of his focus on visible difference – rather than on the historical production of difference – Kang specifically articulated race in the language of aestheticism; he was emphatic that the 'races of India' are 'fierce and ugly', while Blacks (speaking of American Blacks) had 'iron faces, silver teeth, slanting jaws like a pig, front view like an ox, full breasts and long hair, their hands and feet dark black, stupid like sheep or swine'.[34] Yet, this aestheticism derived from a socio-philosophical concern with what he saw as the bases of social injustice, as power that was perpetrated and perpetuated through unchanging ways of seeing rather than historically-produced ways of being.

From today's vantage point, perhaps most remarkable about Kang's view is that he seems not even vaguely concerned with subjectivities and identities as constituted in and through race (or sex or nationality). This absence raises the question of 'culture' quite directly. Indeed, on Kang's view, one of the major obstacles to overcoming boundaries was to equalize civilization across the globe. Yet, his idea of 'civilization' (*wenming* not *wenhua*)[35] is curiously evacuated, or rather is emphatically not articulated in the culturalist vein usually connoted by the term *wen*.[36] Thus, while 'civilization' is articulated as a universalistically unbounded topos, it carries little content. Indeed, as Kang writes:

> When civilizations are equal, when they are the same in their [social] aspects, when [peoples] have become intermingled, [receiving] the same education and the same upbringing so that there is no natural division of the people into high and low, then equality [among men] will be near at hand, and the change will certainly be natural and easy.[37]

Kang's emphasis on civilization as a series of visible or tangible social indices of universal quotidian existence and not as historically constitutive of subjective cultural beings precisely shapes his understanding of 'race' as a both a malleable – indeed, erasable – and an essential category of human unity/division.

On this view, Kang's proposal for abolishing 'race' – along with class, gender and other divisions, which are also mostly articulated in terms of visible signs of inequality and injustice – can only be constructed as plausible if we understand 'race' in his terms: that is, as an abstract spatiality rather than historically specific productivity. For, it is only in this sense that for Kang 'race' could help constitute an understanding of current conflicts without posing an absolute barrier to a global unity envisioned as the erasure of visible bases for the exercise of power. It is hence Kang's contradictory combination of what we might today see as virulently racist and essentialist attitudes (towards Blacks, Indians, or non-whites and non-yellows in general) with the utopian desire for one-world unity that marks not only a crucial global spatial turn in Chinese philosophy in general of the time, but also the possibility for 'race' to become important in such explorations. 'Race' was not a means to instrumentally rationalize the relevance of the outside world to China in contemporary historical terms, but, more important, it was Kang's way to reconceptualize that mutual incorporation as a transformative appropriation aimed at moving beyond the divisiveness of the contemporary world.

Several possible and ostensibly opposed trajectories are present in Kang's incipient philosophy of race and globality: the systematization of divisions in terms of an essentialized racialism combined with national territoriality as global spatial organizational topoi tied to a historically productive sense of spatiality; and, the further refinement of utopian notions of globality. That Chinese 'race' philosophies went in both directions simultaneously at the turn of the century has much to do with the new relevance in Chinese historical consciousness of the modern category of colonialism after 1900 and the initial ways in which Chinese intellectuals came to link Chinese history and its contemporary situation to the world through this new category of analysis.

COLONIALISM, REVOLUTION, AND RACE

At the same time as Kang was working out his one-world philosophy, which, as we have seen, attempted to think the world in a utopian–transformative fashion, other genres of historical writing that combined the world and China into a new unity also arose. Less abstract than Kang's version, one genre in particular, in part adapted from Japan, was the *wangguo shi*, or histories of perished states. These were narratives that largely concerned themselves with recounting the terminal fate of states that had either perished by being eaten up by stronger powers or declined and disappeared because of the fall into corruption of ruling elites. This fate of perishing – not understood as an abstract spatial 'joining' as with Kang but as the disappearance of cultural nations – was most often said to be traceable to a complacently 'enslaved' people, who were unwilling or unable to act to prevent either the swallowings or the corruptions. As such, *wangguo shi* could encompass such distantly past examples as the decline and fall of Babylonia and Rome, and such more recent examples as the 'perishing' of India, Vietnam, Ireland, and Poland, among many others.

Sociologists Hu Fengyang and Zhang Wenjian note that *wangguo shi* made their appearance in China most clearly after the allied occupation of Beijing during the Boxer Rebellion (1900–1).[38] Historian Yu Danshi has characterized them as 'important constituent parts of early twentieth-century Chinese patriotism',[39] because they were written and translated just as nationalist sentiment was stirring among intellectuals. The appearance of the *wangguo shi* as a distinct genre was thus connected to a dramatic increase at the time in journalistic writings and translated books (from the West and Japan) on the world, the latter often called comprehensive world histories (*shijie tongshi*), even though most of these so-called 'world histories', as the prominent journalist and intellectual Liang Qichao complained in 1899, actually were merely histories of Western countries.[40] *Wangguo shi* were hence also intimately connected to contemporaneous efforts being made by Liang Qichao and, from a different direction, Chen Fuchen, among others, to write new national histories of China that departed from the state-dominated dynastic chronicles prevalent in most official Chinese historiographical practice. Indeed, all these histories – the *wangguo shi*, ostensibly about other places and often other times, the 'world' histories and the attempts at national histories – explicitly aimed 'to look anew at China itself from the perspective of the world'.[41]

To grasp the novelty of *wangguo shi* as a genre, it is important to note that, as a term, *wangguo* had first had to be detached from its traditional connotation of the deposing of one dynasty by another. Indeed, by the turn of the twentieth century, *wangguo* had come to refer, not to internal dynastic replacement, but to the colonization of specific places by external powers, where colonization (or *wang*) was understood as more than the usurpation of state power. As Liang Qichao wrote in 1900, in reference to his observations on the colonization of Hawaii by the United States, 'Of old, in the perishing of a state [*wangguo*], the state alone was lost. Today it is different: when the state is destroyed, the race/people follows it [*guowang er zhong ji sui zhi*].'[42] As such, by the first decade of the twentieth century, the weight of the meaning of *wangguo* was decisively shifted from connoting an internal dynastic change to a centrally constitutive moment of modern world history tied to a complex, spatially produced globality. In this guise, the term was increasingly used interchangeably with the contemporaneous understandings of 'imperialism' (*diguo zhuyi*), 'expansionism' (*pengzhang zhuyi*), and 'colonialism' (*zhimin zhuyi*).[43] Moreover, in its compound conjoining with *wangzhong* (perishing of the race), as *wangguo wangzhong*, or as *wangguo nu* (slave of a perished state), it referred to the colonized transformation of whole peoples, including culture, language, organization of labour, and so on.

By the same token and at the same time, the concept used to denote 'revolution' – *geming* – also underwent a sea-change in meaning, in which *geming* provided the flipside to colonization. Previously, *geming* had denoted the withdrawal of the mandate of heaven from a given dynasty/emperor; it was thus, like the older notion of *wangguo*, tied to a paradigm of internal dynastic change and exclusively tied to the state. By the turn of the century, *geming* had taken on the meaning of socio-political revolution, understood both as anti-colonial action against an externalized conquering power – also known as *paiwai* (expelling outsiders/foreigners) – and, as in the case of the French (1789) or Persian (1908) revolutions, as the popular removal of a monarchy in favour of a republican arrangement.[44]

The combination of the popularization of the *wangguo shi*, Qing China's increasingly precipitous decline into social and political chaos, and contemporaneous revolutionary actions erupting throughout the colonized world turned colonialism into the dominant paradigm of historical analysis, while also rendering revolution one of the most hotly debated issues of the first decade of the twentieth century.[45] Of singular importance in constituting these paradigms was the specification of 'difference' and of boundaries; and, with the linked change in the historical connotations of *wangguo* and *geming* – as colonialism and revolution – came a turn in historical consciousness towards an understanding of a politically produced global space of transformative modernity that was to be animated by anti-colonial revolutions across the globe, all connected in global space by the co-temporality of their historical moment, even though each was led by different peoples/races and each sought to reinscribe local boundaries between 'nation' and 'world'.

This turn is noticeable in any number of essays, books, and publications of the time. Here, I wish to discuss briefly the proliferation of popular biographies written at the turn of the century on Chinese and foreign heroes, all of whom were designated heroes of anti-colonial revolutionism. In the first case, Chinese anti-dynastic figures from the past – who had had thriving afterlives in popular prose narratives and local dramatic works, but who were nowhere present as heroes in official histories – were turned into national patriots, with their single most noteworthy patriotic acts said to be their struggles against foreigners (Mongols, Manchus, *et al*, were now understood not as potentially Sinicized and thus legitimate rulers of the empire, but rather into racial outsiders, or colonizers). In this process of historical reinterpretation, many distant figures from the past came to the fore. These included Huang Zongxi, whose 1662 text *Mingyi daifang lu* [The Way of the Prince] was rediscovered in the late-

Qing and promoted as paradigmatic of ethno-nationalism; the late-Ming scholar Wang Fuzhi, who was barely known in his time, yet became well known at the turn of the century 'with the upsurge in anti-Manchu revolutionism';[46] Gu Yanwu, another late-Ming scholar; Yue Fei, a Southern Song general who was executed in the twelfth century despite his struggle against Jurchen invaders, and who, in 1906 was dubbed 'the first Chinese anti-foreign nationalist';[47] and Zheng Chenggong, a.k.a., Koxinga, the Ming restorationist holdout on Taiwan against the Manchu Qing in the mid-seventeenth century;[48] among others.[49]

In the second case, foreign patriots, contemporaneous leaders of anti-colonial struggles across the globe – including the Filipinos Emiliano Aguinaldo and José Rizal; the Transvaal President and Afrikaaner leader in the Boer War, Paul Kruger; the deposed Hawaiian Queen Liliukalani, among others – were rendered not only into patriotic defenders of their people against colonizing outsiders, but, more interestingly, they were also rendered into *tongzhong* (same race) allies with Chinese would-be revolutionaries in the struggle against imperialist modernity. In naming these foreign revolutionaries and anti-colonial activists as racially 'same', 'race' came to signify a common global political project unconnected to skin colour, rather than, as in Kang's sense, a boundary only remedied by wiping away visible signs of difference. While the utopianism encoded in what might be called this incipient Third World solidarity was perhaps no less attainable or realistic than was Kang's utopian vision of the elimination of all visible boundaries – and indeed the moment was quickly swamped by the realities of global revolutionary failure – by the same token, this common political project of 'race' as solidarity was no *posthistoire*. Rather, it was an attempt to imagine and mobilize a different history of modernity that was, however, completely structured and informed by the historicity of the modernist moment. As such, contemporary anti-colonial *paiwai* (expelling outsiders) activism – or, anti-colonial revolution – created an identifiable national/global praxis that could be immediately appropriated for a re-interpretation of the Chinese past and the contemporary historical task, both nationally and globally. In this sense, not only did the immediacy and contingency of global anti-colonial activity lend foreign 'heroes' and their specific spheres of activity contemporary cogency, but, by offering examples of 'patriotism' that were not over-determined by a teleology of completed state-building or by the functionality of symbolic mobilization by an existing state, these anti-colonial figures and resuscitated Chinese heroes were also imbued with a global racial significance informed by an optimistic reading of the dynamics of modern global politics.

For example, in early 1903, Tang Tiaoding [Erhe][50] wrote a series of linked studies of the recently failed Philippine Revolution against the United States.

One study in particular focused on José Rizal, whom Vincent Raphael has called the 'first Filipino'[51] and whose novel, *Noli me Tangere*, forms the opening subject of Benedict Anderson's now classic study of nationalism.[52] Yet, while both Raphael and Anderson concentrate on how Rizal helped create a sense of the Philippine nation in the late nineteenth century for (elite) Filipinos through his rendering of a national–temporal homogeneity, Tang Tiaoding's purpose in introducing Rizal to Chinese readers was to help create a global solidarity amongst different peoples, who were ostensibly linked in contemporary political sympathy. As Tang writes, emphasizing Rizal's resonance not in the Philippines but in the global sphere:

> Alas! This superior talent who was so educated, this Tagalog man, was a great and fierce person of the yellow race [*huangren*]. Indeed, one unique characteristic of our yellow people is that we have a false reputation [in the world] for being primitive [*yeman zhi yuanming*]. Yet, had it not been for the primitive behaviour [*manxing*] of Spain, what would Rizal's contributions have been called? And who would have known [of them]?[53]

At one level, Tang appropriates 'this Tagolog man' for the yellow race, thus placing him in an intimate connection with Chinese, who, when they had written of the Philippines in the past, had generally dismissed Filipinos as uncivilized primitives. At another level, however, Tang's appropriation is not merely a familiarizing gesture or, at least, not a gesture aimed at assimilating the Filipinos into some already understood regime of 'yellowness' that the Chinese (or Japanese) represented. Tang's is, rather, an appropriative gesture aimed at seizing the definition of 'yellowness' away from imperialist epistemologies and their destructive production of the organizing structures of the modern world; and, more interestingly, an attempt to hitch China to this new powerful 'yellowness' represented by the formerly ignored Filipinos.

This point was reinforced, albeit in a different way, by another commentator, who wrote at the same time as Tang of the arms shipment scheme Chinese activists had organized to assist Filipino revolutionaries via Japanese intermediaries, a scheme that was betrayed by those very intermediaries:

> These ever-perfidous Japanese, who speak all the time of a same continent [*tongzhou*], same culture [*tongwen*], same race [*tongzhong*] Asian alliance, who say all the time that the Filipinos are related to them by blood;[54] these very Japanese nevertheless engage in immoral trickery and have forced the Filipinos into horse and cow slavery forever. Alas! Heaven does not oppress yellow people; yellow people oppress each other! With such a race, I wish the world would no longer produce anything in the colour yellow![55]

To be sure, using the very epistemological constructions of racialization mobilized by colonial/imperialist discourses (whether Western or Japanese) in Asia only gets Chinese commentators so far. Nevertheless, the basis upon which Chinese and Filipinos are both 'yellow' (and, in the latter commentary, the basis upon which Japanese are to be excluded from 'yellowness' because of treachery) is understood to be not only the imperialist/colonial ideology of primitiveness that taints China and the Philippines equally in the global sphere, but the Filipinos' falsification of that ideology globally through their political-revolutionary activities.

In particular, in the latter regard, Tang Tiaoding mentions Rizal's 1887 novel, *Noli me Tangere* (whose title Tang translates as *Ru wuchu wo*, or *Don't you touch me!*):

> Although this book was written in the form of a prose narrative [*xiaoshuo*], it actually introduced the problem of the Philippines to the world. It described how the Spanish ruled the Philippines, and how this rule was clearly not designed for the benefit of the Filipinos. [Rizal] loudly protested the position of the Spanish friars in the Philippines and cast doubt upon their supposed righteousness.[56]

Having nothing at all to say about internal racial/class relations among Filipinos themselves –abundantly depicted in Rizal's novel in, for example, the interactions between Spanish-educated, lighter-skinned Filipinos and uneducated, darker-skinned ones; and/or between upper-class, urban Filipinos and rural peasants – Tang is able to concentrate his whole commentary about Rizal, and indeed about the whole revolutionary endeavour, upon the Philippines-in-the-world. This concentration, on the one hand, was most congenial to Tang, who, as with many Chinese elites of his time, was not much concerned with internal bases of social inequity in China (most, other than anarchists, deeming such inequity easily reversible once the global and internal political situations had been settled). Moreover, Tang almost certainly had not read *Noli me Tangere*, at most having heard of it through Filipinos in exile in Japan, where Tang resided briefly in 1902–3. Indeed, as Ma Junwu, another Chinese intellectual in Japan, noted in his translation of some of Rizal's poetry in 1903: 'Those of us living in Japan communicate with one another frequently; in the course of drinking together, we listened carefully to recitations of Rizal [by Filipino revolutionaries], so he became famous [among us].'[57]

Yet, on the other hand, Tang and other commentators' focus on the global production of racialist ideologies for imperialist/colonial purposes was also conditioned by the perceived similarity between the political anti-colonial projects which the Philippines and Chinese intellectuals such as Tang were engaged in fomenting. This latter focus is reinforced in Tang's biographical treatment of Emiliano Aguinaldo, then leader of the Philippine revolution against US colonial occupation. As Tang comments, bringing Paul Kruger of the Transvaal into the narrative at the same time:

> Since the waning years of ancient Greece, no one has resisted the world's strongest states in defence of their own people's independence from the space of a tiny state. The Transvaal's President Kruger is one man with this type of vigorous spirit and determination. Yet, there is another, not yet forty years old, who, from his tiny island no bigger than a grain afloat in the ocean, has led his people in opposition to the world's biggest and wealthiest nation in order to gain his people's independence. Is this not Aguinaldo, the fellow from the Philippines? Although these two are separated by wide oceans and have never met, they have performed moving political dramas on the world stage at the end of the nineteenth century. They can be called jewels of the world.[58]

The contemporaneity of the revolutionary upheavals in the Transvaal – where the Boer War was dominantly understood as an anti-colonial war of independence against Britain – and the Philippines simultaneously creates their respective national and their common global 'stage' of politics. Both stages are racialized, insofar as each participant people separately and all together are engaged in the production of a new globality and a nationalism aimed in part at combatting the racialized primitivism ascribed to them all by imperialist epistemologies. As such, there is no doubt that the condition of possibility for this restructuration of political desire – whether on the national or global 'stage' – is the perceived monolithic production and reproduction of colonial/imperialist race philosophies that seemed to underpin the circulation of representations globally, with their local effectivities and instantiations understood as delimited to the denial of national independence and sovereignty.

Indeed, later in the biography, Tang Tiaoding ostensibly quotes Aguinaldo as declaring:

> if Americans approach our people with unjust arrogance, do not fear: we have shaken off the shackles of Spain and we are now prepared to go against heaven and earth . . . Descendants of Washington: try closing your eyes to examine your conscience! You should be ashamed! The Filipinos have united in order to protect their lives; they have drawn energy and lessons from the pitiful native people [*kelian zhi tumin*], endured battlefields raining

> with canonballs and gunsmoke, and have died in great numbers. Americans have long boasted of their history; I now beg to inquire: where has the great spirit of North America gone?[59]

Here, Tang, via Aguinaldo, is only too happy to conceal internal racial and class division through an appeal to global unevenness and global injustice, an appeal that is globally radical and yet locally blind to its own elitist bases. With this, it is possible to see both the potential and the inherent limitations in the racial formulation of global political solidarity, as this appeal was explicitly conjoined to colonial paradigms of modern history.

THE CHALLENGE OF 'RACE'?

By the time of the failures of the turn-of-the-century anti-colonial revolutionary wave – that is, by 1905 at the latest – historical and contemporary emphasis increasingly turned away from linked global solutions to the solving of local problems. In this turn, the newly adopted colonial paradigm of modern history was mobilized to vilify the Manchu Qing, as much for their Manchu-ness as for their corruption, political failures, and purported 'slavishness' towards the foreign powers. With the racialized understanding of colonialism now in place, Manchus were understood to be the real colonizers of China – rather than being seen as the latest rulers of the millennia-old empire – and the contemporary Chinese task was understood to be anti-colonial revolution aimed against the Manchus, as racially and ethnically 'other' than the Han Chinese. In a longer-term sense, the initial racialization/ethnicization of the Manchus in these years through a colonial paradigm of modernity contributed to the Republican era's proliferating racialization/ethnicization of all non-Han Chinese, inside and outside the borders of China. As a corollary, it also contributed to the racialization of the Han Chinese themselves, most evident in the Republican era turn (and the default return ever since) towards a discourse of a Chinese *minzu* (ethno-nation), whose contemporary historical task was to recapture the greatness of culturalist China's past.[60]

As is evident from the discussion above, 'race' philosophy in China, particularly at the moment of its initial introduction in the late Qing, was tied to a complex and shifting understanding of globality and spatiality. In its more optimistic instantiations, which have returned episodically during China's most revolutionary moments, 'race' was an inclusionist philosophy of defiance, and referred to a global political solidarity. In the language of the late Qing, it was a *tongzhong* (same race) unity, and in its episodic recurrence ever since, this unity was expressed as a shared experience of 'the oppressed peoples of the world' (*bei yapo renmin/minzu*). In its more localist, or narrowly nationalist instantiations, which have also often returned with a vengeance (most recently, in the current era), it was an exclusionist philosophy. Both versions emerged at the same time and have co-existed uneasily for the ensuing century. Yet, the act of remembering the globally radical version is a political challenge, as Ato Sekyo-Otu writes of remembering Fanon in the current moment: a challenge to remember both 'the fledgling promises and prospects' as well as the 'congenital errors and imminent tragedies'[61] of a world history understood as a spatial relationship among peoples brought into being violently and not yet fully confronted or resolved.

CHAPTER 7

Ethnicity and Species: On the Philosophy of the Multi-ethnic State in Japanese Imperialism

NAOKI SAKAI

It has long been forgotten, since Japan's defeat and the loss of its empire, that during the Asia-Pacific war (1931–45) a large number of scholars, journalists and bureaucrats were eagerly engaged in academic and public discussions of racism and colonialism. In contrast to the overall poverty of the critique of racism and ethnic nationalism in post-war Japan, its abundance during the imperial period is striking. While occupying a wide range of political stances, from the total erasure of ethnic differences within the Japanese nation (the Governor's Office in Korea)[1] to a national socialist insistence upon racial purity (Watsuji Tetsurô[2] and Nishitani Keiji)[3], Japanese intellectuals invariably admitted that the issues of racism and ethnicity must be publicly addressed. It is as if the Japanese expeditiously lost interest in the critique of racism as they adjusted themselves to the domestic reality of American occupation and the emerging international order of the Cold War in East Asia. Today, few either in Japan or in North America or Western Europe acknowledge the existence of widely circulated public doctrines in the 1930s and particularly in the early 1940s which claimed that neither scientific racism nor ethnic nationalism was licit in the polity of the Japanese Empire, and that the nation-state of Japan was explicitly created *against* the principle of ethnic nationalism (*minzoku shugi*).[4] The myth of the mono-ethnic society or *tan'itsu minozoku shakai no shinwa* – that, ever since the pre-modern era, Japanese society has been ethnically homogeneous because it is made up mostly of a single ethnic group – is an integral part of this post-war amnesia.[5]

This chapter presents an outline of a philosophical argument about ethnicity and subjectivity in what is often referred to as *Logic of Species* (*Shu no ronri*): a set of essays published in the early 1930s by Tanabe Hajime, a philosopher from Kyoto Imperial University who headed the Kyoto School of Philosophy after the retirement of his mentor and colleague, Nishida Kitarô.[6] It is a summary of a longer, more detailed reading. Let me introduce a warning disclaimer: I deliberately avoid framing Tanabe's texts in terms of a number of binary oppositions, such the West versus the East, and Christian versus Buddhist/Confucian values, because I believe that, by appealing to these binary oppositions in order to foreground one's involvement in the discussion of ethnicity, colonialism, racism and nationality as presented in texts of the 'non-West', one has been solicited to abide by the post-war collective amnesia about wartime Japan. Prejudices and projection mechanisms associated with these binary oppositions inhibit us from calling into question the comfort and security induced by what we wittingly or unwittingly agree to forget for the sake of post-war Japanese national solidarity and the Cold War international configuration.

RACE, ETHNICITY AND SUBJECTIVITY

The variable through which the universalistic nation of multi-ethnic diversity is distinguished from the particularistic nation of mono-ethnic exclusivity is the concept of *minzoku*, translated sometimes as 'nation', sometimes as 'ethnos', 'folk', or even 'race'. The myth of the mono-ethnic society cannot be sustained if this distinction between *multi*-ethnic and *mono*-ethnic nations is not established. In other words, of logical necessity, the myth must embrace an assumption that the unity of the ethnos/nation or *minzoku* must be not only countable but also *accountable*. In Japanese philosophical discourse of the 1920s and 1930s, which certainly did not take the myth of the mono-ethnic society for granted, the concept of the ethnos/nation or *minzoku* was far from self-evident. What was thematically discussed in Tanabe Hajime's series of articles on social ontology, *Logic of Species*, was nothing other than the problematic nature of this concept of *minzoku*. The term *species* was called for because of the inherent ambiguity in such unities as state, nation, ethnos, folk and race, unities without which we cannot comprehend the desires for identity in modern social formations.

Tanabe's social ontology is significant because not only the aforementioned Kyoto School philosophers of world history – such as Kôsaka Masaaki, Kôyama Iwao and Suzuki Shigetaka – but also certain governmental policy-makers such as Murayama Michio, who were concerned with the management of the empire's minority population,[7] appropriated theoretical insights from Tanabe's *Logic of Species*. *Logic of Species* must have been attractive to the Japanese intellectuals of the day because it offered a philosophically rigorous socio-political account of what might have appeared to be the multi-ethnic social reality of the Japanese Empire. Furthermore, it declared itself to be an ethic for the construction of a state embracing political, economic and cultural diversity, an ethic *against* ethnic nationalisms (*minzokushugi*) and separatism. What I find in Tanabe's *Logic of Species* is the most consistent among the philosophical articulations, in the 1920s and 1930s, of an ethico-political thesis on which something like the idea of the Greater East Asian Co-prosperity Sphere could be built.

However, let me issue two disclaimers here. First, Tanabe started publishing articles on the logic of species much earlier than the inauguration in 1940 by the Japanese government of the idea of the Greater East Asian Co-prosperity Sphere. So one cannot argue that Tanabe conceived of *Logic of Species* particularly for the large-scale regional transnational polity, nor that the policies of the Greater East Asian Co-prosperity Sphere were formulated according to the theoretical design found in *Logic of Species*. In this case, too, the relationship between philosophy and politics is over-determined and far from direct. Second, the vision of the multi-ethnic state one can discern in *Logic of Species* was neither the vision officially sanctioned by the government nor the consensus shared by the political and military leaders and bureaucrats. Reading Tanabe's essays, we gain some understanding as to how some scholar-bureaucrats at imperial universities wanted to design Japanese imperialist policies, but argumentations which guided Japanese imperial nationalism did not form a monolith: competing political stances and different debates refuse to be summarized in a single continuous narrative.

Probably the most direct link between the policies of the government and Tanabe's philosophy can be found in an incident that took place at the Second Imperial University – that is, Kyoto Imperial University – on 19 May 1943. As chair of the philosophy department, Tanabe delivered a lecture entitled 'Shi Sei' ('Death and Life', or 'Death in Life'), to an audience that included a large number of volunteer student soldiers who were about to depart for battle.[8] In this infamous lecture, Tanabe unabashedly spoke as a passionate patriot, as an individualist committed to the state's mission, and offered a philosophical justification, in an exceptionally lucid – for Tanabe, indeed – language, for why 'the people [*kokumin*] have to devote themselves to the country'. Yet we should note that, even in this exemplary jingoistic lecture, the individual's devotion to the country is not limited to his participation in the concerted efforts to destroy the enemy and its facilities, and to the execution of his duty, even if it might result in the loss of his own life. 'One's devotion to the country' is not merely the passive subjugation of the individual to the commands issued by the state:

> At the time of emergency, of course, there should be no separation between the country and the individual. But we should at the same time acknowledge that the tendency for such separation exists even more strongly then. This is why [I claim the relationship between the individual and the state (= the country)] is dynamic. By removing separation, some could rather make profit for themselves in such a situation than sacrifice themselves to the country. In an extreme case, some may abhor the war and sympathize with the enemy countries. Knowing there are such facts, we cannot automatically presume that people always adhere to the state. As a matter of course, we must prevent separation from taking place, but, more importantly, we must aspire to create a situation where there is no need for separation, a situation where the state allows the individual to be fully himself and encourages him to act truly and righteously. As I mentioned above, the individual's devotion to the state is premissed on the absolute stance in which we can be with God. Returning from the absolute stance, we must act to make the state accord with the Way of God, and thereby prevent the state from deviating from truth and justice. We are called upon to destroy deception, untruthfulness and injustice within the state because these drive the nation to be alienated from the state and give rise to a separation between the nation and the state. But this cannot be accomplished unless one is determined to sacrifice oneself in this task just as one is in physical warfare. This is one's duty which requires the anticipatory resolution towards one's own death [*kesshi*].[9]

Operative here is Tanabe's basic formula, to which I will later return, according to which a man (the individual, *ko*) is with God (the genus, *rui*) by opposing the species or *shu* (the state). Through devotion to the state and by risking his own life, a man acquires a right to rebel against the state; what the individual aspires to realize even by staking his own life is not the factual content of the state's order or rule, but an idea whose validity goes beyond the existing state, and which, at least in principle, is true and just for entire humanity. This is why the individual's act of devoting himself to the state must be understood to imply not only the movement of the individual's identification with the state but also the movement of the individual's act to pull the state toward some universal principle beyond the existing state. Thus, the idea that is true and just for entire humanity, or the dimension of the genus or *rui*, is indispensable in Tanabe's justification of the self-sacrifice of the individual for the country. This is to say that, for Tanabe, the individual's devotion to the country could possibly take the form of rebellion against the government at any time. It is in this sense that the individual's devotion to the state can be called a duty whose execution requires anticipatory resolution towards one's own death (*kesshi no gimu*).

Tanabe's lecture 'Death and Life' was offered as the first in a series organized in order to deal with the anxiety over death felt by drafted or volunteer students who were about to go to war fronts. Many lectures, including Suzuki Shigetaka's and Kôsaka Masaaki's after Tanabe's, attempted to give a meaning to the probable death of those students by linking their devotion to the world historical mission of the Japanese state. Yet Tanabe also suggested the possibility that, once having anticipatorily put oneself on the side of death, and thereby secured one's loyalty to the country, one could in fact act to transform or even rebel against the existing state under the guidance of the universal idea whose validity is not confined to the existing state. I find it hard to imagine what could have been done in order to 'act to make the state accord with the Way of God' in 1943 when many Japanese intellectuals began to recognize the imminent defeat of the Japanese Empire. As though wittingly overlooking that his philosophical argument could easily be distorted or appropriated to serve unintended political interests, however, Tanabe Hajime presented rather naively a fundamental principle which should regulate the relationship of the individual to the state.

Insofar as the relationship between the state and the individual is seen from the viewpoint of the individual's death, the lecture 'Death and Life' discloses a philosophical insight into the individual's subjectivity and his participation in the state, an insight that was repeated, perhaps unwittingly, seventeen years later in 1960, by Maruyama Masao in his thesis on loyalty and rebellion after the defeat.[10] Here, it is important to stress that, in both Tanabe's and Maruyama's observation, either the individual's identification with the state or rebellion against it would be inconceivable unless the nation-state for the individual is primarily and essentially something to which the individual *chooses* to belong. Let us keep in mind that the problem of loyalty and rebellion would dissipate were the individual thought to belong naturally – or *in itself* – to the country or to the 'species' in Tanabe's terminology. Yet, from this, does it not follow that the species can be divided into natural and non-natural ones? What is at stake in Tanabe's observations is that the individual is always able to posit an existing social grouping she belongs to as something not naturally inherent to her, as something for her choice. Her belonging to it is never her natural property.

Therefore, it is clearly stated that the individual belongs to a social grouping as a result of her wishing to belong to it and that the individual's belonging to the nation, for instance, must be 'mediated' by *her freedom*. One can identify oneself with the country because freedom is available for one not to do so. Only by giving up the possibility of not identifying with or of separating oneself from the nation can one gain one's belonging to it. So, in order to belong to it, one must choose to *give up* the possibility of not belonging to it. It is a closing that must be intentional. It is an investment in a negative form, and as a reward for this investment the individual gains the ground on which to justify her act which would otherwise appear treasonable, an act 'to make the state accord with the Way of God, and thereby prevent the state from deviating from truth and justice'. The closing is a scheme to translate the fact of the individual's belonging to a social grouping into a matter of choice, and the freedom of separating oneself from it must be granted in order for this scheme to operate. Needless to say, separation from the nation need not be physical. Subsequently, one cannot belong to the nation naturally or without 'mediation'. This is to say that no body among the Japanese nation is, naturally and immediately, Japanese.

Underlying Tanabe's emphatic stress on the individual's freedom and negativity is a philosophical thesis that neither nation nor ethnos could possibly be conceptualized as a particularity within the generality of humanity; that the arborescent taxonomy of the Linnaean type, of the species and the genus, is not only utterly inadequate to but also politically and morally misleading for an understanding of how humans form their collectivities and thereby divide humanity into many ensembles. Yet, strangely enough, Tanabe continued to base his argument on the concepts of the species and the genus.

Outside the discipline of formal logic to which the name Aristotle is attributed, the term 'species' is most often used in biological taxonomies as a median term in the series: individual (*ko*), species (*shu*), genus (*rui*). Individuals are always members of some class, just as individual humans are also members of the subset, species, of that genus, and each subset distinguishes itself by its *specific difference* from other subsets. Because of its association with biological taxonomy, which in essence preserves the dictates of classical logic, Tanabe Hajime has to establish, in the domains of knowledge of the social and historical, a new use of the term 'species' which clearly differs from its uses in the botanical and zoological sciences and natural history. In a sense, Tanabe introduced his concept of species in his social ontology in order to disqualify the validity of the old Linnaean classification in the domain of the social. And in so far as the category of race is associated with the discourse of Linnaean taxonomy and eighteenth- and nineteenth-century biology, it can be said that he introduced his concept of species in place of the racialized one. By no means, however, do I imply that Tanabe's *Logic of Species* is therefore outside racism. Rather, it is with the acknowledgement of the fundamental inadequacy of the logical taxonomy of the species and the genus that Tanabe's social ontology begins. Concurrently, let me note, the notion of the individual or *kotai* can no longer be conceived within the Linnaean classification, either.[11]

This is to say that the term *kotai*, which I have to translate into 'the individual' for the lack of a more appropriate word, cannot be directly equated to the individual as an indivisible unit of life.

In applying a term that is widely accepted in the classical taxonomies of creatures to inquiries into the social, however, there are two main dangers to be warded off by deliberately demarcating the concept of 'species' from the classical comprehension of the term. The first danger is an obvious one, in that the social sense of belonging to a group must never be confused with the biological and physiological facts of some creature belonging to a specific class.

Going back to the issue of the *minzoku* (nation, ethnos, folk or race), let me redefine it with regard to the question of taxonomy in general. First of all, the *minzoku* is not an immediate given unless it gains its reality through the individual: only when an individual *belongs* to it does the *minzoku* acquire its own reality. But how can we define an individual's belonging to a specific *minzoku*? Does the belonging to a specific *minzoku* mean that the individual shares the habits and mores of other members of the same group? Does it mean the sharing of the same language, of the same tradition, of the same culture? Or does it imply that the individual is blood-related to other members, lives in the same region, or shares the same physiognomic features?

All these attempts to define the individual as belonging to a specific *minzoku* externally and objectively seem inadequate precisely because none of them meets the following criterion.[12] In a social formation, the individual's belonging to a group is an essential part of his self-awareness or *jikaku*, so that an individual can never be classified into a species unless he is *aware of belonging to it*. In other words, unless he identifies himself with a *minzoku*, he cannot be said to belong to it. Furthermore, this belonging is not a matter of epistemic consciousness but a mode of praxis in the social. 'Self-awareness is not a lived experience (*taiken*); it is a mediation.'[13] Here, Tanabe uses the term 'mediation' in the Hegelian sense of *Vermittlung* of the subject's *self-othering with itself*. In social ontology, what one is, is simultaneously what one ought to be. Therefore, for Tanabe Hajime, the logical must ultimately be the ethical. Accordingly, his social ontology is called the logic of species, which is at the same time the ethics of species.

As Tanabe reiterates, self-awareness should, in the first place, not be problematized with regard to *understanding* (*Verstehen*) but in the context of *inference*, which involves the shift from one utterance to another, from one speaking voice to another, so that self-awareness must necessarily be conceptualized dialogically and dialectically.[14] In contrast, the biological taxonomy classifies an individual into a species without regard to the individual's self-awareness. This is to say that a subject (or *shukan*) who classifies the individual in a biological taxonomy does not return to the very individual that is classified.

The fact of the individual's belonging to a species is established irrespective of its freedom, of the freedom for the individual to refuse to belong to it. In this conception of belonging which the supposition of a totemic community assumes, there is no inner relation between the individual and the species so that the individual does not exert any influence over the way the species is. In other words, the individual in this case is not a subject, or is without self-awareness, because of the lack of an inner split or negation which is an essential moment in mediation; this mode of belonging does not constitute a social praxis. Not being autonomous, the individual unwittingly would do what it is accustomed to doing. It would simply obey given dictates, without being conscious of a gap between what ought to be and what is.[15] For the individual, therefore, the species is not a reality but a transparent irrelevancy.

The second danger is also related to the individual's freedom. Tanabe has clearly to distance himself from such a conception of the species as follows:

> The notion of moral or collective personality – in which 'personality' has *proper analogical* value – applies to the *people* as a whole in a genuine manner: because the people as a whole (a *natural whole*) are an ensemble of real individual persons and because their unity as a social whole derives from a common will to live together which originates in these real individual persons.
>
> Accordingly, the notion of moral or collective personality applies in a genuine manner to the *body politic*, which is the organic whole, composed of the *people*.[16]

In this typically corporatist comprehension of national community and the state, heterogeneity or discontinuity hardly exists between the 'real individual person' and 'the body politic'. An assembly of 'the people' is supposed to form some communion and constitutes itself as an organic whole. Tanabe emphatically distances himself from the corporatist conception of the social whole or of the species, and insists on *an essentially discordant relation* between the individual and the species. In this respect, Tanabe's social ontology from the outset assumes the undecidability inherent in modern subjectivity that is caused by the disappearance of the *body politic* in modern social formations.[17] This undecidability is preserved – partially if not fully – in the term 'negativity' and, as we will see, it plays the central role in Tanabe's social ontology.

The individual does not belong to the species in the same way that a part is embraced by and absorbed into the whole. In the corporatist conception of the social, which is still under the spell of pre-dialectical and therefore pre-modern logic, Tanabe argues, the part and the whole are understood as a relationship between two terms which are continuous with one another, that is, the particular and the general.[18] Here, I must hasten to add that the individual is not the general that is most particularized; it remains essentially heterogeneous to the opposition of the general and the particular. A human individual does not belong to a nation, for example, just as a cat belongs to the genus of cats or as a potato does to the class of tubers. By no means can the species be conceived of by analogy to an organism or in terms of an analytical relation between two terms.[19] So, how should we understand the state of affairs depicted in the statement 'an individual *belongs* to a nation, an ethnos, a *minzoku*, and so forth, that is, a species'?

It is important to keep in mind that, in one phase leading to a further elaboration on the concept of the species, Tanabe refers to the discussion of totemic organization by Durkheim and Lévy-Bruhl and gives high praise to their insight that the reign of a society over an individual must be understood according to the logical relationship of the general and the particular. Yet, the point most forcefully put forth by Tanabe is – contrary to Durkheim's sociologization of Kantian ethics – that the individual's belonging to the species cannot be characterized by its conformity to the totemic belief of a given group, whether that group is clannish, ethnic or national;[20] it must be premissed upon the *negation* of it. Tanabe's critique of French anthropological approaches to totemism shows that the supposition of the totemic community in which an individual *immediately* accepts its maxims without being aware of its belonging actually makes it impossible for an individual to act morally. Only where there is freedom on the part of the individual to negate and disobey the imperatives imposed upon it by the totemic beliefs can it be said to belong to it. In other words, *only as a subject* can the individual be said to *belong to* the species. Therefore, for the individual to be in the species is to be *mediated* by its negativity, and what is misleading about the corporatist conception of the species lies in the fact that it overlooks and suppresses negativity, without which the species would be a matter of no significance for the individual. What entails the transfer of the term from the domains of knowledge on natural beings to those on the social is that the social would be inconceivable without taking human negativity into account. So, if modernity is defined in terms of the negativity inherent in the constitution of a subject, the domain of the social itself is of modernity; the very possibility of thinking about the social is already marked by modernity.[21] Moreover, negativity could imply the discursive mediation of antagonism from the viewpoint of social practice, so the social would be incomprehensible once deprived of negativity and antagonism.

THE INDIVIDUAL, THE SPECIES, THE GENUS

Tanabe Hajime discerns two moments without which no relationship between the individual and the species can be thought, and outside of this relationship the recognition of one's belonging to the species cannot ensue: the first moment is the individual's factual participation in the given species, and the second is its negation of it. The first moment can be said to be that of *facticity*, whereas the second is that of negativity. Indeed, this very splitting of the moments is facilitated by negativity and a process of the subject's *self-othering with itself* or *mediation*.[22] At the same time, negativity opens up space not for a factual but for an active participation in the species. But, at this stage, that which the individual actively and wittingly decides to belong to does not remain the species as it used to be. For negativity and the first stage of mediation alter the nature of a social grouping in which one once was blindly and immediately placed.

Whereas, in immediacy, the individual would never constitute itself as a subject, it becomes a subject by returning to itself after reflecting upon and distancing itself from its immediate inheritance, through self-negation. Tanabe's exposition of the self-negational contradictory and heterogeneous relation between the individual and the species is at the same time an attempt to construct a logic of social praxis by rearticulating the logical (not analytic but dialectical) relations among individuals, the species and the genus (*ko*, *shu*, *rui*) in terms of the Hegelian triplicity of individuality, particularity and universality. Yet, one must instantly note that, up to this stage of development, the individual has not returned to itself and that, therefore, mediation has not completed its circle.

The species is not an entity, like a human body, a tree or a book, and one cannot designate it unless one mistakes its representative, or symbol or schema for it (I will return to this point). In order to deal with the reality of the species, therefore, we must start with the process of thematization in which its reality is brought into awareness. One comes to an awareness of its existence by negating and calling into question what has been taken for granted in one's own behaviour and customs. The thematization of the species is accompanied by a self-awareness on the part of the individual that it has been nurtured and cultivated in that substratum which it now wants to abandon. For the individual, the species is *its own* past and an other at the same time. In so far as it is a past from which the present is distinguished, the past is an other to and of the present. In this respect, the individual sheds its past and objectifies and distances itself from it.[23] But, as it recognizes the past as its own, it must subsume the species in itself. Accordingly, for the individual the species is constitutive of its facticity or thrownness (*Geworfenheit*), in Heideggerian terminology, in *Dasein*'s 'projective existence' (*Entwurft*) into the future. The thematization of the species is intertwined with the self-transcending or ecstatic *jikaku* or self-awareness as *geworfener Entwurft*, which is a mode of social practice by which to project oneself into the future and to bring about something which does not exist yet, rather than a mere epistemic recognition.[24]

Thus, the reality of the species is an institutional reality *par excellence*. It manifests itself as an assemblage of the universals which regulate individuals' behaviours, and can by no means be ascribed to the whimsy of an individual. It is a reservoir not of the individual but rather of collective habits. It is always of trans-personal and publicly habituated rules just like a language. Yet it is not ubiquitous or general in the sense of the genus that every member of humanity should be subsumed under the definition 'homo sapiens'. It is at this stage that Tanabe introduces the concept of *rui* or the genus and thereby indicates how one's belonging to the species inevitably leads to a participation in the genus of humanity.

Unlike the individual and the species, which possess reality in their respective senses, the genus is not a positive institutional reality. It follows that it is pointless to talk about the individual's refusal or disobedience of the genus. If the genus is discussed in this manner, as if it constituted a positive institutional reality, it invariably suggests the absolutization of a particular species, of which ethnocentrism is the best example, and leads to denying the individual its negativity. In other words, the genus is not the positive reality one could revolt against or disobey. Rather, it exists as something like a problematic. Nonetheless, it signifies an infinitely open society for the totality of humanity, the only society which encompasses every member of humanity. Yet:

> To dissolve [into the genus] particular societies which oppose one another is to neglect the concreteness of social being. It amounts to erasing the problems for social beings rather than solving them. History has proven how disrupting for the progress of humanity and how numbing to one's conscience it is to entrust all to religion's absolute affirmativeness.[25]

(History would prove this point again, in Tanabe's own career in the late 1930s and 1940s. Can you think of a better example of 'religion's absolute affirmativeness' than his lecture 'Death and Life'?) The genus is an essential moment in mediation between the individual and the species. The genus is not the general that underlies a *specific difference* between one particular species and another as in Aristotelian logic. The genus is called for in the individual's refusal and disobedience of the edicts of the given social institutions which have been internalized by individuals. The individual negates and deviates from the species by appealing to something higher than the rules whose validity is specific and limited.

If I lived in a community in which, for instance, the locality of my residence is predetermined by my racial status, I could either take such a state of affairs for granted or call it into question, thereby risking fragmenting and dividing the putative unity of that community. According to Tanabe, my belonging to that community becomes an issue for my self-awareness only when I act to disagree or disobey such a custom, thereby risking fragmentation and division of that community. In other words, I do not belong to that community naturally because of my birth or another innate accident, but *only when I try to negate and change it will I begin to belong to it*. Yet my belonging to it is potentially a divisive moment which might result in a schism in the putative coherence of the community. So, I would have to appeal to an authority beyond the dictates which are immediately sanctioned by that community in order to call that custom into question. I can act to change it only by introducing and adhering to an imperative, whose execution is impossible within the given dictates of that community, and the implementation of which will bring about something that does not exist as yet. Nevertheless, the imperative thus introduced cannot be my own; even if I am absolutely alone in my commitment to it, the imperative I volunteer to abide by must be collectively valid. I would have to postulate the principle of equality, which I believe to be not only higher than the dictates of the community but also acceptable by *everyone in the world* in principle.[26] In the name of this principle, I would engage in an antagonistic relation with the members of the community who refuse to agree with the transformation of the community in this direction. This is a struggle in which one can be destroyed by the majority of the community or can destroy it. It can be a struggle of life or death. Yet, one has to postulate beyond this given community a collectivity for whom this principle of equality is a rule by which to live. But, as we can realize instantly, this collectivity is not a positive reality because we cannot find any factually existent community of people which actually lives according to it anywhere in the world. Perhaps this is why Tanabe felt justified in using such terms as God, for instance, in 'Death and Life' when he said 'we must act to make the state accord with the Way of God, and thereby prevent the state from deviating from truth and justice'.[27]

A collectivity defined by the dictate in which one engages to change the species does not exist positively; it is the genus. The genus is not a positively existing institutional reality; it exists in the individual's struggle with the species. Furthermore, if each dictate positively demands a different collectivity, different dictates beyond any community could postulate different genera which could be the totality of humanity at the same time. In other words, the genus must be mediated by the individual's negativity, but it cannot be a positive reality such as the species. The totality of humanity is inexpressible in any institutional form, and, consequently, often called God by Tanabe.

It is in relation to the genus that the individual is independent of the species:

> Unlike the species it [the genus] does not directly oppose the individual; instead, it liberates the individual from the constraints of the species and lets it assume a free stance as an individual. Thereby the genus comes into being, mediated by the negativity of the individual's relation to the species.[28]

So the genus is neither a generalization of many species, nor an ideal representative of them. Simply, the genus is in the element not of generality but of universality. Again the term 'genus' betrays the conceptual economy of the particularity–generality framework which many of us take for granted. It is the absolute totality which is expressed in human *historical* action but which cannot be represented conceptually. For it is *an idea*. Tanabe agrees with Max Scheler in that the individual's moral action expresses the eternal absolute and, therefore, that historical practice based upon the individual's autonomous will can be understood as an action contributing itself teleologically toward the absolute totality.[29] In this respect, too, we cannot think of the genus as commensurate with differences and commonnesses among species. The genus cannot be posited in the register of conceptual opposition or what Gilles Deleuze calls 'differen*c*iation'.[30] By virtue of the fact that the genus is radically heterogeneous with and negative to the species, every individual can be recognized as equal under the genus (equality only in the negative sense, that is, of the absence of a hierarchical ordering), irrespective of its factual belonging to a particular species. For this reason, the ultimate totality of humanity must be *mu* in the sense of being an absolute negativity.[31]

Thus the individual returns to itself only when it also participates in the genus and distances itself from the species. But it does not follow that the individual would then cease to belong to the species. Negative mediation also transforms the species, so that the individual's negativity indicates the basic mode of social practice by which to work on social reality. 'Praxis [*jissen*] whereby the species is renewed puts the individual and the species in correlation.'[32] (The liberal notion of voting in a general election which allows the individual to participate in the process of transforming a social formation might fit this idea of praxis, but Tanabe does not specify it.) Accordingly, the sense of one's belonging must be altered. Through social praxis, which is negative in regard to the given formation, the individual belongs to the species by actively transforming it, according to the dictates of universal humanity. Thus, only as a practical subject or *jissen shutai* can the individual belong to it. At the same time, though, the species which the practical subject works to transform cannot remain immediate.

Here, too, Tanabe recognizes two moments inherent in the mediation of self-negational contradiction, this time from the viewpoint of the species: one concerning the ethnic and factual constraints from which no individual can escape; and another which mediates both antagonisms among the individuals within the same species, and contradictions between the individual and the species. These two moments are explained in a variety of ways: for example, in reference to Tönnies' distinction of *Gemeinschaft* (*shuteki kyôdô shakai*) and *Gesellschaft* (*koteki keiyaku shakai*) and the Bergsonian opposition of the closed society and the open society. According to Tanabe, in this process a clear distinction is made possible between the substratum as that on which the individual *is*, and the subject which acts socially towards other individuals. But this distinction applies only within mediation. This is the point to be remembered in the following exposition.

In this regard, let me note the complexity of the term 'subject' or *shutai* as Tanabe adopts it here, since this term was used by many at that time in slightly different ways. In history, an individual acts to transform the given community by believing in the universality of a certain idea. Therefore, in so far as an individual's action can be regarded as a historical practice (*rekishiteki jissen*) that embodies the conviction that its action will be justified not because it is an action based upon its particular whim but because it *ought* to be sanctioned by the genus – that is, the totality of humanity (which does not exist positively) – it is also an action of that idea. Thus, an individual acts in history to constitute itself as a subject, but the same historical practice is the process in which the idea realizes itself as a Subject or Spirit. Therefore, in historical practice, the subject's will to act is already and always the Subject's will,[33] just as 'The *labour* of the individual for his own needs is just as much a satisfaction of the needs of others as of his own, and the satisfaction of his own needs he obtains only through the labour of others.'[34]

> As the individual in his *individual* work already *unconsciously* performs a *universal* work, so again he also performs the universal work as his *conscious* object; the whole becomes, as *a* whole, his own work, for which he sacrifices himself and precisely in so doing receives back from it his own self.[35]

Even if one is not sanctioned by anybody in the positive sense and has to act alone and in absolute isolation, as was the case with Jesus, historical practice is the action of the Subject whereby the individual returns to itself.[36]

Thus the individual comes across the genus only when it cannot abide by the imperatives of a given species. In relation to the genus, the individual is singular and independent of the species as substratum in which it is supposed to be embraced. In other words, the individual is then alienated from the immediate community and stands alone. It is in this solitude that the individual is able to encounter the genus, and this insight is consistently emphasized throughout Tanabe's writings. Thus Tanabe argues that his concepts of the individual, the species, and the genus correspond to the Son, the Holy Ghost and the Father, respectively, in the Holy Trinity.[37] As an isolated singular abandoned by the Father, the individual is the Son. The individual as the Son encounters the genus as the Father precisely in the absence of the Father. And through the anticipatory resolution towards its own death – as we have already seen in Tanabe's lecture 'Death and Life' – the individual can work to change the species.

Thus the reality which the individual obtains through negativity and historical practice is at the same time a species and a work as the Subject. Tanabe calls this reality the 'kitai *soku* shutai', or 'substratum *that is* Subject'. Through the participation of the genus, a society – or an ethical substance in Hegelian terminology – which is called the *minzoku kokka* or nation-state emerges, and this society is not directly the species because it embodies the dictates of universal humanity. It is the synthesis of the individual's factual belonging to a given community of customs and mores and its belonging to universal humanity. Therefore, the state in the nation-state in this formulation implies the moment of the agent as a *Subject*,[38] while the nation in the nation-state means the unity of the work as a *community* which individuals create collectively by transforming the given social reality. Thus it was possible for Tanabe to argue:

> 'To be a member of the state is the highest right [and obligation] for the individual.' If the subject of this proposition simply means that any individual is born and dies within the state or that the life of the individual becomes possible only when it is incorporated into the variety of state organizations, the proposition would not be able to take the predicate 'the highest right'. That it is thus predicated should mean that the proposition does not state a mere [observable] fact but that it refers to the state of affairs which has to be realized by the individual's will and action. In other words, it implies that, while the individual could will to refuse it, the individual is obliged to will and, following such a will, to promote the realization of such a state of affairs . . . Therefore, membership in the state should not demand that the individual sacrifice all its freedom and autonomy for the sake of the unity of the species. On the contrary, the proposition would not make sense unless the state appropriates into itself individual freedom as its essential moment.[39]

Therefore the view which equates the nation–state with one ethnic community cannot be accepted at all. Hence, Tanabe criticizes Hegel for his ethnocentricity: 'Hegel never completely rid himself of the tendency to regard the State as the ethnic spirit of an ethnic community.'[40] The claim that to be a member of the state is the highest right and obligation *for the individual* would not be accepted unless the individual negates the ethicality (*Sittlichkeit*) of a specific community and actively endorses the morality (*Moralität*) for the individual to transcend the particularity of a specific community toward the universality of generic humanity. Absolute loyalty to the state can be legitimated only when the state is an actualization of the universalistic logic of mediation which goes beyond the ethnically specific and towards the state that grounds the individuality of the individual returning to itself through universality. One might suspect a complicity between universalistic nationalism and cosmopolitan individualism in Tanabe Hajime's *Logic of Species*.

IN PLACE OF A CONCLUSION

As we have seen above, Tanabe's *Logic of Species* was intended to refute and dissuade *Minzoku-shugi* or ethnic nationalism, which was perceived to be the most immediate menace to Japanese imperial nationalism in the 1930s, by taking into account the historical conditions that drove people to ethnic nationalism and the social antagonisms that made ethnic nationalism so attractive to the people under colonial rule.[41] If seen from the viewpoint of ethnic nationalism, *Logic of Species* would appear to comprise a series of meditations that attempt to undermine any political and philosophical discourse that would legitimate a particularistic rebellion against universalism in the name of which imperialism dominates. Tanabe's argument is conspicuous for its almost obsessive emphasis on negativity and for its rather religious notion of universal humanity, which, one can sense, must have had a certain appeal to Marxist activists and other leftists, many of whom in fact supported ethnic nationalism and separatism in Japan's annexed territories and who later had to undergo the traumatic experience of conversion or what is known as *tenkô*.[42] On the other hand, as the term *shu* clearly indicates, he was also concerned with the particular historical and cultural conditions of the time. Given these cursory observations and the outline of his philosophical project, how should we understand the connections between his philosophy and nationalism?

In the 1920s and 1930s, the Japanese Empire covered many overseas territories, including Hokkaidô, Taiwan, Korea, the southern part of Sakhalin, Manchuria, the Pacific Islands, and so forth. The population under the jurisdiction of the Japanese state could not be viewed as linguistically and culturally homogeneous by any account. Although I have serious doubts about the validity of the distinction between mono-ethnic and multi-ethnic societies, we may use the term 'multi-ethnic' in order to draw attention to the composition of the Japanese Empire at that time. It was simply impossible to assume a simple overlapping between the state and the ethnos or any 'natural' community, although those minorities in the Empire were rendered somewhat invisible. The state had to represent and incorporate a multitude of the populace which did not share any single national language or ethnic culture in so far as 'language' or 'culture' is understood to be a closed unity.

Tanabe never ignored this historical situation: his conception of the state in the nation-state reflected his awareness of it in the following:

> The opposition of a species against another species necessarily contains a duality: it is the exclusionary relationship between plural species on the one hand, and the opposition of the individual to the species on the other hand. The state is the synthesis of the individual and the species. Therefore it must necessarily mediate the opposition between the conquering species and the conquered species and thereby sublate that opposition into a generic synthesis by recognizing the freedom of the members of the conquered species *to a certain extent* and by appropriating the former enemy.[43]

Thus, Tanabe seeks the historical origin of the state in the conquest of one species over another. 'Though not related to the conquered through blood ties, the conquering species allows the conquered to survive, and unifies it into itself through the mediation of the shared land.'[44] Ethnic conflicts are mediated by the state's recognition of a minority's freedom just as it recognizes the individual's freedom that facilitates collaborative economic activities among those opposing groups. Or, since the species could signify the social class, inter-specific conflict could be a class conflict. But this recognition must be limited; it is permitted only *nanrakano teidono* or *to a certain extent* because the ethical substance is also a political sphere where struggles cannot be absent.

It is evident that the species is not an ahistorical entity. It is a moment in mediation which goes on in world history. But the individual belonging to the conquered species can continue to negate a given social reality and work for its transformation. In this respect, it is not the immediate species but the state that provides the individual with opportunities for justice that is valid beyond the confines of a specific community. For the species, in so far as it is the ethical substance which is mediated by the genus – that is, *kokkateki minzoku* or state nation – is always in a dialectical process in which it continues to split itself and appropriate other specific communities. But, by the same token, the existence of the state already implies that the society reigned over by the state consists of a plurality of specific communities.[45] Unless there is ethnic or class conflict, the state would not be called for, so there the state would never be. Internal antagonism dialectically gives rise to the state just as the individual's negativity invites the moment of universal humanity into the species. In the ambivalent hyphenation between the nation and the state, one thing is certain: *there is no necessity for the state unless the nation is multi-specific (or multi-ethnic)*. Where there is no multiplicity of species in the state, that state cannot exist in the modern world. In order for the nation–state of Japan to exist, therefore, the Japanese nation must be multi-ethnic, though what is signified by multi-ethnicity in this instance is far from clear. A logical corollary of this insight, which Tanabe Hajime would never have pronounced publicly, was that no modern nation-state could possibly exist except as *a trace of colonial violence* that necessarily gave rise to social antagonism among the species.

Since I have to omit a detailed examination of how *Logic of Species* could have served and justified Japanese colonial rule and total mobilization policies during the Asia-Pacific war, let me state the following in place of a conclusion to this article. When seen from the viewpoint of the minority population in the Empire who were mobilized for Japan's war efforts, *Logic of Species* was nothing but an endorsement of colonial violence. Because of its universalistic aspiration and the sense of national mission, it was exceptionally aggressive and violent. Just as it was one of the sources for the philosophy of world history, it also gave rise to the philosophy of world war.

ACKNOWLEDGEMENT

This chapter was first published in *Radical Philosophy*, 95, May/June 1999. It is reproduced here (with minor amendments) with permission.

CHAPTER 8

On Chineseness as a Theoretical Problem

REY CHOW

My main concern in this chapter is with ethnicity not simply as a sociological fact, seemingly evident everywhere, but rather as a problematic in the production, organization, and transmission of knowledge – a problematic that requires theoretical analysis rather than empiricist assertion.[1] What this means, within the parameters of academic intellectual inquiry, is that we need to make a fundamental critique of the practices of pedagogical dissemination, including the assumptions, long held as givens, about language, literary genres, stylistic conventions, and so forth – things that have not hitherto been understood in close relation to the ethnic as such. The field of China study – in particular the study of the Chinese languages, literatures, and cultures – serves as an excellent case in point for several reasons. First, due to the Western imperialism and colonialism of the past few hundred years, sinology as it is pursued in European and American institutions very much, to this day, partakes of the discursive politics of orientalism, a politics that often includes impassioned denials of biased representation by its white practitioners, who as a rule believe that they have specialized in a non-whites culture out of love. Second, as is often the case with reactions to orientalism, there exists in the China field the familiar claim, held by many who are ethnically Chinese as well as by their non-Chinese colleagues, of a unique, original ethnic tradition, as though the violence of a continuing Western domination must be offset with an equally violent nativist rebuttal, a determined (re)construction, in the postcolonial aftermath, of a virginal past. Third, the presence of a Chinese diaspora in almost every part of the contemporary world inevitably complicates matters: these displaced populations, many of whom have nothing any more to do with China, its languages, or its cultures, but who are nonetheless identifiable as

Chinese, obviously problematize the grand narrative of a continuous ethnic heritage. Yet in the controversies over cultural identity, the signs of the times are that the diasporic is fast becoming the norm.

Although all of these issues can be and have been studied sociologically or historically, the point of my discussion, as mentioned, is rather how such issues are inseparable from epistemological, linguistic, literary – in short, representational – considerations. Without the academic and scholarly forces that rationalize, consolidate, and reproduce it, would the ethnic as such remain viable? To this extent, the systematic cultivation, rewarding, and empowerment of uncritical thinking among those who inhabit the China field – including the persistent reluctance on the part of most of its practitioners to speak against the racism embedded in the pedagogical practices they have inherited, and the resolute silence on the part of many contemporary Chinese intellectuals, inside and outside China, *vis-à-vis* Chinese cultural chauvinism – are simply some of the more readily recognizable symptoms of this particular regime of ethnicity production.

THE ETHNIC SUPPLEMENT AND THE LOGIC OF THE WOUND

For several years now, with much fanfare and controversy, what is generally known as theory – by which is really meant post-structuralist theory even though other types of discourses are sometimes included – has made its way into modern Chinese literary (and of late, cultural) studies. Numerous publications, issued by university presses such as Stanford, Duke, California, and others, seem to respond to the consensus, among the younger generations of scholars at least, that some use of or reference to theory is a necessity.[2] While the most prominent example is probably feminist theory and its corresponding investigations of women,[3] buzz words such as *postcolonial*, *postmodern*, *the body*, *the subject*, *interdisciplinarity*, and so forth also seem ubiquitous and popular. The hostility toward 'Western theory', which merely a decade ago was still predominant in the field of China studies, has apparently become all but marginalized to the point of insignificance.

This enthusiasm for theory coincides, in many ways, with enthusiasm at a different, though not unrelated level – that of *Realpolitik*. With the modernization campaign introduced by Deng Xiaoping after he resumed political centrality in the late 1970s, the People's Republic of China (PRC) has been undergoing rapid, radical economic reforms, so much so that, by the early fall of 1997, a massive plan to convert most of China's state-owned enterprises into 'share-holding' ones was announced in the Fifteenth Communist Party Congress, leaving many to wonder exactly what would still be left of the

Chinese government's avowedly socialist or communist ideological commitment. Taken in the broad sense of the word *economy*, such openness toward economics may be understood, though with much debate, of course, as a pragmatic acceptance of an order that is capable of managing things so that they *work*. For China at this historical juncture, the economic order that works is one that is capable of successfully transforming the existing, stored-up power of labour into energy that mobilizes and propels – into capital.

Much the same can be said about theory. As speculative labour, theory, too, seems to have acquired in the field of China studies something of the aura of a managerial economy that works, an economy that can transform the substantial accumulation of labour – in the form of knowledge – into a new type of force: cultural capital, the chief characteristic of which is its fluidity, its capacity for bypassing the cumbersome gravity of iron-clad boundaries, be those boundaries national, racial, sexual, or disciplinary. If both economics and theory share a common new goal of turning things around where they have become stagnant, it is because they also share the telos of 'progress', a rationalistic aspiration toward acceptance, recognition, and active membership on the global scene.

The parallel between academic and political economies does not stop at the level of what works, be it in the form of cultural or financial capital. Both are marked, as well, by a recurrent symptom, the habitually adamant insistence on *Chineseness* as the distinguishing trait in what otherwise purport to be mobile, international practices. Just as socialism, modernization, or nationalism at the level of *Realpolitik* has been regularly supplemented by the word *Chinese*, so, in the much smaller sphere of the academic study of China, is the word *Chinese* frequently used to modify general, theoretical issues such as modernity, modernism, feminism, poetic tradition, novels, gay and lesbian issues, film theory, cultural studies, and so forth. One can almost be certain that, once a new type of discourse gains currency among academics at large, academics working on China-related topics will sooner or later produce a 'Chinese' response to it that would both make use of the opportunity for attention made available by the generality of the theoretical issue at hand *and* deflect it by way of historical and cultural characteristics that are specific to China.

This collective habit of supplementing every major world trend with the notion of 'Chinese' is the result of an over-determined series of historical factors, the most crucial of which is the lingering, pervasive hegemony of Western culture. 'The West', in this instance, is, as Naoki Sakai writes, 'not merely a geographic particular: it is an ambiguous and ubiquitous presence of a certain global domination whose subject can hardly be identifiable'; the West is what 'peoples in the so-called non-West have to refer to and rely on . . . so as to construct their own cultural and historical identity'.[4] Against the systematic exclusivism of many hegemonic Western practices, the ethnic supplement occurs first and foremost as a struggle for access to representation while at the same time contesting the conventional simplification and stereotyping of ethnic subjects as such.[5] Nevertheless, even when such access is achieved, the mainstream recognition of non-Western representations is not necessarily, often not at all, free of prejudice. As I have pointed out in my discussion of contemporary Chinese cinema, there remains in the West, against the current façade of welcoming non-Western 'others' into putatively interdisciplinary and cross-cultural exchanges, a continual tendency to stigmatize and ghettoize non-Western cultures precisely by way of ethnic, national labels.[6] Hence, whereas it would be acceptable for authors dealing with specific cultures, such as those of Britain, France, the United States, or the ancient Greco-Roman world, to use generic titles such as *Women Writers and the Problem of Aesthetics*, *Gender Trouble*, *Otherness and Literary Language*, *The Force of Law*, *The Logic of Sense*, *This Sex Which Is Not One*, *Tales of Love*, and so on, authors dealing with non-Western cultures are often expected to mark their subject matter with words such as *Chinese*, *Japanese*, *Indian*, *Korean*, *Vietnamese*, and their like. While the former are thought to deal with intellectual or theoretical issues, the latter, even when they are dealing with intellectual or theoretical issues, are compulsorily required to characterize such issues with *geopolitical realism*, to stabilize and fix their intellectual and theoretical content by way of a national, ethnic, or cultural location. Once such a location is named, however, the work associated with it is usually considered too narrow or specialized to warrant general interest. That this vicious circle of discriminatory practice has gone largely uncontested even by those who are supposedly sensitive to cultural difference is something that bespeaks the insidious hypocrisy of what purports, in North America at least, to be an enlightened academy. To this extent, authors who feel obliged to comply with this convention (of categorizing intellectual subject matter by way of ethnic labelling, which is deemed unnecessary in the case of whites and imperative in the case of nonwhites) are not personally responsible for the situation even as they perpetuate the problem by adhering to the convention. Such authors often have no choice.

In the case of China, the problematic of the ethnic supplement predates the current trends in North American academe. For a continuous period between the mid-nineteenth and the early twentieth centuries, China was targeted for territorial and military invasions by numerous Western powers as well as Japan, invasions that led to the signing of a series of what were known as unequal treaties between the Chinese government and various foreign nations, which were granted major monetary indemnities, territorial concessions, trading privileges, and legal exemptions (known as extraterritoriality) on Chinese soil. The unspoken rule of the Scramble for China at the turn of the twentieth century was simple: attack China, then proclaim you're being attacked and demand heavy compensation; if China fails to pay up, attack it some more, demand more compensation, and so forth. The recent historic return of the British Crown Colony of Hong Kong to the People's Republic was, for Chinese populations all over the world, regardless of their political loyalties, a major watershed that put an end to this 150-year history of aggression and violence against China. And yet, even as the history of humiliation that officially began with the Treaty of Nanking (signed as the result of the First Opium War, which led to the ceding of Hong Kong Island to Britain in 1842) formally closed on 1 July 1997 – without violence or bloodshed – the media in the West, led by Britain and the United States, continued their well-worn practice of broadcasting all news about China as a *crisis*, picking on the smallest details in a militant goading-on of so called democracy in order to demonize China and thus affirm Western moral supremacy.[7]

While this is not exactly the place to recapitulate modern Chinese history in detail – interested readers will be able to find volumes devoted to the topic easily – I highlight it for the purpose of underscoring the historicity behind the issue of ethnic supplementarity. Chinese intellectuals' obsession with China and their compulsion to emphasize the Chinese dimension to all universal questions are very much an outgrowth of this relatively recent world history.[8] In the face of a pre-emptive Western hegemony, which expressed itself militarily and territorially in the past, and which expresses itself discursively in the present, Chinese intellectuals in the twentieth century have found themselves occupying a more or less reactive, rather than active, position. The subsequent paranoid tendency to cast doubt on everything Western and to insist on qualifying it with the word *Chinese* thus becomes typical of what I would call *the logic of the wound*. Beginning as a justified reaction to aggression, and gathering and nurturing means of establishing cultural integrity in defence, the logic of the wound is not unique to China. Nonetheless, it is something modern and contemporary Chinese culture seems enduringly reluctant to give it up.

In the habitual obsession with 'Chineseness', what we often encounter is a kind of cultural essentialism – in this case, sinocentrism – that draws an imaginary boundary between China and the rest of the world. Everything Chinese, it follows, is fantasized as somehow better – longer in existence, more intelligent, more scientific, more valuable, and ultimately beyond comparison. The historically conditioned paranoid reaction to the West, then, easily flips over and turns into a narcissistic, megalomanic affirmation of China; past victimization under Western imperialism and the need for national 'self-strengthening' in an earlier era, likewise, flip over and turn into fascistic arrogance and self-aggrandizement. Among the young generations of Chinese intellectuals in the People's Republic, the mobilization of an unabashedly chauvinistic sinocentrism – or what I would call, simply, sino-chauvinism – has already taken sensationally propagandist forms, typified by the slogan 'China can say no'.[9]

This paradoxical situation in which what begins as resistance to the discriminatory practices of the older Western hegemony becomes ethnicist aggression is part and parcel of what Etienne Balibar describes as the general displacement of the problematic of racism in the post-Second World War period. From the older racism based on biology and genetics, Balibar writes, the decolonized world has steadily shifted into a new, 'differentialist racism', which finds its justification no longer in the absoluteness of blood but in the insurmountability of cultural difference. Ironically, this new, second-order racism has been encouraged in part by the ideologically humanistic, indeed antiracist, arguments of the post-war phenomenon of anthropological culturalism, which is 'entirely oriented towards the recognition of the diversity and equality of cultures'. Such an emphasis on cultural differentials has led to a situation in which 'culture' itself and the aggressive racist conduct that is adopted to fortify cultural boundaries have become naturalized. Balibar argues:

> What we see here, is that biological or genetic naturalism is not the only means of naturalizing human behaviour and social affinities . . . [C]*ulture can also function like a nature*, and it can in particular function as a way of locking individuals and groups *a priori* into a genealogy, into a determination that is immutable and intangible in origin.[10]

As China emerges as a world power at the end of the twentieth century and the beginning of the twenty-first, these volatile realities of ethnicity will inevitably have to become a central part of modern Chinese studies. It is in this context that we should rethink the use of the label 'Chinese', which occurs as frequently as its status remains untheorized and taken for granted. In recent years, as various alternative forces gather momentum, we have begun to see a gradual epistemic shift that seeks to modify the claim of a homogeneously unified, univocal China. Among such alternative forces are studies of China's minority populations (for example, the Huis, or Chinese Moslems), continual demands for the liberation of Tibet, intermittent protests from Xinjiang and Inner Mongolia, repeated assertions of political and national autonomy by Taiwan, and concerted efforts for democratic government and the rule of law in post-British Hong Kong. As well, in the relatively new area of cultural studies, the notion of Chineseness as a monolithic given bound ultimately to mainland China has been interrogated and critiqued by scholars such as David Yen-ho Wu, Ien Ang, and Allen Chun, attentive to issues of the Chinese diaspora.[11] However flawed and unsatisfactory, the modes of inquiries made under the rubric of identity politics have indisputably opened up new avenues of engaging with ethnicity, which is, strictly speaking, an unfinished process. (Conversely, it is because traditional literary studies have not provided tools for understanding the politics of ethnicity – even while such studies are fully inscribed in ethnicity's fraught articulations – that the foregrounding of identity constructions may help lead to new ways of reassessing literary theories and practices themselves.) As Stuart Hall writes:

> We still have a great deal of work to do to *decouple* ethnicity, as it functions in the dominant discourse, from its equivalence with nationalism, imperialism, racism and the state . . . What is involved is the splitting of the notion of ethnicity between, on the one hand the dominant notion which connects it to nation and 'race' and on the other hand what I think is the beginning of a positive conception of the ethnicity of the margins, of the periphery.[12]

It is such 'splitting' of the notion of ethnicity that will, I believe, be instrumental to the reimagining of a field such as modern Chinese studies. Insofar as it deals with the politics of literary culture and representation, modern Chinese studies has, all along, we may say, been constructed precisely on the very ambiguity of the ethnic supplement – of the victim-cum-empire status of the term *Chinese*. Once ethnicity is introduced consciously as a theoretical problem, the conventions of understanding practices that are not explicitly about ethnicity as such take on new and provocative implications. For instance, what is Chinese about the Chinese language and Chinese literature? If *language* and *literature* in the narrow sense have been fundamentally dislocated in poststructuralist theory by way of the 'differences' inherent to signification, *Chinese* language and literature must now be seen as a further dislocation of this fundamental dislocation, requiring us to reassess 'ethnicity' (as a site of difference) not only in terms of a struggle against the West but also, increasingly, in terms of the permanently evolving mutations internal to the invocation of ethnicity itself, in particular as such mutations bear upon the practices of writing.

Within the institutional parameters of Chinese literary studies in the West, however, there is an additional ethnic factor that prohibits the problematization of ethnicity as I have suggested. This is the persistent orientalist approach adopted by some white China scholars toward their objects of study. Even at a time when race and ethnicity have become ineluctable issues in academic inquiry, such orientalism often continues bald-faced under the guise not only of 'objective' but also of morally 'progressive', indeed 'theoretical', discourses.[13] To fully confront the issue of Chineseness as a theoretical problem, therefore, it is not sufficient only to point to the lack of attempts to theorize Chineseness as such. It is equally important for us to question the sustained, conspicuous silence in the field of China studies on what it means for certain white scholars to expound so freely on the Chinese tradition, culture, language, history, women, and so forth in the postcolonial age; it is also important for us to ask why and how one group of people can continue to pose as the scientific investigators and moral custodians of another culture while the ethnic and racial premises of their own operations remain, as ever, exempt from interrogation. The theorization of Chineseness, in other words, would be incomplete without a concurrent problematization of *whiteness* within the broad frameworks of China and Asia studies.[14]

Having raised these general issues of ethnicity that pertain to the field of China studies as a whole, I will now move on to a brief analysis of the more specific aspects of the relation between Chineseness and the study of Chinese language and literature.

THE LANGUAGE ISSUE

One assumption that binds the discipline of Chinese studies is that of a so-called standard language, by which is meant the language *spoken* in Beijing, Mandarin, which has been adopted as the official 'national language' since the early twentieth century. Known in the People's Republic by its egalitarian-sounding appellation Putonghua (common speech), the hegemony of Mandarin has been made possible through its identification more or less with the written script, an identification that lends it a kind of permanence and authority not enjoyed by other Chinese speeches. Even in the instrumental uses of language, though, Chineseness – just what is Chinese about 'standard Chinese' – inevitably surfaces as a problem. As John DeFrancis writes, 'the "Chinese" spoken by close to a billion Han Chinese is an abstraction that covers a number of mutually unintelligible forms of speech'.[15] The multiple other languages – often known subordinately as 'dialects' – that are spoken by Chinese populations in China and elsewhere in the world clearly render the monolithic nature of such a standard untenable.[16]

In the West, meanwhile, this untenable standard is precisely what continues to be affirmed in the pedagogical dissemination of Chinese. When there are job openings in the area of Chinese language and literature in North American universities, for instance, the only candidates who will receive serious consideration are those who have verbal fluency in Mandarin. A candidate who can write perfect standard Chinese, who may have more experience writing and speaking Chinese than all the Caucasian members of a particular East Asian language and literature department combined, but whose mother tongue happens to be (let's say) Cantonese would be discriminated against and disqualified simply because knowledge of Chinese in such cases really does not mean knowledge of *any* kind of Chinese speech or even command of the standardized Chinese written language but, specifically, competence in Mandarin, the 'standard' speech that most white sinologists learn when they learn to speak Chinese at all.

Such, then, is the fraught, paradoxical identity of a non-Western language in the postcolonial era: Mandarin is, properly speaking, also *the white man's Chinese*, the Chinese that receives its international authentication as 'standard Chinese' in part because, among the many forms of Chinese speeches, it is the one inflected with the largest number of foreign, especially Western, accents. Yet, despite its currency among non-native speakers, Mandarin is not a straightforward parallel to a language such as English. Whereas the adoption of English in non-Western countries is a sign of Britain's colonial legacy, the enforcement of Mandarin in China and the West is rather a sign of the systematic *codification and management of ethnicity* that are typical of modernity, in this case through language implementation. Once we understand this, we see that the acquisition of the Chinese language as such, whether by environment or by choice, is never merely the acquisition of an instrument of communication; it is, rather, a participation in the system of value production that arises with the postcolonized ascriptions of cultural and ethnic identities.

In a context such as British Hong Kong, for instance, it was common for Chinese people in Hong Kong to grow up with a reasonable command of the Chinese language even as they were required to learn English. Nonetheless, with the systematically imposed supremacy of English in the colony, the knowledge of Chinese possessed by the majority of Chinese people, however sophisticated it might be, was not generally regarded as having any great value to speak of.[17] But the same was not true of Westerners: the rare instance of a Westerner knowing a few phrases of Chinese, let alone those who had actually learned to speak and read it, was instead usually hailed with wonderment as something of a miracle, as if it were a favour bestowed on the colonized natives. Similarly, in the West, knowledge of Chinese among non-Chinese sinologists is often deemed a mark of scholarly distinction (in the form of 'Wow, they actually know this difficult and exotic language!'), whereas the Chinese at the command of Chinese scholars is used instead as a criterion to judge not only their ethnic authenticity but also their academic credibility. For the white person, in other words, competence in Chinese is viewed as a status symbol, an additional professional asset; for the Chinese person, competence in Chinese is viewed rather as an index to existential value, of which one must supply a demonstration if one is not a native of Beijing. And, of course, if one is not a native of Beijing and thus not *bona fide* by definition, this attempt to prove oneself would be a doomed process from the beginning. Those who are ethnically Chinese but who for historical reasons have become linguistically distant or dispossessed are, without exception, deemed inauthentic and lacking.[18]

There are, in sum, at least two sets of urgent questions around the language issue. The first has to do with the 'other' Chinese languages that have so far remained incidental realities both in terms of state policy and in terms of pedagogy. As the polyphony of these other speeches and their respective ethnicities is likely to become louder in the decades to come, it will be increasingly impossible to continue to treat them simply as the negligible aspects of a canonized discipline. Officials and scholars alike will undoubtedly need to respond to the plurality that has hitherto been suppressed under the myth of 'standard Chinese'. But such a response cannot simply take the form of adding more voices to the existing canon. The second set of questions, therefore, has to do with a much-needed effort not only to multiply the number of languages recognized but also to theorize the controversial connections among language possession, ethnicity, and cultural value. These latter questions, which I believe are even more important than the first, have yet to begin to be raised in the field of modern Chinese studies.[19]

'CHINESE' LITERATURE: A LITERARY OR ETHNIC DIFFERENCE?

Another major assumption that binds the discipline of Chinese studies is that of an unproblematic linkage between Chineseness as such and Chinese *literary* writing. In such linkage, what is Chinese is often imagined and argued as completely distinct from its counterparts in the West, even as such counterparts are accepted in an *a priori* manner as models or criteria for comparison.

To use a classic example in this systematically *reactive construction of a fictive ethnicity in literary studies*,[20] let us take the prevalent belief among some sinologists that ancient Chinese writing is distinguished by a non-mimetic and non-allegorical (as opposed to a mimetic and allegorical) tradition. This belief, I should emphasize, is fundamentally akin to the premise of post-war anthropological culturalism, namely, that there is a need to recognize cultural difference in a world still run by the erasure of such difference. At the same time, the assertion of the Chinese difference tends often to operate from a set of binary oppositions, in which the Western literary tradition is understood to be metaphorical, figurative, thematically concerned with transcendence, and referring to a realm that is beyond this world, whereas the Chinese literary tradition is said to be metonymic, literal, immanentist, and self-referential (with literary signs referring not to an other-worldly realm above but back to the cosmic order of which the literary universe is part). The effort to promote China, in other words, is made through an *a priori* surrender to Western perspectives and categories.[21] Accordingly, if mimesis has been the chief characteristic of Western writing since time immemorial, then non-mimesis is the principle of Chinese writing.[22] Haun Saussy captures the drift and implications of these arguments in the following. According to the sinologists, he writes:

> Without 'another world' to refer to, no Chinese writer can possibly produce allegories. There are only contextualizations . . . The secret of Chinese rhetoric is that there is no rhetoric. The seeming allegories, metaphors, and tropes of Chinese poets do no more than report on features of the Chinese universe . . . Metaphor and fiction, instead of being dismissed or bracketed as constructs of Western ontology, have now been promoted (as categories) to the status of realities. It is an astonishing conclusion.[23]

Such arguments about the Chinese difference, as Saussy points out, have been made with great erudition. In referring to them, my point is not to challenge the technical mastery and historical knowledge that unquestionably accompany their formulation. Rather, it is to foreground the fact that, in the insistent invocation of a Chinese tradition – and with it Chinese readers with Chinese habits, sensibilities, perspectives, points of view, and so forth – seldom, if ever, has the question been asked: what exactly is meant by *Chinese*? Why is it necessary at all to reiterate what is Chinese in Chinese poetry by way of so-called Western attributes of poetic writing? What does it mean to supply this particular *copula* – to graft a term that is, strictly speaking, one of ethnicity onto discourses about literary matters such as allegory? If such erudite and authoritative accounts have succeeded in explaining the formal details of texts (by expounding on literary and historical commentaries that deal with the various uses of poetic conventions, for instance), little, if anything, has been done about the non-literary term *Chinese* even as it is repeatedly affixed to such studies. The (rhetorical) status of the term remains external to the formal issues involved, and the question of cultural difference, which such discussions of literary matters are supposedly addressing, simply refuses to disappear because it has, in fact, not yet been dealt with.

What happens as a result of latching the investigation of literary specificities to this unproblematized, because assumed, notion of Chineseness is that an entire theory of ethnicity becomes embedded (without ever being articulated as such) in the putative claims about Chinese poetics and literary studies. For instance, when it is assumed that poets, literati, commentators, and readers engage in literary practices in the Chinese way, the discourse of literary criticism, regardless of the intentions of the individual critic, tacitly takes on a cross-disciplinary significance to resemble that of classical anthropology. And, once classical anthropology is brought in, it becomes possible to see that the practitioners of Chinese writing – or the Chinese practitioners of writing – are, in effect, read as ethnics, or natives, who are endowed with a certain *primitive logic*. As the paradigm of anthropological information retrieval would have it, such treasures of primitive thought, however incomprehensible to the contemporary mind (and precisely because they are so incomprehensible), must be rescued. The Western sinologist thus joins the ranks of enlightened progressives engaged in the task of salvaging the remains of great ancient civilizations. Since it is no longer possible to interview the natives of ancient China – the writers of classical Chinese narratives and poems, and their contemporary readers – the texts left behind by them will need to be upheld as evidence of their essential ethnic difference.

But what *is* this essential ethnic difference? As I already indicated, it is, according to these sinologists, non-mimeticism, a way of writing and reading that is said to be natural, spontaneous, immanentist – and, most important, lacking in (the bad Western attributes of) allegorical, metaphorical, and fictive transformation. While ostensibly discussing literary matters, then, these sinologists have, *de facto*, been engaged in the (retroactive) construction of a certain ethnic identity. The Chinese that is being constructed is, accordingly, a non-mimetic, literal-minded, and therefore virtuous primitive – a noble savage.

The implications of this are serious and go well beyond the study of an esoteric literary tradition. The characterization, however well intended, of an entire group of people (the Chinese of ancient China) in such cognitive, psychological, or behavioural terms as a disposition toward literalness, is, in the terms of our ongoing discussion, racist. Even though it takes the benevolent form of valorizing and idealizing a projected collective 'difference',[24] such racism is, to use the words of Ang, 'reinforced precisely by pinning down people to their ethnic identity, by marking them as ethnic'.[25] In Balibar's words again, this is a racism 'whose dominant theme is not biological heredity but the insurmountability of cultural differences'. Culture here functions as 'a way of locking individuals and groups *a priori* into a genealogy, into a determination that is immutable and intangible in origin'.[26]

From this it follows that it is antiquity that remains privileged as the site of the essence of Chineseness, which appears to be more bona fide when it is found among the dead, when it is apprehended as part of an irretrievable past. Within the field of Chinese, then, the dead and the living are separated by what amounts to *an entangled class and race boundary*: high culture, that which is presumed to be ethnically pure, belongs with the inscrutable dead; low culture, that which is left over from the contaminating contacts with the foreign, belongs with those who happen to be alive and can still, unfortunately, speak and write. It is not an accident that one of the most memorable studies of the ancient Chinese is R.H. Van Gulik's *Sexual Life in Ancient China*, a fascinating account in which, at the crucial moments, highly metaphorical passages about sexual activities, written in classical Chinese – already a challenge to the imagination with their allusions to dragons, phoenixes, cicadas, jades, pearls, clouds, and rain – are translated into Latin.[27] If the trends of modern and contemporary society move in the direction of fluidity and translatability between cultures, the sinologist, on the contrary, finds his vocation rather in the painstaking preservation of savage thought. He does this by rendering such thought indecipherable except to the learned few, West and East. Primitive logic, here in the form of the art of the bedchamber, is thus museumized and dignified, gaining its exotic value and authority at once through a punctilious process of fossilization.

Ridden with the contradictions of a modernist, rationalist attempt to redeem the past, Western sinology seems ultimately unable to extricate itself from a condition of captivity in which the only kind of specialty it can claim is, by logic, 'hypotheses inimical to [its own] conclusions'.[28] With the passage of time, sinology has hardened into an obstinate elitist practice with the presumption that Chineseness – that very notion it uses to anchor its intended articulation of cultural difference – is essentially incomparable and hence beyond history. One could only surmise that, if sinology had been a little more willing to subject the belief in Chineseness to the same fastidious scrutiny it lavishes on arcane textual nuances, the intellectual results produced would perhaps have been less ephemeral.

LITERATURE AND ETHNICITY: A COERCED MIMETICISM

The ideological contradictions inherent in the study of premodern Chinese writing are not exactly resolved in modern Chinese studies, but because of the conscious efforts to politicize historical issues in modernity, scholars of modern Chinese literature are much more sensitized to the inextricable relation between formal literary issues and non-literary ones such as ethnicity. In modernity, the equivalence between Chinese literature and Chineseness enjoys none of the comfortable security of the dead that it has in sinology. Instead, it takes on the import of an irreducibly charged relation, wherein the historicity of ethnicity haunts even the most neutral, most objective discussions of *style*, resulting in various forms of mandated reflectionism.[29]

In his book *Rewriting Chinese*, Edward Gunn demonstrates how, in modern Chinese writing, style – a presumably formal matter involving rhetorical conventions that may be rationally explained through numerical analysis – has never been able to separate itself from tensions over *regional* diversities.[30] Since the early twentieth century, every attempt to stake out new ground in Chinese literature through recourse to more universal or global linguistic principles has, in turn, been weighed down and derailed by a corresponding set of demands about addressing specificities of native, local, rural, disenfranchised, and downtrodden voices, which, according to their defenders, have been left out and need to be given their place on the new stylistic ground. We think, for instance, of the May Fourth Movement of the late 1910s to the 1930s, with its advocacy of adopting Western linguistic styles in Chinese writing; the urbane Modernist Movement in the 1950s and 1960s in Taiwan, initiated by the Chinese elites who had left the mainland; and the renewed attempts at modernizing Chinese fiction and poetry in the People's Republic in the 1970s and 1980s after the climax of the Cultural Revolution. In retrospect, it is possible to say that the politics of style, like the standardization of language, is as much an index to the organization of ethnicity inherent to nation building as more overt bureaucratic measures, and that even the People's Republic's official strategies to *stylize* Chinese writing – to the extent of sacrificing the aesthetic value of the unpredictable – for the purpose of political cohesion must be seen as symptomatic of a postcolonial global modernity marked, as always, by massive ethnic inequalities.[31]

Interestingly, if we read such *political* strategies (to stylize and stabilize language) from a *literary* perspective, we would have to conclude that in the global scene of writing (understood as what defines and establishes national identity), Third World nations such as China have actually been *coerced into a kind of mimeticism*, into a kind of collective linguistic/stylistic mandate under which writing has to be reflectionist, has to be an authentic copy of the nation's reality. From the standpoint of the Chinese state, it was as if Chineseness had, in the twentieth century, become the burden of an ethnicity that was marginalized to the point of unintelligibility and the only way to be intelligible, to regain recognition in a world perpetually ignorant of and indifferent to Chinese history, is by going realist and mimetic: to institute, officially, that writing correspond faithfully to the life of the Chinese nation as an ethnic unit.

In other words, the administering of writing in modernity, whether at the level of native intellectuals' advocacy for large-scale formal changes or at the level of explicit intervention by the revolutionary state, is always, ultimately, a regimenting or disciplining of ethnicity as a potentially disruptive collective problem. To this we may add the work of cultural critics (outside China) who are intent on arguing for the Chinese difference.[32] It is in this light – in the light of the politics of Chinese writing in modernity – that we may finally appreciate the full implications of sinological arguments about ancient Chinese writing. Like the Chinese political state, the sinology that specializes in Chinese poetics/narratology, insofar as it attempts to ground Chineseness in specific ways of writing, can also be seen as a kind of ethnicity–management apparatus. Once this becomes clear – that is, once the attempt to ground Chineseness is understood to be, in fact, a managerial operation dictated by extra-literary circumstances – the idealistic assertion of a non-mimetic, non-allegorical tradition that distinguishes Chinese writing, that makes Chinese literature *Chinese* literature, can only crumble in its own theoretical foundations. For isn't equating a definitive classification (the non-mimetic) with what is Chinese precisely a mimeticist act – an act that, even as it claims to resist mimesis, in fact reinscribes literary writing squarely within the confines of a special kind of reflection – the reflection of a reality/myth called Chineseness?

Mimeticism here is no longer simply a literary convention, however. Rather, it is a type of representational copulation forced at the juncture between literature and ethnicity, a reflectionism that explicitly or implicitly establishes equivalence between a cultural practice and an ethnic label – in the form of 'this kind of poetic/narrative convention *is* Chinese'. In this equation, this act intended to validate a particular kind of writing *as* ethnic difference *per se*, mimeticism, chastised though it may be at the formal level as an evil Western tradition, returns with a vengeance as *the* stereotyped way to control and police the reception of literary writing. In the hands of the sinologists, even ancient poems and narratives, it turns out, are documentaries – of what is Chinese. In the study of modern Chinese literature, such mimeticism between writing and ethnicity, which has all along been foisted on Third World literature in general, would receive a different name – national allegory – soon to be adopted widely even among Chinese critics.

Meanwhile, the émigrés who can no longer claim proprietorship of Chinese culture through residency in China henceforth inhabit the melancholy position of an ethnic group that, as its identity is being 'authenticated' abroad, is simultaneously relegated to the existence of ethnographic specimens under the Western gaze. Worth mentioning in this context is the work of Tsi-an Hsia, who in the 1950s attempted, in Taiwan, to reinvigorate Chinese writing by advocating – borrowing the principles of the Anglo-American New Critics – serious attitudes toward 'new poetry'. One of the results of this attempt to rediscover the true poet's voice, however, was a further displacement of the ethnicity that such literary efforts were supposed to consolidate – the trend among Chinese students from Taiwan to study abroad in the United States, eventually bringing the habits of New Criticism to bear upon their reading of Chinese literature overseas.[33] As Gunn comments, 'it is tempting to conclude that T.A. Hsia and his students had not brought modern literature to Taiwan but had moved Chinese literature to the United States'.[34]

In exile, Chinese writing (first in Taiwan, then in the United States) is condemned to nostalgia, often no sooner reflecting or recording the 'reality' of Chinese life overseas than rendering Chineseness itself as something the essence of which belongs to a bygone era.[35] Even so, the coerciveness of the typical mimeticism between representation and ethnicity continues.[36] No matter how non-mimetic, experimental, subversive, or avant-garde such diasporic writing might try to be, it is invariably classified, marketed, and received in the West as Chinese, in a presupposed correspondence to that reality called China. As in the case of representations by all minorities in the West, a kind of paternalistic, if not downright racist, attitude persists as a method of categorizing minority discourse: minorities are allowed the right to speak only on the implicit expectation that they will speak in the documentary mode, 'reflecting' the group from which they come.[37]

REIMAGINING A FIELD

Although the abstract notion of the field of modern Chinese literary studies has hitherto been harnessed to the fantasy of an essentialized ethnicity, a standardized language, and a coercive equivalence between literary writing and Chineseness *per se*, even the most reactionary of the field's practitioners cannot be blind to the fact that, in the past decade or so, there has been an increasing non-coincidence between Chinese literary studies as such and what is actually taking place under its rubric. More and more scholars are turning to texts and media that are, strictly speaking, non-literary (including film, television dramas, radio programmes, art exhibits, and pop music), while non-China-related publications dealing with modernism, modernity, feminism, gay and lesbian studies, postcoloniality, philosophy, history, and so forth regularly fill China scholars' bibliographical lists. Against the rigidity of the norm of Chinese studies, then, a considerable range of discourses that are not Chinese by tradition, language, or discipline is making a substantial impact on the study of Chinese literature and culture. With the invasion of these foreign elements, how can the legitimating disciplinary boundary of Chinese versus non-Chinese be maintained? And, if we should attempt to redefine the field from Chinese language and literature to Chinese literary studies or Chinese cultural studies, what is the precise relation among these words – *Chinese*, *literary*, *cultural*, *studies*? Do Chinese literary studies and Chinese cultural studies mean the literary studies and cultural studies that are Chinese – in which case we would be confronted once again with the essentially external status of *Chinese* as an ethnic qualifier; or, do these designations mean the studies of Chinese literature and Chinese culture – in which case we would face the same problem, which was in the past circumvented by a grounding in language and ethnicity, a grounding that must nonetheless no longer be taken for granted? (The same pair of questions can probably be asked of similar claims about British, French, or American literary and cultural studies.) In either configuration, what remains to be articulated is what, after the formulations of literature, culture, and literary or cultural studies, constitutes the ethnic label itself.

The essays collected in the volume *Modern Chinese Literary and Cultural Studies in the Age of Theory* make it clear that the old model of area studies – an offshoot of the US Cold War political strategy that found its anchorage in higher education[38] – can no longer handle the diverse and multifaceted experiences that are articulated under the study of Chineseness, be that study through texts of fiction, film, history, art, subtitling, stand-up comedy, criticism, geographies of migration, or cultural studies. Instead, in the age of theory, new linkages and insights that may be at odds with more acceptable or naturalized conventions of interpretation continue to emerge, extending, redrawing, or simply traversing and abandoning existing boundaries of the field as such. The interior of Chinese studies is now not so distinguishable from its exterior. If there is one feature that all the essays in the aforementioned volume have in common, it is not so much China itself as a sense of the mobility, permeability, and continuity between the inside and the outside of modern Chinese studies.

Readers will form their own judgements as to whether the effort at reimagining the field of modern Chinese studies constitutes any significant intervention in the long run. What is finally noteworthy, in my view at least, is that even as the notion of Chineseness is implicitly or explicitly deconstructed and critiqued, and thus becomes more and more of a catachresis in any readings, one cannot assume that it is simply empty or arbitrary. Instead, we are confronted with the following questions: if, following Ien Ang's bold, diasporic reconceptualization, we may indeed say that Chineseness can no longer be held as a monolithic given tied to the mythic homeland but must rather be understood as a provisional, 'open signifier',[39] should we from now on simply speak of Chineseness in the plural – as so many kinds of Chineseness-es, so many Chinese identities? Should Chineseness from now on be understood no longer as a traceable origin but in terms of an ongoing history of dispersal, its reality always already displaced from what are imaginary, fantasmatic roots? As is evident in other intellectual movements, the course of progressivist anti-essentialism comprises many surprising twists and turns, and the problem of Chineseness is, one suspects, not likely to be resolved simply by way of the act of pluralizing. (White feminism, which has taught us that the problems inherent in the term *woman* have not disappeared with the introduction of the plural, *women*, is the best case in point here.) And it is at this juncture, when we realize that the post-structuralist theoretical move of splitting and multiplying a monolithic identity (such as China or Chinese) from within, powerful and necessary as it is, is by itself inadequate as a method of reading, that the careful study of texts and media becomes, once again, imperative, even as such study is now ineluctably refracted by the awareness of the unfinished and untotalizable workings of ethnicity. The study of specific texts and media, be they fictional, theoretical, or historical, is now indispensable precisely as a way of charting the myriad ascriptions of ethnicity, together with the cultural, political, and disciplinary purposes to which such ascriptions have typically been put.

Only with such close study, we may add, can Chineseness be productively put under erasure – not in the sense of being written out of existence but in the sense of being unpacked – and re-evaluated in the catachrestic modes of its signification, the very forms of its historical construction.

CHAPTER 9

Race and Slavery:
The Politics of Recovery and Reparation

FRANÇOISE VERGÈS

In January 2001, there was a preliminary meeting in Senegal to discuss calls for compensation for the slave trade and colonialism. The meeting laid the ground for the UN-backed world conference on world bigotry and injustice to be held in South Africa in September 2001. At the Dakar meeting, some delegates wanted the slave trade to be defined as a crime against humanity and the current economic situation of the poorest nations to be seen as economic racism from the West.[1] Delegates were thus shocked when they heard Abdoulaye Wade, Senegal's president, declare that 'racism against Africans in places such as Europe was "marginal" when compared to ethnic and fratricidal conflicts within Africa' and that 'campaigns to demand compensation for slavery and colonialism were childish'. Wade argued that lack of democracy in Africa was a far bigger problem, and ethnic violence on the continent a far more damaging phenomenon than discrimination and violence against Africans on foreign continents. Delegates, in their majority, rejected Wade's remarks and argued that the slave trade and colonialism shared the greatest responsibility for current ethnic strife. The goal set for the conference in the following September was to have the West offering an apology and compensation. This is not surprising. The terms are familiar, as is the discourse. Apology, compensation, reparation for the individual and the community, the *devoir de mémoire* (duty to remember) and the search for an external culprit frame most current discourses on past violence, present responsibility and possible grounds for a better future.

Against this apparent consensus Wade's characterization of the demand for compensation as 'childish' might appear flippant, but his remarks should not be too easily rejected. In this chapter. I wish to explore how race has come to be inextricably connected to a politics of reparation and recovery and with a narrative that insists on wounds and damages. I am not looking at the European philosophies that have promoted racism or at colonial racism. Here, I investigate the discourse, elaborated by the descendants of slaves and colonized peoples, of the politics of recovery and reparation. I will focus more specifically on the debate on slavery and reparation in the post-slavery French territories, the Creole societies of Martinique, Guadeloupe and Réunion.[2]

To be sure, the West's responsibility for the current state of African countries must still be underlined, analysed and explored.[3] Its philosophies of race must still be exposed for what they were and are. We must pursue that project. However, it is important – in fact, essential, I think – for those who are 'on the other side', those whose ancestors have suffered from European organized slavery and colonialism, to examine carefully the motives, desires, and intentions that support demands for apology and compensation. What is the *mise-en-scène* of the theatre of apology and compensation? Why would Europe's apology serve if we do not look at local and regional complicity with the slave trade and slavery? Would Europe's apology replace the necessary work on the linguistic, cultural and social legacy of slavery in the African world? Should we not confront as well the desire to incarnate the good that the demand for apology implies? To enjoy the prestige of our heroic parents or to commiserate with the suffering of our victimized parents is normal, but when these sentiments support a political demand we must ask whether we are acting in our own interests rather than in the name of morality. As Tzvetan Todorov has argued, 'The public reminder of the past has an educative dimension only if it also questions our own actions and shows that we (or those with whom we identify ourselves) have not always been the good incarnate.'[4]

Past suffering comes down to us as a narrative that exercises a powerful attraction because it conjures up images of loss, misfortune, and tragedy. In the current discourse of recovery and reparation, these images echo the Christian pathos, albeit secularized (though not always, as Bishop Tutu demonstrated during the Truth and Reconciliation Commission in South Africa). One might ask, with Avishai Margalit:[5] what if the Christian-inspired discourse of guilt, atonement and pardon does not resonate for a group? And, what would justify the universalization of a Christian discourse and iconography? Not everyone is a Baptist president who delights in asking for forgiveness. However, a secularized Christian eschatology does indeed shape the discourse of reparation. The amount of suffering in the past determines the amount of rights in the present. The victimized group receives an open line of credit. No debt, no responsibility; or rather, as philosopher François Flahault has characterized the problematic of the debt: 'Everything is owed to me, you are forever indebted to me.'[6] The debt is, of course, not only material but also symbolic. But does an ethics of responsibility not demand that we abandon thinking in terms of being owed everything, that we think ourselves too in the position of debt? What is bad cannot be merely excluded from the self and the body and projected onto the other. A critical examination of the non-European active participation in the slave trade, slavery, and colonization according to the ethics of responsibility is necessary and contributes to the project of 'provincializing Europe', a project in which the notion of periphery is reworked and peripheries of peripheries begin to appear.

We are currently witnessing what seems to be an inexorable movement towards the demand for apology, reparations and compensation for the past. The model for those who wish to receive apologies and compensation for slavery and colonialism is obviously the campaign which has been led, for the past 20 years, by Jewish organizations against the European states, banks, museums, and individuals who took advantage of Nazi laws against the Jews to increase their wealth. An ethical and legal framework has emerged, with its own metaphors and tropes. Time has become a central issue: it is urgent that compensation occurs *now*, because there are fewer and fewer survivors; because it will constitute a warning against those who might be tempted to re-establish policies of racial discrimination; because it will have, alongside an ethical dimension, an educational one. Recent publications by Rony Brauman, Peter Novick, and Norman Finkelstein have pointed to the *political* problems raised by this approach.[7] I do not wish here to enter into the general debate surrounding their controversial conclusions. I do, however, agree with much of their particular discussions of victimhood and righteousness, commemoration and the apolitical position. The processes of the identification with victims produces, it seems, a righteous, pure and innocent identity. Virtue is thought to be unambiguously on the side of the victims, evil on the side of the victimizers. Historical and political analyses of the social forces at work, of the passions that are sometimes unleashed, of the power of hatred and envy as social practices, disappear behind a moralistic condemnation that hopes to constitute a strong enough barrier against present and future racial discriminations. The moralistic condemnation resonates powerfully with a doctrine that connects 'suffering and truth, suffering and redemption, suffering and spiritual purity, suffering as a gateway to the sacred'.[8] However, the moralistic condemnation appears to constitute a very weak barrier against new explosions of ethnic violence. It is not that a moral condemnation is not needed, but that it must be done in connection with a series of reflections on the constitution of the Other as a mortal threat to my being, and on the processes (psychological, social, cultural and political) that pave the way to the destruction of these Others.

In the discourses of wound, recovery and reparation, the African world and its margins are ruled by the signifier 'slave', and by the history of the Atlantic slave trade. But why should the Atlantic experience represent the experience of the entire continent? What about North Africa, East Africa and the Indian Ocean world, in which forms of slave trade and slavery gave birth to different memories, cultures and languages than the Black Atlantic? Why should wound, damage and harm define the African, or Afro-Creole, self? In the discourse of recovery and reparation, the self has been damaged to the extent that only a politics of recovery could heal the self. Only a politics of reparation by the West could heal the continent. Recovery is seen here as the recovery of an enchanted past, as the reinscription of the multifarious forms of subjectivity in an objective totality. Reparation means to restore a 'world of before', whose seamless life was interrupted by external forces. It is, of course, not totally incomprehensible that the desire to restore harmony and concord would be so attractive, or would capture the imagination. The African world is confronted by a rapid erosion of social and economic infrastructures, with the violence of capitalist global deregulation, and with the collapse of borders, regimes and institutions. The dream of the recovery of a world in which markers and meanings do not shift constantly, in which the outcomes of actions are not always dictated by accident and hazard, is entirely understandable. People do invent ways to deal with the disorder of everyday life.[9] When that dream becomes, however, a fantasy that shapes politics, one must pause for thought. Both recovery and reparation as a 're-enchantment of tradition' (borrowing Achille Mbembe's apt formulation) imply that there is a core to retrieve.[10] Collective identity and collective memory are entangled in a circular relationship. Certain memories are selected to express what is central to collective identity; those memories reinforce that form of identity, which in turn selects the memories that support its claims, and so on. Thus, the common denominator of 'African identity' is the trauma of the slave trade and slavery, a trauma which has wounded the self, that same self who turns to memories of slavery and colonialism to explain present neuroses, nightmares, weaknesses, and existential problems of all kinds. Race (its discourse, practice, laws, and representations) has directly wounded the Self. Therapeutic practices are required. As Mbembe has remarked, in this discourse of recovery African selfhood is entirely contained within the field of victimhood and, furthermore, generalizes the Atlantic experience as a representation of the experience of the entire continent.

COLONIZED CITIZENSHIP AND CREOLIZATION

In the post-slavery French territories in recent years, a politics of recovery and reparation has also framed the debates around identity, albeit within the specific framework of the French politics of commemoration and memory. As I have said elsewhere, the commemoration (in 1998) of the 150th anniversary of the abolition of slavery in the French colonies is a good example. The official discourse of the commemoration constructed a clear historical rupture. Monarchy had established slavery; the Republic had abolished it. It was a clear-cut narrative of teleological progress, a struggle between good and evil, between *les forces du futur* and *les forces du passé*. 1848 had accomplished the promise of the French Republic when Robespierre had declared '*Périssent les colonies plutôt que nos principes.*' The beautiful revolution had integrated the slaves into the family of French citizens. Abolition was a *gift* of Republican France, and the emancipated were thereafter forever indebted to France. The debt, however, had been honoured and it was now time to celebrate the creativity of Creole societies and their contribution to the culture of humanity.[11]

In order to counter the French republican discourse of abolition as gift, Creoles turned to the kind of discourse of debt and reparation described above. Within that framework, the construction of identity is dependent upon the capacity to find harm in the past and upon the belief that the past entirely defines the present. It is important to clarify this relationship between past and present at work in the reparation/recovery discourse. Despite current work on the ways in which traditions are invented and the past recreated to support political claims, memory in the reparation/recovery discourse functions as a sacred repository of collective identity. The connection between collective memory and collective identity is, as I said above, circular: each elaborated to reinforce the other. But what exactly is meant by the phrase 'collective memory'? To the French sociologist Maurice Halbwachs, who coined the expression, the present determines what of the past we remember and how we remember it as collective memory. Collective memory, Halbwachs argued, is thus profoundly anti-historical: it does not accept multiple perspectives; it rejects the ambiguous, the uncertain and the indeterminate. The temporality of collective memory is a timeless present, that is, a time in which the past and present form a continuous sign-chain.

The past of slavery becomes the *present* of Creole societies and the figure of the slave is re-enacted as a traumatic presence. The experience of slavery is both past and present. Such a vision then paradoxically relegates the system of slavery to a pre-history, a pre-modern period, but one whose pre-modernity still determines the postcolonial world. The outcome is an unfortunate 'history' in which there is no slave rebellion, no abolitionist politics, and no creation of a new culture, a new people – in this case, a Creole culture and people. Slavery is thus no longer one system of exploitation of human beings by other human beings but something outside of history, outside the realm of the thinkable, something 'evil'. Hence the moralistic tone still largely used to denounce current forms of enslavement. The surprised 'how can such things exist in our world?' reveals the strength of a certain narrative, that of a *universal abolition* (extinction, eradication) of slavery effected in the mid-nineteenth century within the 'civilized world and beyond' by European powers. Historians have, nonetheless, qualified that narrative. They have shown how abolitionism produced new forms of discipline and punishment that were often as violent as their precedents; how it displaced (willingly or unwillingly) the blame for slavery onto others (feudal aristocrats in Europe, Muslims or local tyrants abroad); and how abolition (willingly or unwillingly) supported the 'civilizing mission' of European imperialism (with the claim to be saving peoples from barbarian practices).[12] This, in any case, does not deny the emancipatory dimension of abolitionism but points to the dangers of the 'temptation of goodness'. The rhetorics of slavery and abolitionism answer each other, each seeking to challenge the foundation of the other. Abolitionism holds as a universal law that no human being can enslave another, slavery that there are justifications for enslavement. Enslavement does not belong to a pre-modern history. It recurs in our so-called postmodern global world under new aspects (for example, the traffic in human beings, the profit from which is becoming as important as that of the drug trade), though the foundation remains the same: the transformation of a human being into a thing that can be bought, sold and disposed of. Furthermore, looking at the history of slavery only in terms of the traumatic experience that for many it no doubt reduces different histories and geographies (East, West, Islands, linguistic territories, and so on) to *one* history and geography, which constitute the *very foundations* of a certain identity. One signifier – slavery – dominates the world of this Symbolic.

To be sure, the affirmation of the hegemony of the sign of slavery has also constituted a counter-hegemonic strategy in French Creole post-slavery societies, for the discourse of recovery and reparation seems to be the only one to which the French Republic will listen. French republicanism, as is well known, strongly rejects any reference to 'race' in the creation of the republican Nation and of French identity. Fraternity and equality are the two pillars of French republicanism and only equal brothers are said to inhabit republican France.[13] In this narrative, the slave trade and slavery become two 'irrational' events connected with the feudalism and backwardness of the *ancien régime*.[14] But even so, when slavery was abolished in 1848 a paradoxical form of citizenship emerged: a colonized citizenship, in which equality was qualified. The brother in the colony was equal, *but not quite*. Not only did French abolitionism transform slaves' emancipation into a debt owed to the French Republic, 'colonial' citizenship imposed a space of lack that put the new citizens in the position of beggars. Creoles had to beg to be included within the political community of French citizens. The political demand 'on which basis are we not your equals?' was translated into a demand for love and recognition: 'What do we lack that explains your exclusionary practices?' As equality was both offered and postponed, the colonized (male) Creole citizen became alienated, dependent on the (of course unsatisfied) desire of the French colonizer. The public space produced by colonized citizenship was not democratic. It encouraged a binary structure: acceptance through unconditional love for France or rejection. Those who questioned the persecutive character of colonized citizenship (the Republic's demand: 'show me over and over your love') and the paranoid structure imposed by the hegemony of the vocabulary of love in the political space of colonial relations were demonized.

In fact, to be accepted into the body of the republican Nation, the Creole citizen had to operate a double denial: to reject enslavement as the matrix of their world and to absolve France of its responsibilities for participation in the slave trade and slavery. Thus, inequalities produced by *colonialism* were denounced, but the connection between slave society, colonial society and French republican ideology was not made. However, the political discourse became detached from the cultural and social world in which race and ethnicity framed the processes of identification. In Réunion Island, after the abolition of slavery in 1848, thousands of indentured workers were brought from India, Malaysia, China and Africa to work in the sugar fields. A new racial typology emerged, influenced by European racial 'science': *Kaf* (descendants of slaves, of African origin) were described as 'lazy, violent, childish'; *Malbar* (people of Indian origin) were 'cunning and hypocrites'; *Zarab* (Muslim Indians) could not be trusted; *Sinwa* (of Chinese origins) were 'dirty, liars, thieves'; *Yab* (poor whites, victims of the land restructuring after 1848) were poor but white and thus 'good Catholics'. Thus, Réunion's white elite borrowed the lexicon of 'scientific' racism to describe the island's creolized multi-ethnic society. Its racial discourse was an answer to the fear of post-slavery social chaos and its desire to contain the emergence of a Creole identity, rooted in the history of the slaves' resistance, in the syncretism of African, Malagasy and Asian beliefs and rituals, the Creole languages invented by slaves, and the processes of creolization which each ethnic group experienced. The population, that is, *ought* to be French, Catholic and colonized.

When in the 1930s, a new elite emerged in the Colonies, it was republican and secular, educated in the French universities, not tied to land ownership, and influenced by the ideals of European socialism (equality, non-racial societies, the fight against capitalism). It rejected any reference to ethnicity and race, a discourse adopted by trade unions as well. In 1946, the colonial status of the Old Colonies (Martinique, Guadeloupe, Réunion, Guyana) was abolished by the French Parliament, and they became French Overseas Departments (Départements d'Outre-Mer, or DOM). However, it would be unfair to claim that anti-colonialists did not acknowledge the role of slavery in the making of the Creole world. Aimé Césaire, in his *Return to My Native Land* and *Discourse on Colonialism*, described slavery as the *matrix* of the Creole society. In *Discourse on Colonialism*, written after the Second World War, Césaire even compared the practices and racism of European slavery and colonialism to Nazi practices and racism. Slavery and colonial racism challenged the European ideal of its civilizing mission, pointing out the extent to which violence, inhuman practices and philosophies of terror inhabited its heart. Yet, it would be the emergence of the politics of identity in the 1970s that would bring back to the Creole societies the problematic of the past as a lasting wound and damage that colonized the present. It was partly an answer, as I have argued, to the difficulty of transforming a cultural difference into a political difference. Slavery and colonialism had created a Creole society, political assimilation has been fought for and won. A difficulty remained: what form of political association can be invented between a people constituted by slavery and colonialism and its former master? Some Creoles turned then to the idiom of recovery and reparation. They were victims because their ancestors had been victims and victimization was handed down from generation to generation.

The politics of apology and recovery in Creole societies is, however, not quite about the restoration of harmony. Harmony is not really something that belongs to the repertoire of the Creole societies, built as they are upon destruction (of family and of social and cultural ties) and erasure (of native languages). There were either no natives on the land (Réunion Island) or they were destroyed (Martinique, Guadeloupe). Slaves from diverse cultures, languages and traditions (Asia, Madagascar, Africa) were thrown together. They invented a language, a culture and rituals that were the product of processes of creolization (imitation, translation, substitution, creation). Predatory, violent and inhuman practices constituted the grounds upon which Creole societies developed their creativity. What could restoration mean in this context? Here, demands for recovery and reparation are addressed to a power that has marginalized (or ignored) the contribution of Creoles to politics and culture. In this scenario, recognition and reparation would both be performed through apology and reparation. France would apologize for having participated in the slave trade and slavery and would recognize the Creole world.

And this is in fact what happened in 1998. The French government admitted the wrong of the slave trade and slavery, but rejected demands for financial or material reparation: recognition, it was implied, *was* reparation. But what has concretely changed since then? The role of France in the slave trade and slavery is still extremely marginal to schools' curricula; relations between France and its post-slave territories are still formulated through an idiom of debt; deep inequalities persist in Creole societies; dependency is still the frame that shapes social and economic relations.

BEYOND DEPENDENCY?

Frantz Fanon famously refused to bear the burden of slavery. In *Black Skin, White Masks*, he declared that he did not wish to fight for compensation for his ancestors' victimization. A free man could not exist through the past, the traditions, the ethnic characteristics and the categories of the colonizer. In *Black Skin, White Masks*, Fanon ridiculed the alienation of the Antillean, his and her desire to become 'white', to speak 'white', to think 'white'. The Antillean was a prisoner of the white's gaze, forever seeking an approval that the white either did not want or did not bother to give. To be free meant to liberate oneself from that neurotic embrace. A new identity could not be built on a return to the past or on carrying the past. Emancipation meant, first, getting rid of the aspiration to become white; and, second, to rise above the binarism of racism – white vs black – in order to build a 'new humanism'. Fanon's conclusions echoed those of the colonized then engaged in the movement of decolonization. Albert Memmi, in *The Colonizer and the Colonized*, concurred when he declared: 'The former colonized will have become a man like any other.'[15] The tradition of the dead should not weigh upon the living, the ghosts of the slaves should have been laid to rest. The present could not be sealed in what Fanon called the 'materialized Tower of the Past'.[16] Recovery and reparation were about rupture, de-alienation and reconstruction – tearing the shroud of the past. The past should not be a burden, Fanon claimed; let us go free from the ruins, the spectres and the phantoms which bar the road to the future and hinder the present.

Elsewhere I have challenged Fanon's belief that it is possible to erase the past in such a radical way, or to start anew as if on the basis of a *tabula rasa*.[17] This aspect of Fanonian psychology seemed to me to be based not only on the (admittedly widely shared) illusion of self-creation, but also on the belief that there exists a 'core' self, a 'truer' self that would be uncovered by tearing the mask. I will not repeat my critique here, but I will qualify it. There is in Fanon's affirmation an insight into the apolitical nature of the politics of recovery and its narcissistic use of the past to compensate for a troubling present, responsibility for which cannot possibly – according to this account – be mine. Fanon foresaw in the politics of recovery a politics of 'projection': projecting outside of the (national, cultural) body the deep ambiguities, the passions, the sentiments of hatred and animosity that nonetheless animate the (post)colonial unconscious and consciousness. As such, the politics of recovery is an ideology that seeks to protect individuals from loss and mourning and to transform politics into a field in which conflicts are regulated by moralistic condemnation rather than through a confrontation with the plurality of positions.

I wish to propose another politics of recovery and reparation, in which my demand for recognition of the past is not entirely dependent on the recognition of guilt by the One who I have put (justly or unjustly) in the position of having damaged my past and thus my self. There is an inevitable loss that I must mourn, a time and space that are irretrievable, while the past yet constructs a web of debts and filiations in which I am caught. Memories and expectations constitute the threads of this web, the context of these memories and expectations *colour* the fabric of the web and draw a pattern upon it. I am attached to the world of others and to those who constitute my world (family, relatives, characters of my family romance) by this fabric. The process of reconstructing and recovery means disentangling the threads of the fabric in order to weave it anew. If the fabric is not to constitute a straitjacket, I might need to undo the knots that hinder my movements and construct new knots that tie me to others. To Creoles today, an ethics of responsibility might do more towards emancipating us from the idiom of debt that ties us in an unhealthy relation with 'France'. To Creoles today, a politics of reparation could mean first opening their horizon: rather than a fixation on France and Europe, developing relations with their region (African-Asian for Réunion, Caribbean-American for Martinique and Guadeloupe). Second, a politics of reparation could mean transforming their insularity into an advantage rather than an obstacle, and last but not least, challenging the relation of dependency on France with its related sentiments, resentment and rage. In other words, a new politics of reparation might entail renouncing what the current politics of recovery and reparation has transformed into a requirement: having the Other demanding forgiveness, performing atonement, enacting guilt. For there are – there must be – moments when recovery and reparation are also about forsaking the demand to the Other.

CHAPTER 10

Rewriting the Black Subject: The Black Brazilian Emancipatory Text

DENISE FERREIRA DA SILVA

How are we to interpret articulations of black desire in the postmodern burial grounds where many attempt to put to rest the liberal subject and its once most promising foe, the proletarian vanguard? I pursue this question out of a concern that available mappings of the postmodern field have not sufficiently included the concept of the racial in their critiques of modern representation.[1] More particularly, I worry about the currency of gestures that are critical of essentialism and authenticity in discussions of black cultural politics and the ease with which 'hybridity' and rejections of race in grandiose defences of humanism have been advanced as unproblematic strategies to situate black conditions. My aim here is to map the signifying terrain on which black Brazilian activists articulated an emancipatory project during the 1980s. Although the concept of 'freedom' is problematized, this discussion does not forfeit 'emancipation' as the privileged trope (principle of organization) in articulations of black subjectivity. To insist on the idea of emancipation as constitutive of a certain black desire is, here, not an unreflective appropriation of a liberal, Hegelian or Marxist heritage, because the idea of an emancipatory project is mediated by a refusal to see a conception of positive freedom as the sole condition for emancipation. Conceiving black desire as an effect of its own articulation and context, emancipation is defined as an effect of *resignification*, in which strategies deployed in various of the moments of the articulation of the racial as a nexus of power/knowledge are appropriated and re-articulated to enable the emergence of the subaltern as an active and productive subject.

This is part of an attempt to move discourse away from interpretations of raced subjectivities as teleologies of a subject whose desire for freedom is but an attempt to achieve self-transparency. Instead, I read projects of black emancipation as constrained by their historico-epistemological conditions of emergence, a *textual–historical* context constituted by the deployment of various products of the racial knowledge and various versions of the hegemonic Brazilian text, as well as by articulations of black subjectivity deployed elsewhere. What follows is a response to a discomfort with contemporary attempts to account for 'the black subject'. I hope it makes a convincing case for displacing the yearning for transparency that often underlies concerns with authenticity, essentialism, and hybridity.

BLACK NOSTALGIA AND THE PROBLEM OF SELF-TRANSPARENCY

While many critiques of essentialism and authenticity have rendered Africanity a less appealing signifier of black desire, displacement remains a central trope in the attempt to describe the trajectory of the black subject.[2] Many contemporary writings on black subjectivity seek, in the cultural products of materially dispossessed blacks in the USA, the Caribbean and Europe, expressions of a discrete black desire – unmediated signifiers of blacks' particular condition as both 'insiders' and 'outsiders', unwanted and unwilling participants in the adventure of modernity. In the assumption of the category of 'the outsider', the ghost of authenticity haunts several of the intellectual articulations of black subjectivity. Some interpret what materially dispossessed blacks do and say as a true and authentic articulation of a black desire;[3] others call attention to the hybrid character of these formulations[4] or denounce the fact that only highly commercialized masculinist or hetero-normative elements are taken to signify blackness.[5] In any case, regardless of the position taken in this debate, there seems to be a shared yearning to find in urban black youth culture the traces of a black subjectivity, whose trajectory does not coincide with the flux of modernity, though it takes place within it.

Some early and contemporary black critical intellectual undertakings seem to be haunted by a nostalgia for self-transparency precisely because they conceive of black consciousness as fundamentally split, emerging under conditions of displacement and constituted in or through terror and material deprivation. Although they are written against hegemonic narratives of blackness, these accounts seem to repeat a movement characteristic of them, imagining the black subject as a self-transparent entity, similar to the dominant articulation of the (European) Western subject.[6] My contention here is that blackness does not carry within itself this longing for transparency. On the contrary, the longing for transparency is an effect of the categories deployed in the attempt to capture the particularity of the active black subject. The historical idea of self-consciousness as self-presence plays a crucial role. Even when seen to be an effect of particular material and ideological conditions, self-consciousness is conceived as independent of external (spatial) determinants, as the result of internal processes through which the mind takes itself as an object of reflection in time.[7] In effect, then, such discourses retain the idea that the self-conscious subject is undetermined, unsituated and unmediated, and that 'true consciousness' is the realization of 'freedom'.

My reading of black Brazilian emancipatory texts of the 1980s recognizes that this yearning for self-transparency is constitutive of the strategies deployed in the attempt to examine the contemporary condition of black subjects. This is, in part, because they were formulated within the spatio-temporal, historical–epistemological, framework of modernity. This recognition that blackness exists within the historical and epistemological boundaries of modernity goes beyond the recognition that it delimits a particular experience of being modern, such as Gilroy's view of black cultural products and political statements as the expression of a commonality that immediately reflects the ambivalence instituted/reflected by blacks' positioning in modernity.[8] Such a perspective, I believe, entails a conception of the black inscription in modernity in which the latter remains exterior, an object (to be either fully appropriated or forfeited) of black desire, in relation to which the historical trajectory of blackness in modernity emerges as the trajectory of a lack.[9] It seems to me that Gilroy's account remains haunted by the nostalgia for self-transparency both in his interpretation of black emancipatory narratives as either demanding inclusion as the only possibility for fulfilling the project of modernity or as the imagining of (and attempts to bring about) a condition that lies beyond the spatial/temporal boundaries of modernity. It also suggests that a conception of 'culture' is central to the articulation of this yearning for transparency. This conception has – perhaps unwittingly – inherited some of the presuppositions of an early twentieth-century anthropological formulation of culture: Boas's (1911) notion of the 'primitive mind', which endowed the 'Others of Europe' with a certain *historicity* while simultaneously placing them outside the unfolding of universal history.[10] Boas conceived of the 'native (Other) mind' as a prisoner of 'traditional' elements – an effect of its natural and social environment – a condition that apparently prevented 'primitive' consciousness from reaching the same degree of abstraction, complexity and fluidity achieved in 'modern civilization'. The postmodern move in which the Other's cultural enunciations have been constructed as hybrid, fluid, and relational has not eliminated the essentialist assumptions inherent in Boas's account of non-European culture. That is, it retains the presupposition that even these fluid, relational, and complex cultural products express a discrete, collective being.

In a critique of some anthropological and sociological accounts of black urban culture, Robin Kelley argues that they deploy a monolithic, essentialist view of black culture by selecting just a few aspects of cultural production with which to associate cultural norms, values and behaviours. In common with many contemporary black cultural critics, Kelley's project is to implode such views by highlighting the complex, hybrid, and fluid character of black urban culture. To this end Kelley's study examines various urban cultural manifestations – including soul, hip hop, dozen, basketball and double dutch – arguing, among other things, that the elimination of employment opportunities influenced urban black youth to seek means for creating economic opportunities in 'play'.[11]

Kelley successfully achieves his objective. He provides a convincing and rich account of how cultural practices and sports played a central role, in the 1970s and 1980s, in black urban youth's attempt to overcome material deprivation. But even if the black cultural productions or expressions Kelley highlights are indeed complex and hybrid, the concept of culture behind his analysis cannot account for complex, hybrid, and fluid black identities. In Kelley's account, as soul and hip-hop are appropriated as 'black things', they signify blackness as produced and expressed at a given temporal and spatial juncture: Harlem in the 1970s and the Bronx in the 1980s, respectively. But merely to state that the cultural products are fluid, complex, and hybrid does not avoid the presumption of the ontological and epistemological category of culture according to which the products, practices, and ideas of a people express a discrete consciousness. That is, this concept of culture constitutes the space of emergence of a group's consciousness as too detached, unaffected by the consciousness of the groups inhabiting the larger social space. It seems, then, that the recurrence of the ideal of transparency in interpretations of black subjectivity is the result of a notion of black culture that presumes, among other things, an immediate connection between consciousness and its embodied manifestations.

This is intimately connected to an understanding of race as a pre-historical and pre-conceptual referent, indicating either what is outside of or excluded from modernity. It thus becomes virtually impossible to account for (and perhaps conceive of the possible) different black trajectories in modernity. In fact, variations in black historical and social trajectories have been explained primarily in terms of whether the racial operates as a cultural or ideological principle of exclusion in different social formations. As a result, the kind of black consciousness described by Du Bois, which has become the model for black consciousness, is expected to emerge only in social formations in which racism is an unequivocal dimension of the cultural or ideological context.[12]

How then to conceive of, and to understand, a non-Du Boisian black consciousness?

READING HISTORICAL-EPISTEMOLOGICAL MODES OF RACIAL SUBJECTION

The first formulations of modern racial knowledge deployed ontological categories of racial difference, the primary productive effect of which was the production of the globe as a *modern* space.[13] That is, they populated it with bodies and places whose configurations signify distinct forms of consciousness. These categories of racial difference (blackness, whiteness, Asianness, and so on) and the meanings attached to them were appropriated to justify various social-economic apparatuses of racial subjection, such as Jim Crow in the USA, apartheid in South Africa, and racial democracy in Brazil. But more importantly, they were also appropriated in the production of various social-symbolic apparatuses – hegemonic national texts in which the national subject was articulated through its racial difference from blacks and other subaltern (raced) subjects. In response to this I shall trace the articulation of one black desire, in black Brazilian narratives of the 1980s, as an effect of strategic resignifications attempting to recuperate blackness and Africanity from within the hegemonic narrative of the Brazilian nation.[14]

Whether advancing a liberal or a Marxist conception of politics, studies of racial politics share the assumption that race is only politically significant in social formations where it operates as an exclusionary principle. That is, they privilege racism as either a cultural or an ideological component in social practices of exclusion that result in the subjection of people of colour. Contemporary studies of Brazil tend to deploy this view of race as a political category in their portrayal of 'whitening' and 'racial democracy' as hegemonic cultural or ideological constructs whose primary effect has been to hide from blacks (and from all Brazilians for that matter) the fact that notions of race and racial difference operate as principles of, and bases for, exclusion.[15] More precisely, racial democracy, and the underlying celebration of miscegenation, are often cited as the cultural or ideological cause of the failures of the black Brazilian movement. These failures include: the movement's inability to convince blacks, and Brazilian society more generally, that race operates as a social category; the co-option of activists by political parties who have incorporated the race question into their agendas as an electoral strategy;[16] an inability to mobilize the black Brazilian population; and the deployment of a culturalist strategy in which the emphasis on racial identity finds in the pervasiveness of the ideology of racial democracy a virtually invincible enemy.[17] It is commonly argued that even in the light of obvious indicators of black economic dispossession and political subordination, the black movement's claims and demands are not heard because the hegemonic national narrative successfully recalls the fact of miscegenation to argue that social subjection in Brazil results from class and not racial exclusion. The evidence of race mixture is even taken to indicate that Brazilians are adverse to race prejudice and racial discrimination.

But we do not need to conceive of the racial as operating as a purely exclusionary principle. Conceiving of it instead as a productive strategy of power/knowledge displaces the conceptions of the 'political' underlying these examinations of black Brazilian emancipatory narratives. On the one hand, it displaces the liberal conception of politics, according to which individuals face each other in a context of interaction ruled by universal and abstract principles. My primary target is the formulation that racial politics refers to those circumstances in which social interactions are ruled by 'racist beliefs', that is, circumstances in which bodily characteristics named racial define the nature and consequences of these interactions.[18] On the other hand, I attempt to displace certain Marxist formulations of racial politics that reduce racial subjection to a moment of class subjection,[19] also conceiving of racism as an ideological mechanism of exclusion and exploitation.[20] Without denying the fact that exclusion constitutes an important moment in processes of racial subjection, I am targeting another level, analytically prior to the social relations captured with the notion of racism.

My interest here is in the historical–epistemological conditions of possibility for the emergence of the subaltern as a subject of self-representation. These are also the conditions of the possibility of the articulation of projects of emancipation. In what follows I assume that the subaltern, racial ontologies articulated in postmodern celebrations are not expressions of a previously silenced subjectivity but have been historically and epistemologically produced in particular regimes of power in response to particular political-symbolic strategies of subjection. So how does the concept of the racial as a *productive* construct of power/knowledge work in the particular case of Brazil?

ARTICULATING BLACK DESIRE

In the context of the nineteenth-century science of man, the white body and the space of Europe were written as unmediated signifiers of modern consciousness. In the final decades of the nineteenth century 'nation' and 'race' became the fundamental symbolic entities in accounts that aimed to constitute a given collectivity as a modern political subject, capable of fulfilling the cultural and material projects of modernity.[21] For intellectuals and politicians in the 1880s, attempting to articulate a Brazilian subject in the light of the project to reorganize the country as a modern capitalist nation-state, the main challenge was to counter the eschatological argument that miscegenation resulted in the constitution of a physically, morally and intellectually degenerate people and that the tropics did not provide adequate environmental conditions for building a 'modern civilization'.[22] The problem, then, was how to write the emerging history of a tropical nation of *mestiços* and blacks as the unfolding of a modern subjectivity.

Out of the efforts to respond to this challenge two versions of what would become the hegemonic Brazilian text emerged: *whitening* and *racial democracy*. These ideologies appropriated blackness and Africanity to inscribe the particularity of the Brazilian subject, but without producing Brazil as a black nation. Instead, the resignification of miscegenation as necessary for the fulfilment of the modern project in the tropics enabled the writing of Brazilian history as the teleology of a – somewhat tanned – European subject, whose success was a result of the colonizer's ability to appropriate from the subjugated Africans and Indians the physical and technological elements necessary to survive and thrive south of the Equator.[23] The materiality of miscegenation thus resides not in the specific bodies that combine signs of blackness, Indianness and whiteness, but in the effects of a strategy of racial subjection, appropriating and resignifying miscegenation to write the temporality and spatiality of the Brazilian subject.[24] This, I believe, constituted the main challenge that faced the Black Brazilian political projects after Emancipation in 1888.

In this attempt to specify the re-signifying strategies deployed by the black Brazilian movement, I consider some of the statements that characterize the particular configuration of black Brazilian emancipatory texts in the 1980s. What has been called the second wave of black politics in Brazil was part of a reconfiguration of Brazilian politics, in the mid-1970s, following ten years of military dictatorship in Brazil marked by the attempts, in many cases armed struggles, against the repressive regime. The creation of the *Movimento Negro Unificado Contra a Discriminação Racial* (Unified Black Movement against Racial Discrimination) in 1978 inaugurated a new era in Brazilian racial politics.[25] Throughout the 1970s the agenda of the *Movimento Negro Unificado* (MNU), as the organization was later renamed, incorporated questions on issues such as employment discrimination and police violence to situate the particular modes of racial subjection operating in Brazil.[26] This emphasis on political–economic processes did not preclude a sense of the importance of cultural practices in the constitution of a separate black subject: denunciations of employment discrimination were accompanied, for example, by demands for the protection of Afro-Brazilian religious practices.[27] Yet, as Hanchard argues (in *Orpheus and Power*), in the 1980s black political narratives were dominated by what he calls a 'culturalist' trend. According to Hanchard, the privileging of culture had a negative impact on black Brazilian politics because it limited the possibility of forming alliances with other subaltern groups. Unquestionably, in the 1980s, culture played a crucial role in the writing of the black Brazilian subject. However, as I argue below, this was not achieved at the expense of a consideration of politico-economic processes.

Black Brazilian emancipatory narratives of the 1980s reject black subaltern positioning while highlighting the importance of blacks in Brazilian history. In the writing of black Brazilian subjectivity two elements are crucial in the attempt to demonstrate how blackness captures a distinct historical trajectory, a resignifying move necessary for the articulation of a black desire: the attempt to recuperate Africanity (African cultural practices) and a demarcation of the subaltern region resulting from the temporal historical oppression of blacks in Brazil. The resignifying strategies that would distinguish this particular configuration of the black Brazilian emancipatory text appear in interventions at a National Meeting of Black Organizations in Rio de Janeiro, 29 July–1 August, 1982.[28]

> The history of the black people in Maranhão has yet to be written, and this is one of the objectives of the Centre of Black Culture. Our bibliographic research has shown that the material (chronicles and poetry) in the press and official historiography is a product of a slave society and as such is partial and racist. The authors speak for the system and its interests. Even the so-called progressive, and humanitarian or paradoxically abolitionist authors . . . show in their works the ideas they have about Indians and blacks and the negative influences of these races on Brazilian culture.[29]

The re-writing of Brazilian history was more than a gesture of inclusion. The focus on the violence of slavery did more than offer counter-explanations of racial democracy as an outcome of mild slavery. It was also needed to write the slave as an active subject by recuperating acts of resistance, which up to that moment were absent from Brazilian historiography:

> We search here for the historical roots of racial prejudice and discrimination against blacks and the historical factors that lead this or that ethnic group to develop more than others; moreover we do a critical revision of the historiography of the black Brazilian . . . [R]especting the official historiography, it always placed the black in a disadvantaged position, giving him a negative image as passive, lazy, without a perspective and revolutionary initiative. We cite as examples the quilombos, the males and palmares revolution, which the official history always tried to minimize or marginalize, as historical episodes of political and revolutionary struggle against the patriarchal regime.[30]

This articulation of a discrete black subject questions the major premises of racial democracy. It attempts to trace an always already there but hidden active presence of blacks. That is, the critique of racial democracy was also a challenge to the first version of the hegemonic national narrative, whitening, and its explicit desire for whiteness:[31]

> The pressures we suffer in a society which has different values – beauty standards different from ours, behaviour standards distinct from ours – lead us to wish to imitate the dominant race. And, without noticing the subtleties of this ideology of domination, we black women pass into the future generations we are forming the practice of miscegenation though marriage and pressed hair, as a negation of our racial characteristics.[32]

While black Brazilians have challenged racial democracy since the 1940s, the 1970s black movement's appropriation of the findings of sociological studies of the modern Brazilian space enabled a challenge to racial democracy coupled with the demarcation a black space[33] – a space necessary for the articulation of a productive and active black subject in a region lacking (racially demarcated) geographical boundaries. Because, unlike African Americans, black Brazilian activists could not write a black history unfolding in segregated spaces, this demarcated raced space was signified through actual and past political–economic processes and Africanity. Blackness could then be articulated as a racial difference, which signified both a subaltern social position and an *authentic* black culture.

Recourse to sociological investigations supported the claim that blacks occupied a subaltern position in the social structure,[34] suggesting an account of the emergence of the black subject in terms of the circumscription of the subaltern region – an effect of the temporal unfolding of political-economic processes – occupied by blacks in the Brazilian social space:

> Racial discrimination is more obvious in terms of employment and the distribution of wealth. It belongs to the very socio-economic structure of Brazilian society, where the obstacles to [black] social mobility, at the educational and professional level, are politically amplified . . . [T]he geographical distribution of blacks (and mulattoes) and whites [is such that] 70% of non-whites are situated in the less developed demographic areas (47.7% in the Northeast, 14.1% in Minas Gerais and Espirito Santo), while 70% of the whites are in the Southeast region.[35]

Sociological investigations of Brazil's racial conditions provided the scientific 'truth' of racial subalternity, and the task of the black movement was to use that 'truth' as a tool for dismantling racial democracy. It was also deployed to re-write Brazilian history, with the pedagogical objective of teaching black Brazilians of their particular social situation:

> This process of the demystification of reality . . . was oriented toward the search for an explanation for . . . the evidence that, 94 years after emancipation, the black remains discriminated against, oppressed, on the margins of Brazilian society . . . attempting to go beyond the immediate appearances that cover the black question in Brazil and searching to demonstrate the underlying aspects of this problematic, as a initial step to the development of a process of consciousness raising and of the comprehension of the history and the situation of the black people.[36]

The effort to draw the boundaries of blackness in Brazil also demanded such space be associated with a particular spirit, a culture that could not be sublated into the national culture.[37] Thus, as the black subaltern space was characterized as a region of subalternity, black culture (Africanity) could be recuperated and redefined as an oppressed culture. In that movement, blackness was reconstructed not solely as what gives continuity and unity to a black subject, but also as the attribute necessary to resist subordination. Though an association with other slaves' forms of rebellion – such as the quilombos, communities of runaway slaves – Africanity was deployed as a signifier of resistance, indicating a refusal to occupy the position the hegemonic national narrative attributed to blacks.

Unquestionably, this reappropriation of African culture as a signifier of black desire reflected the centrality given to cultural identity in approaches to modern subaltern conditions in the last three decades. But because this African culture had already been incorporated in the articulation of the national (culturally and physically mixed) subject, the early anthropological notion of *resistance*, rather than authenticity or purity, would organize this account of black subjectivity.[38] In the period between 1978 and 1989, the reappropriation of African culture required the reclaiming of Afro-Brazilian cultural products as a site of cultural resistance. This was also a demand to reclaim Africanity from within the national subjectivity, by characterizing African cultural products as expressions of the consciousness of a subaltern group which should be not only valued as such but also protected from commercialization and cooptation.

Rewriting Brazilian history with an emphasis on resistance became central to the articulation of a black Brazilian subject. It inaugurated a narrative of the historical trajectory of the black subject in which the contemporary black movement was figured as a self-conscious expression of this history and culture of resistance. But more importantly, in the project of raising the consciousness of black Brazilians as a whole, black institutions, activists, and intellectuals took upon themselves the task of articulating a productive and active black desire, to produce its unique spatiality and temporality. In this process, sociological investigations that demonstrated that blacks occupied a subaltern region in Brazilian society played a crucial role, providing 'scientific' evidence for their claims which could be deployed to counter the prevailing 'ideological' formulations. This enabled the black emancipatory narratives to draw parallels with those other forms of resistance to racial subjection that sociological and historical accounts of the role of the racial in modernity define as properly political, for example, the US Civil Rights movement and the independence wars in Africa.[39]

Examinations of racial politics in Brazil understand the various resignifying strategies there as non- or pre-political because they fail to recognize that the political significance of the racial precedes the historical social relations and institutional arrangements in which people of colour participate as subaltern subjects. Race emerged as a modern political category in the nineteenth-century science of man. Connecting bodies, (continent) places of origin, and forms of consciousness, it enabled the delineation of the territory in which the modern cultural principles of universal equality, rationality and justice would be deployed by construing whiteness and the European space as the unmediated signifiers of modern consciousness. The modern concept of the racial occupies a central place in the hegemonic national narratives within which people of colour emerged as subaltern modern subjects. Non-European 'multiracial' nations – such as the United States, Brazil, and South Africa – deployed narratives that produced the national subject and social space as unmediated signifiers of modern consciousness by writing their non-white members either outside of the national consciousness or occupying subaltern position in relation to it.[40]

The problem with assessments of racial politics in Brazil stems from the deployment of a conception of consciousness that, like other contemporary constructions of the subaltern, conflates two aspects of representation, representation as being-in-itself and representation as being-for-itself,[41] and privileges the latter as the condition of possibility of emancipation. Furthermore, examinations of racial politics in Brazil and elsewhere assume a doubly determined conception of being-for-itself, or self-consciousness. Not only do they assume that self-consciousness requires the recognition of a collectivity's subaltern social position and their emergence as revolutionary subjects, they inherited from the formulation of race as a sociological category the assumption that racial difference always already signifies cultural – material and mental – differences that emerged and were consolidated outside the temporality and spatiality of modernity.[42] This entails a conception of race consciousness which assumes that the raced body itself is an unmediated (pre-political and pre-conceptual) signifier of oppression and exclusion.

In Brazil, the raced subaltern Other is also an effect of textual conditions, the hegemonic narratives which produced the Brazilian subject as the embodiment of the cultural and material projects of modernity. But, unlike those of the United States and South Africa, the hegemonic Brazilian narrative needed to articulate the subaltern raced Other in the national text in order to narrate the nation's history as the process of elimination, via miscegenation, of these Others as a necessary step toward the building of a modern nation outside the European space. This defines the context of articulation of black Brazilian desire. Because this subaltern raced subject does not exist outside the text which produced its alterity, the most immediate political act of black Brazilian activists in the 1980s was to engage critically with the hegemonic construction of the nation and its appropriation of black culture in the construction of the national subject and the national space as a particular expression of the cultural and material projects of modernity.

The black Brazilian emancipatory narratives of the 1980s constitute a textually and historically specific articulation of race as a political category, or better, they reflect particular historical-epistemological conditions of production of meanings of the racial. In this sense, this emancipatory text is radically distinct from those which have become the model for black consciousness: the articulations of African-American desire. These latter have been deployed against a strategy of racial subjection that located blackness outside the temporality and spatiality of the US national subject and against the primary effect of this signification of blackness. Segregation drew the symbolic line demarcating the boundaries between the white national subject and a subaltern black (social and cultural) space. This symbolic line has been appropriated in sociological theorizing of race as empirical evidence of black subjugation.[43] Because black intellectual investments also take this line to signify black conditions in modernity, it has never become an object of examination. This, I believe, has been the crucial obstacle to the examination of the racial as a product of modern modes of representation and a productive strategy of power/knowledge. Examining the strategy of racial subjection that constitutes the condition of possibility of the black intellectual investment in transparency will contribute to interpretations of black subjectivity which, while recognizing that they emerge within the modern historical and textual matrix, will no longer reduce them to black versions of the modern desire for self-transparency.

Notes

Introduction: Philosophies of Race and Ethnicity

1. For the distinction between 'error' and a type of 'illusion' that 'does not cease even though it is uncovered and its nullity is clearly seen', see Immanuel Kant, *Critique of Pure Reason* (1781; 1787), trans. Paul Guyer and Allen W. Wood, Cambridge University Press, Cambridge, 1997, pp. 384–7 (A293–8/B249–55). Kant's concept of transcendental or 'objective' illusion is the philosophical basis of the concept of ideology.
2. Anthony Appiah, 'The Uncompleted Argument', *Critical Inquiry* 12, 1985, p. 35. See also, K. Anthony Appiah, *In My Father's House: Africa in the Philosophy of Culture*, Oxford University Press, Oxford, 1992.
3. K. Anthony Appiah, 'Race, Culture, Identity', in K. Anthony Appiah and Amy Gutmann, *Color Conscious: The Political Morality of Race*, Princeton University Press, Princeton, NJ, 1996, especially pp. 74–105. The reference to 'dynamic nominalism', a term Appiah borrows from Ian Hacking, is on p. 78.
4. See also, Linda Martín Alcoff, 'Towards a Phenomenology of Racial Embodiment', *Radical Philosophy* 95 (May/June 1999), pp. 15–26.
5. See Lewis R. Gordon (ed.), *Existence in Black: An Anthology of Black Existential Philosophy*, Routledge, New York and London, 1996; Lewis R. Gordon, *Bad Faith and Anti-black Racism*, Humanities Press, Atlantic Highlands, NJ, 1995. With regard to the question of the 'masculinism' of Fanon's existentialism, feminist readers have, in turn, engaged in critical dialogue with Fanon's texts.
6. See, for example, Cornel West, *Keeping Faith: Philosophy and Race in America*, Routledge, New York and London, 1993.
7. Lucius T. Outlaw Jr, *On Race and Philosophy*, Routledge, New York and London, 1996, p. 11: 'I worry that efforts of this kind [Appiah's advocation of 'racial identitification' without a commitment to the existence of 'race'] may well come to have unintended side effects that are too much of a kind with racial and ethnic cleansing in terms of their impacts on raciality and ethnicity

as important means through which we construct and validate ourselves.' For a succint revision of the Introduction to *On Race and Philosophy* and a statement of Outlaw's general position see 'On Race and Philosophy', in Susan E. Babbitt and Sue Campbell (eds), *Racism and Philosophy*, Cornell University Press, Ithaca and London, 1999.

8. See Appiah and Gutmann, *Color Conscious*, pp. 97–9.
9. See Gayatri Chakravorty Spivak, 'In a Word: Interview', in *Outside in the Teaching Machine*, Routledge, New York and London, 1993, pp. 1–23. Spivak argues that the critique of essentialism should be understood 'not as an exposure of error, our own or others', but as an acknowledgment of the dangerousness of something one cannot not use' (p. 5). For political arguments against a strategic essentialism of 'race' (in favour of a 'strategic universalism'), see Paul Gilroy, *Between Camps: Race, Identity and Nationalism at the End of the Colour Line*, Allen Lane/Penguin, London, 2000. (US imprint: *Against Race: Imagining Political Culture Beyond the Color Line*, Harvard University Press, Cambridge, MA, 2000.) For a recent sociological defence of the realist rejection of 'race' as an explanatory category, see Bob Carter, *Realism and Racism: Concepts of Race in Sociological Research*, Routledge, London and New York, 2000.
10. See, for example, Ivan Hannaford, *Race: The History of an Idea in the West* Johns Hopkins University Press, Baltimore and London, 1996; Nancy Stepan, *The Idea of Race in Science: Great Britain 1800–1960*, Macmillan, Basingstoke, 1982; Michael Omi and Howard Winant, *Racial Formation in the United States from the 1960s to the 1980s*, Routledge, New York and London, 1994; Robert Bernasconi and Tommy L. Lott (eds), *The Idea of Race*, Hackett, Indianapolis, 2000; Robert Bernasconi (ed.), *Race*, Blackwell, Oxford, 2001.
11. See Robert Bernasconi, 'Who Invented the Concept of Race? Kant's Role in the Enlightenment Construction of Race', in R. Bernasconi (ed.), *Race*, pp. 11–26; and Bernasconi 'Kant as an Unfamiliar Source of Racism', in Julie K. Ward and Tommy L. Lott (eds), *Philosophers on Race: Critical Essays*, Blackwell, Oxford and Malden MA, 2002, pp. 145–66; Emmanuel Chukwudi Eze, 'The Color of Reason: The Idea of "Race" in Kant's Anthropology', in Emmanuel Chukwudi Eze, (ed.), *Postcolonial African Philosophy: A Critical Reader*, Blackwell, Cambridge, MA and Oxford, 1997; pp. 103–40; Thomas E. Hill Jr and Bernard Boxill, 'Kant and Race', in Bernard Boxill, (ed.), *Race and Racism*, Oxford University Press, Oxford and New York, 2001, pp. 448–71.
12. See, for example, the new international cross-disciplinary quarterly journal *Ethnicities* (vol. 1, no. 1, April 2001) in which the term functions to transcode what would often previously have been 'racially' conceived conflicts into the dual discourse of nationalism and liberal multiculturalism. Michael Omi and Howard Winant identify 'ethnicity' as one of three paradigms within 'racial theory' itself. Although introduced as a sociological category in the 1920s in opposition to the dominant biologically conceived conception of race, the 'ethnicity paradigm', according to Omi and Winant, with its analogical basis in white immigrant assimilation in the USA, was constituitvely unable to account for different historical experiences (histories including slavery and

colonization, for example) and in fact covered over the forms of specifically *racial* discrimination. See Omi and Winant, *Racial Formation in the United States*, pp. 9–23.

13. See Margaret Simmons, 'Richard Wright, Simone de Beauvoir, and *The Second Sex*', in her *Beauvoir and the Second Sex: Feminism, Race, and the Origins of Existentialism*, Rowman and Littlefield, Lanham, MD, 1999; and 'Beauvoir and the Problem of Racism', in Ward and Lott (eds), *Philosophers on Race*, pp. 260–84.
14. See in particular, Stuart Hall *et al.*, *Policing the Crisis: Mugging, the State, and Law and Order*, Macmillan, London and Basingstoke, 1978, and CCCS (eds), *The Empire Strikes Back*, Hutchinson, London, 1983. The location of the Centre for Contemporary Cultural Studies in Birmingham, down the road from Enoch Powell's Wolverhampton constituency had a determining effect upon its cultural–political orientation.
15. That this is the case in contemporary discourses on 'race' is clear. The best-known British exponent of the argument is Paul Gilroy. See Gilroy, *There Ain't No Black in the Union Jack: The Cultural Politics of Race and Nation*, Routledge, London, 1991 (first published by Unwin Hyman, 1987). The hugely influential but rather less hegemonic articulation of the argument with regard to discourses of 'sex' is exemplified by Judith Butler's *Gender Trouble: Feminism and the Subversion of Identity*, Routledge, London and New York, 1990.
16. Stuart Hall, 'New Ethnicities', in James Donald and Ali Rattansi (eds), *'Race', Culture and Difference*, Sage (in association with the Open University), London, 1992, p. 257. In this essay Hall himself notes (p. 256) the inevitable imbrication of questions of ethnicity with questions of gender (and sexuality).
17. See the autobiographical sketches in George Yancy (ed.), *African-American Philosophers: 17 Conversations*, Routledge, New York and London, 1998. The still overwhelmingly white constitution of philosophy departments in the UK, and the dominance there of the Oxbridge tradition, goes a long way in explaining the glaring lack of philosophical work on race and ethnicity in the UK.
18. The focus on 'African philosophy', and the character of the debates about it, are, to some extent, an effect of this dominance. See Emmanuel Chukwudi Eze (ed.), *African Philosophy: An Anthology*, Blackwell, Oxford, 1998.
19. Aijaz Ahmad, *In Theory: Classes, Nations, Literatures*, Verso, London and New York, 1992, p. 17. See also, especially, Chapter 8, 'Three Worlds Theory: End of a Debate'. As Ahmad points out, there were actually three distinct versions of the notion of a Third World: the Nehruvian, the Soviet and the Chinese, each with a different political inflection.
20. See Homi Bhabha, *The Location of Culture*, Routledge, London and New York, 1994, Chapter 4. For an early overview of these developments from a standpoint sympathetic to a deconstructive version of colonial discourse theory, see Robert Young, *White Mythologies: Writing History and the West*, Routledge, London and New York, 1990.
21. Benedict Anderson, *Imagined Communities: Reflections on the Origin and Spread of Nationalism*, Verso, London and New York, 1983; Benedict Anderson, *The Spectre of Comparison: Nationalism, Southeast Asia and the World*, Verso, London

and New York, 1998, Chapter 3; Chetan Bhatt, *Liberation and Purity: Race, New Religious Movements and the Ethics of Postmodernity*, UCL Press, London, 1997, Chapter 2.

22. In the Anglo-American context, see, for example, Paul Gilroy, *The Black Atlantic: Modernity and Double Consciousness*, Verso, London, 1993.

Chapter One: Philosophy and Racial Identity

1. David Theo Goldberg, *Racist Cultures: Philosophy and the Politics of Meaning*, Blackwell, Oxford, 1993; Cornel West, *Prophesy Deliverance!*, Westminster Press, Philadelphia, 1982.
2. West, *Prophesy Deliverance!*, p. 55.
3. Goldberg, *Racist Culture*, p. 6.
4. Michel Foucault, *The Archeology of Knowledge*, trans. A.M. Sheridan Smith, Pantheon, New York, 1982, p. 45.
5. Michel Foucault, *The Birth of the Clinic*, trans. A.M. Sheridan Smith, Vintage Books, New York, 1975, p. 30.
6. See also Adrian Piper, 'Passing for White, Passing for Black', *Transitions* 58, pp. 4–32.
7. Anthony Appiah, *In My Father's House: Africa in the Philosophy of Culture*, Oxford University Press, New York, 1992, pp. 32, 45, and Chapters 2 and 3 generally.
8. Richard Rodriguez, *Days of Obligation: An Argument with My Mexican Father*, Viking, New York, 1992, p. 1.
9. See, for example, the special issue of *Identities: Global Studies in Culture and Power* on '(Multi)Culturalisms and the Baggage of "Race"', edited by Virginia Dominguez, vol. 1, no. 4, April, 1995.
10. Richard Rorty, *Philosophy and The Mirror of Nature*, Princeton University Press, Princeton NJ, 1981; Martin Jay, *Downcast Eyes: The Denegration of Vision in Twentieth-Century French Thought*, University of California Press, Berkeley, 1993; Frederic Jameson, *Signatures of the Visible*, Routledge, London and New York, 1992, p. 1.
11. Iris Young, 'The Ideal of Community and the Politics of Difference', in Linda Nicholson (ed.), *Feminism/Postmodernism*, Routledge, New York, 1990, pp. 303–5.
12. For a recent development of this idea, see Paul Ricoeur, *Oneself as Another*, trans. Kathleen Blamey, University of Chicago Press, Chicago, 1992.
13. Dan Danielson and Karen Engle, 'Introduction', in D. Danielson and K. Engle (eds), *After Identity: A Reader in Law and Culture*, Routledge, New York, 1994, pp. xiii–xix.
14. Michael Steinberg, '"Identity" and Multiple Consciousness', paper delivered at the workshop 'Identity: Do We Need It?', sponsored by the Internationales Forschungszentrum Kulturwissenschaften, Vienna, Austria, May 1995.
15. Gary Peller, 'Race Consciousness', in D. Danielson and K. Engle (eds), *After Identity*, p. 74.
16. Ibid., p. 76.

17. Lewis Gordon, *Bad Faith and Antiblack Racism*, Humanities Press, Atlantic Highlands, NJ, 1995, especially Chapter 14.
18. Charles Mills, 'Non-Cartesian Sums: Philosophy and the African-American Experience', *Teaching Philosophy*, vol. 17, no. 3, October 1994, p. 228.
19. Ibid., p. 228.
20. Ibid.
21. Ibid., p. 226.
22. Ibid., p. 225.
23. Hannah Arendt, *On Violence*, Harcourt, Brace Jovanovich, New York, 1969, pp. 18–9, quoted in Gordon, *Bad Faith and Antiblack Racism*, pp. 88–9.
24. Paul Gilroy, *The Black Atlantic: Modernity and Double Consciousness*, Verso, London, 1993 and Harvard University Press, Cambridge, MA, 1993.
25. Ibid., p. xi.
26. Ibid., p. 15.
27. Ibid., p. 56.
28. See Mills, 'Non-Cartesian Sums', p. 226.
29. Gilroy, *The Black Atlantic*, p. 49. Frederick Douglass, *Narrative of the Life of Frederick Douglass, an American Slave, Written by Himself*, Yale University Press, New Haven, 2001.
30. See my 'Cultural Feminism vs. Poststructuralism: The Identity Crisis in Feminist Theory', *Signs*, vol. 13, no. 3, 1988, pp. 405–36, for further elucidation on this point.
31. Gilroy, *The Black Atlantic*, p. 52.
32. Ibid., p. 53. Gilroy calls Hill Collins's account of knowledge 'experience centred', meaning to differentiate it from theoretical critique, but I would take issue with this characterization. One could have an experience-centred account of knowledge, or at least one that emphasizes the importance of experience, without either a transparent view of experience or an anti-theoretical disposition. The complex history of twentieth-century radical empiricism as well as the phenomenological tradition are counterexamples to this assumption.
33. Ibid., pp. 32, 49.
34. Gilroy, *The Black Atlantic*, p. ix.
35. Ibid., p. x.
36. For a similar argument against setting *a priori* limits on the plasticity of social practices, see Judith Butler's review essay 'Poststructuralism and Postmarxism' in *Diacritics*, Winter 1993, pp. 3–11. Here she is criticizing Ernesto Laclau's 'description of the logical features by which any social practice proceeds' on the grounds that it postulates 'a logic to which social practices are subject but which is itself subject to no social practice' (ibid., p. 9). I would make a related claim that we cannot determine in advance, outside of social practice, the 'logic' of identity concepts, or their inevitable political effects.
37. Kobena Mercer, *Welcome to the Jungle: New Positions in Black Cultural Studies*, Routledge, New York, 1994.
38. Robert Fernandez Retamar, *Caliban and Other Essays*, trans. Edward Baker, University of Minnesota Press, Minneapolis, 1989, pp. 16, 19.
39. For an attempt at such a phenomenology see my 'Towards a Phenomenology of Racial Embodiment', *Radical Philosophy* 95, May/June 1999, pp. 15–26.

Chapter Two: Fanon, Phenomenology, Race

1. Frantz Fanon, *Peau noire, masques blancs*, Collection Points, Seuil, Paris, 1975, p. 187.
2. *Black Skin, White Masks*, trans. Charles Lam Markmann, Grove Press, New York, 1967.
3. Fanon, *Peau noire*, p. 7.
4. Ibid., p. 155.
5. Ibid., p. 89.
6. To take only one example; Fanon uses the expression *souventefois* (ibid., p. 73), which to a French reader looks like either a misprint or an odd condensation of *souvent* and *mainte fois*. It is quite simply the Martinican–Guadeloupean Creole form of *souvent* (often).
7. Ibid., p. 120.
8. T.W. Adorno, *Minima Moralia*, trans. E.F.N. Jephcott, Verso, London, 1978, p. 110.
9. Fanon, *Peau noire*, p. 98.
10. Ibid., p. 90.
11. Sigmund Freud, *Jokes and their Relation to the Unconscious*, Pelican Freud Library, vol. VI, Penguin, Harmondsworth, 1976, p. 143.
12. Cited in Alain Ruscio, *Le Credo de l'homme blanc*, Editions Complexe, Brussels, 1995, p. 256.
13. Frantz Fanon, 'Antillais et Africains', in *Pour la Révolution africaine*, Maspéro, Paris, 1969, p. 26.
14. Henri Bergson, *Le Rire: Essai sur la signification du comique*, PUF, Paris, 1969, pp. 31–2.
15. Fanon, *Peau noire*, p. 90.
16. Françoise Dolto, *Correspondence I 1913–1938*, edited by Colette Percheminier, Hatier, Paris, 1991, pp. 44–5, 53, 58–9, 64.
17. Claude McKay, *A Long Way from Home*, Pluto Press, London, 1985, p. 74.
18. On the iconography of the advertisements for Banania, see Jan Nederven Pieterse, *White on Black: Images of Africa and Blacks in Western Popular Culture*, Yale University Press, New Haven, CT and London, 1995, pp. 162–3.
19. Fanon, *Peau noire*, p. 132n.
20. Maurice Merleau-Ponty, *La Phénoménologie de la perception*, Gallimard, Paris, 1945, p. 466; *Phenomenology of Perception*, trans. Colin Smith, Routledge, London, 1989, p. 407.
21. Jean-Paul Sartre, *L'Etre et le néant*, Collection Tel, Gallimard, Paris, 1972, p. 265; *Being and Nothingness*, trans. Hazel Barnes, Routledge, London, 1972.
22. Jean-Paul Sartre, *Saint-Genet: Comédien et martyr*, Gallimard, Paris, 1952, p. 23.
23. Pieterse, *White on Black*, p. 161.
24. Fanon, *Peau noire*, p. 27.
25. Merleau-Ponty, *La Phénoménologie de la perception*, pp. 114, 117; *Phenomenology of Perception*, pp. 98, 101.

26. Jean Lhermitte, *L'Image de notre corps*, Editions de la Nouvelle Revue Critique, Paris, 1939, p. 11.
27. Frantz Fanon, *Sociologie d'une révolution*, Maspéro, Paris, 1968, p. 42.
28. Fanon, *Peau noire*, pp. 89–90.
29. Ibid., p. 92.
30. Ibid., p. 33.
31. Abdoulaye Sadji, *Nini, mulâtresse du Sénégal*, Présence africaine, Paris, 1988, pp. 177–8.
32. Mayotte Capécia, *Je suis Martiniquaise*, Editions Corréa, Paris, 1948, pp. 202, 131.
33. See, for instance, Gwen Bergner, 'Who is that Masked Woman? Or, The Role of Gender in Fanon's *Black Skin, White Masks*', *Publications of the Modern Language Association of America*, vol. 110, no. 1, January 1995.
34. Fanon, *Peau noire*, pp. 179 n.2, 181.
35. 'Le Syndrôme Nord-africain' (1952), in *Pour la Révolution africaine*; 'Guerre coloniale et troubles mentaux', in Fanon, *Les Damnés de la terre*, Maspéro, Paris, 1961.
36. Fanon, *Peau noire*, p. 123.
37. David Macey, 'The Recall of the Real: Frantz Fanon and Psychoanalysis', *Constellations*, vol. 6, no. 1, 1999.
38. Octave Mannoni, *Prospéro et Caliban: Psychologie de la colonisation*, Editions Universitaires, Paris, 1984 (first published as *Psychologie de la colonisation* in 1950).
39. Fanon, *Peau noire*, p. 67.
40. Ibid., p. 78.
41. Ibid., p. 8.
42. Sigmund Freud, 'Five Lectures on Psychoanalysis', *Standard Edition of the Complete Works of Sigmund Freud*, vol. 11, Hogarth, London, p. 14; Fanon, *Peau noire*, p. 117.
43. George Lamming, 'The Negro Writer and his World', paper presented to the *Présence Africaine's* First Congress of Black Writers and Artists, 1956, p. 321.
44. Sartre, *Réflexions sur la question juive*, Gallimard, Paris, 1969, pp. 83–4.
45. Fanon, *Peau noire*, p. 93.
46. Jean-Paul Sartre, 'Orphée noir', in Léopold Sédar Senghor, *Anthologie de la nouvelle poésie nègre et malgache de langue française*, PUF, Paris, 1948.
47. Fanon, 'Antillais et Africains', p. 31.
48. Fanon, *Sociologie d'une révolution*, p. 29.
49. Fanon, *Peau noire*, p. 92.
50. Ibid., p. 106.
51. Aimé Césaire, *Cahier d'un retour au pays natal*, in *Poésies*, Seuil, Paris, 1994, p. 31.
52. bell hooks, *Wounds of Passion*, Women's Press, London, 1998, p. 54.
53. Fanon, *Peau noire*, p. 122.
54. Aimé Césaire, *Une Tempête*, Seuil, Paris, 1969, p. 83.
55. Francis Affergan, *Anthropologie à la Martinique*, Presses de la Fondation Nationale des Sciences Politiques, Paris, 1983, p. 177.

Chapter Three: Primordial Being

1. G. Spivak, *A Critique of Postcolonial Reason*, Routledge, London, 1999, p. 8, emphasis added.
2. A. Schopenhauer, *The World as Will and Representation* vol. I (1818), trans. E.F.J. Payne, Dover, New York, 1969, p. xv.
3. Voltaire, *The Philosophy of History* (1766), Philosophical Library, New York, 1965, pp. 9, 69, 73.
4. Voltaire used an existing argument that Abraham derived from the Indian idea of 'Bram'. Ibid., p. 69.
5. The text was the Ezourvedam procured by the library at Paris, which Voltaire believed was translated by a Brahmin and was not 'the Vedam itself' but a sequel. Ibid., p. 77.
6. J.G. Herder, *Reflections on the Philosophy of the History of Mankind* (1784–91), Book VI, in J.G. Herder, *On World History*, ed. H. Adler and E.A. Menze, trans. E.A. Menze and B. Palma, M.E. Sharpe, New York, 1997, pp. 220–1.
7. R. Schwab, *The Oriental Renaissance*: *Europe's Rediscovery of India and the East, 1680–1880*, Columbia University Press, New York, 1984, p. 59.
8. See, for example, J.W. Sedlar, *India in the Mind of Germany*, University Press of America, Washington, DC, 1982, p. 30.
9. 'It is also incontestable that the Brahmins formed their people to such a degree of gentleness, courtesy, temperance and chastity, or at least have so confirmed in them these virtues, that Europeans, compared to them, frequently appear as impure, inebriated and deranged.' Herder, *Reflections*, Book VI, p. 241.
10. J.G. Herder, 'Fragment of an Essay on Mythology' (*c.* 1782–92), in J.G. Herder, *Against Pure Reason: Writings on Religion, Language and History*, trans. M. Bunge, Fortress Press, Minneapolis, 1993, p. 80.
11. R. Taylor, 'The East and German Romanticism', in R. Iyer (ed.), *The Glass Curtain Between Asia and Europe*, Oxford University Press, London, 1965, p. 190.
12. J.G. Herder, *Reflections on the History of the Philosophy of Mankind* (1784–91), Book VII, ed. F.E. Manuel, University of Chicago Press, Chicago and London, 1968, p. 5.
13. J.G. Herder, 'Ideas Towards a Philosophy of History', in Herder, *Against Pure Reason*.
14. 'Thus we can judge with probability that the intermixture of races . . . which gradually extinguishes their characteristics, does not seem beneficial to the human race – all pretended philanthropy notwithstanding.' I. Kant, *Anthropology from a Pragmatic Point of View* (1796–98), trans. V.L. Dowdell, Southern Illinois University Press, Carbondale and Edwardsville, 1978, p. 236.
15. Herder, *Reflections*, Book VI, p. 241.
16. Quoted in L. Poliakov, *The Aryan Myth: A History of Racist and Nationalist Ideas in Europe*, Heinemann, London, 1971, p. 186.
17. Schwab, *The Oriental Renaissance*, p. 349.
18. W. Halbfass, *India and Europe: An Essay in Understanding*, State University of

New York Press, Albany, 1988, pp. 60–1. This has been a very useful source of ideas for some of the directions taken below.

19. Compare Schelling's mobilization of Hindu creation metaphors in attacking the presuppositions of Hegel's philosophy in F.W.J. Schelling, *On the History of Modern Philosophy* (*c.* 1833–87), trans. A. Bowie, Cambridge University Press, Cambridge, 1994, pp. 147–8.
20. G.W.F. Hegel, *Lectures on the Philosophy of World History – Introduction: Reason in History* (1822–31), trans. H.B. Nisbet, Cambridge University Press, Cambridge, 1975, pp. 132–3, emphasis added.
21. F. Schlegel, 'On the Language and the Wisdom of the Indians', in *Aesthetic and Miscellaneous Works* (1808), trans. E.J. Millington, Henry G. Bohn, London, 1849.
22. F. Schlegel, *The Philosophy of History*, trans. J.B. Robertson, Henry G. Bohn, London, 1847 (fifth, revised edition), p. 93.
23. The Indian texts that Hegel knew and used were extensive and included the work of Jones, Colebrooke, Wilkins and Halhed as well as Wilhelm von Humboldt's essay on the Bhagavad Gita on which Hegel made an extensive commentary that is seen as definitive of his view of Indian philosophy and its possibility for ethics. See I. Viyagappa, *G.W.F. Hegel's Concept of Indian Philosophy*, Università Gregoriana, Rome, 1980, pp. 266–74, for a full list of Hegel's sources; Halbfass, *India and Europe*, pp. 85–6. See also M. Hulin, *Hegel et l'Orient: Suivi de la Traduction Annotée d'un Essai de Hegel sur la Bhagavad-Gita*, Vrin, Paris, 1979.
24. M. Foucault, *The Order of Things: An Archaeology of the Human Sciences*, trans. Alan Sheridan-Smith, Tavistock, London, 1970, p. 219.
25. Hegel, *Lectures on the Philosophy of World History*, p. 135.
26. Foucault, *The Order of Things*, p. 233.
27. G.W.F. Hegel, *The Philosophy of History*, trans. J. Sibree, Prometheus Books, New York, 1991, pp. 141–2, emphasis added.
28. For an assessment of Western critiques of Indian conceptions of time and historicity, see R. Thapar, *Time as a Metaphor of History: Early India*, Oxford University Press, Delhi, 1996.
29. Both Hegel and Marx used the opium metaphor to describe, respectively, Brahminism and religion in general. The drugged religious bliss in *The German Ideology* is perhaps the superstructure to the base of 'the Asiatic mode of production' in the *A Contribution to the Critique of Political Economy*.
30. Hegel, *The Philosophy of History*, p. 9.
31. See Halbfass, *India and Europe*. We can also read this as two antagonistic sides of 'the active principle' in which Hegel could criticize Romantics like Schlegel for a celebration of Oriental stasis, while the Romantics saw their mission as one of dynamic vitality. See also C. Schmitt, *Political Romanticism*, trans. G. Oakes, MIT Press, Cambridge, MA, 1986.
32. J. Derrida, *Specters of Marx: The State of Debt, the Work of Mourning and the New International*, trans. P. Kamuf, Routledge, London, 1994, p. 51.
33. J.L. Nancy, *The Birth to Presence*, trans. B. Holmes *et al.*, Stanford University Press, Stanford, CA, 1993, p. 189.
34. J. Derrida, *Dissemination*, trans. B. Johnson, Athlone Press, London, 1981, pp. 70–1. At least India was a remedy for Schlegel, for a period. He, like

many of his Romantic peers, converted to Catholicism. We find the Indian metaphor as poison, drug and remedy in turn-of-century thinking about Western decline, of which Oswald Spengler and René Guenon are important markers.

35. On Maier, see A.L. Willson, *A Mythical Image: The Ideal of India in German Romanticism*, Duke University Press, Durham, NC, 1964, pp. 93–104.
36. It can also be easy to forget that Saussure's work was as a Sanskritist and scholar of Indo-European languages in both Paris and Geneva. While now known principally for his *Cours* as the founding text of structuralism, the only book he wrote was the *Mémoire sur le système primitif des voyelles dans les langues indo-européenes*, Teubner, Leipsick, 1878.
37. R. Safranski, *Schopenhauer and the Wild Years of Philosophy*, Harvard University Press, Cambridge, MA, 1991, pp. 201–2.
38. A. Schopenhauer, *Parerga and Paralipomena*, vol. II, trans. E.F. Payne, Clarendon Press, Oxford, 1974, p. 397.
39. Sedlar, *India in the Mind of Germany*, p. 47.
40. A. Schopenhauer, *Parerga and Paralipomena*, vol I, trans. E.F. Payne, Clarendon Press, Oxford, 1974, p. 422.
41. A. Schopenhauer, *The World as Will and Representation*, vol. II, trans. E.F. Payne, Dover, New York, 1969, p. 169.
42. B. Magee, *The Philosophy of Schopenhauer*, Clarendon Press, Oxford, 1997, p. 15.
43. Safranski, *Schopenhauer*, p. 201.
44. Magee, *The Philosophy of Schopenhauer*, p. 15. See also Sedlar, *India in the Mind of Germany*, p. 232.
45. See Halbfass's discussion, *India and Europe*, pp. 113–20.
46. *The World as Will and Representation*, vol. I, p. 3.
47. Ibid., p. 25.
48. Ibid., p. 100.
49. Ibid., p. 149.
50. *The World as Will and Representation*, vol. II, p. 350.
51. Ibid., pp. 321, 323.
52. *The World as Will and Representation*, vol. I, p. 195.
53. *The World as Will and Representation*, vol. II, p. 581.
54. *The World as Will and Representation*, vol. I, p. 199.
55. *The World as Will and Representation*, vol. II, pp. 488–9.
56. Ibid., pp. 507–8.
57. *Parerga and Paralipomena*, vol. II, p. 397.
58. Ibid.
59. *The World as Will and Representation*, vol. I, p. 232.
60. Spivak, *A Critique of Postcolonial Reason*, Chapter 1; G. Spivak, 'Response to Jean-Luc Nancy', in J.F. MacCannell and L. Zakarin (eds), *Thinking Bodies*, Stanford University Press, Stanford, CA, 1994.
61. Spivak, *Critique of Postcolonial Reason*, p. 8.
62. Spivak 'Response', pp. 37, 39–43.
63. There are many possible references here, but see D. Upadhyaya, *Pandit Deendayal Upadhyaya – Ideology and Perception* Part II: *Integral Humanism*, compiled by V.V. Nene, trans. M.K. Paranjape and D.R. Kulkarni, Suruchi

Prakashan, New Delhi, 1991; S.R. Goel, *Defence of Hindu Society*, Voice of India Press, New Delhi, 1993.

Chapter 4: Race and Language in the Two Saussures

1. Ferdinand de Saussure, *Cours de linguistique générale*; publié par Charles Bally et Albert Sechehaye avec la collaboration de Albert Riedlinger; édition critique préparée par Tullio de Mauro; postface de Louis-Jean Calvet Payot, Paris, 1995; *Course in General Linguistics*, ed. Charles Bally and Albert Sechehaye in collaboration with Albert Riedlinger, trans. Wade Baskin, Collins, London, 1974; Jean Starobinski, *Words Upon Words: The Anagrams of Ferdinand de Saussure*, trans. Olivia Emmet, Yale University Press, New Haven, CT, 1979. Unless otherwise stated, all references to Saussure's *Course* will be to the Payot edition, followed by the Collins. (I have also consulted Ferdinand de Saussure, *Course in General Linguistics*, ed. Charles Bally and Albert Sechehaye; with the collaboration of Albert Riedlinger; trans. Roy Harris, Duckworth, London, 1983.)
2. Ferdinand de Saussure, *Mémoire sur le système primitif des voyelles dans les langues indo-européennes*, Teubner, Leipsick, 1879.
3. Ananya Vajpeyi, '"Les semences du temps": F. de Saussure and the Role of Sanskrit in the Construction of a "Modern" Linguistics'. MPhil University of Oxford, 1996. See also Gayatri C. Spivak, 'Neocolonialism and the Secret Agent of Knowledge', an Interview with Robert J.C. Young, in *Neocolonialism, Oxford Literary Review*, 13 (1991), pp. 220–51.
4. *Cours*, p. 166; *Course*, p. 120.
5. *Cours*, p. 167; *Course*, p. 121.
6. Jindrich Toman, *The Magic of a Common Language: Jakobson, Mathesius, Trubetzkoy, and the Prague Linguistic Circle*, MIT Press Cambridge, MA., 1995. For an exception, see Samuel Weber, 'Saussure and the Apparition of Language: The Critical Perspective', *Modern Language Notes*, 91 (1976), pp. 913–38.
7. Anna Morpurgo Davies, *History of Linguistics*, ed. Giulio Lepschy, Longman, London, 1998, p. 185.
8. *Cours*, p. 286; *Course*, p. 209.
9. *Cours*, pp. 41, 262; *Course*, pp. 20, 191.
10. *Cours*, p. 304–5; *Course*, p. 222–3.
11. *Cours*, p. 286; *Course*, p. 209.
12. *Cours*, pp. 316, 272; *Course*, pp. 231, 198–9.
13. Centre de Recherche pour un Trésor de la Langue Française, *Trésor de la langue français. Dictionnaire de la langue du XIXe et du XXe siècle, 1789–1960*, Éditions du C.N.R.S., Gallimard, Paris, 1971–94.
14. *Robert, Dictionnaire alphabétique et analogique de la langue française*, Société du Nouveau Littré, Paris, 1960.
15. Ferdinand de Saussure, *Cours de linguistique générale* (1967–74), Éd. critique par Rudolf Engler, Harrassowitz Wiesbaden, III, 438/3.
16. *Cours*, p. 305; *Course*, p. 223.

17. Saussure, *Cours de linguistique générale* (1967–74), IV, 497/1.
18. *Cours*, p. 317; *Course*, p. 232. Saussure's emphasis.
19. *Cours*, pp. 202–3; *Course*, p. 147.
20. *Cours*, p. 310; *Course*, p. 227, translation modified.
21. *Cours*, p. 312; *Course*, p. 228, translation modified.
22. *Cours*, p. 317; *Course*, pp. 231–2.
23. Léopold de Saussure, *Psychologie de la colonisation française dans ses rapports avec les sociétés indigènes*, Félix Alcan, Paris, 1899.
24. Joseph Arthur comte de Gobineau, *Essai sur l'inegalité des races humaines*, 4 vols, Firmin Didot, Paris, 1853–55; Gustave Le Bon, *Les lois psychologiques de l'évolution des peuples*, F. Alcan, Paris, 1894.
25. Jacques Lacan, *The Four Fundamental Concepts of Psycho-Analysis*, trans. Alan Sheridan, Hogarth Press, London, 1977, p. 151; Léopold de Saussure, *Les origines de l'astronomie chinoise*, Librarie orientale et américaine, Maisonneuve frères, Paris, 1930.
26. Some sections of Saussure's *Psychologie de la colonisation française dans ses rapports avec les sociétés indigènes* (1899) are translated in Philip D. Curtin (ed.), *Imperialism*, Macmillan, London, 1972. This translation is used when available, and page numbers are cited as Curtin. *Psychologie de la colonisation française dans ses rapports avec les sociétés indigènes*, p. 300; Curtin, p. 88.
27. Saussure, *Psychologie de la colonisation française*, pp. 299, 108.
28. Saussure, *Psychologie de la colonisation française*, p. 302; Curtin p. 89.
29. Saussure, *Psychologie de la colonisation française*, pp. 165, 170–3.
30. Ibid., p. 10.
31. Ibid., pp. 4, 16.
32. Ibid., p. 307; Curtin, p. 91, translation modified.
33. Saussure, *Psychologie de la colonisation française*, p. 305; Curtin, p. 90. See also Robert J.C. Young, *Colonial Desire: Hybridity in Culture, Theory and Race*, Routledge, London, 1995.
34. See Winfried Baumgart, *Imperialism: The Idea and Reality of British and French Colonial Expansion, 1880–1914*, Oxford University Press, Oxford, 1982.
35. See Raymond F. Betts, *Assimilation and Association in French Colonial Theory 1890–1914*, Columbia University Press, New York, 1961.
36. Jules Harmand, *Domination et colonisation*, E. Flammarion, Paris, 1910, p. 156; Curtin, pp. 294–5.
37. See, for example, *Cours*, pp. 261, 268; *Course*, pp. 191, 195.
38. I am indebted to my research student Ananya Vajpeyi for this information, drawn from her reading of Saussure's manuscripts. See also *Cours*, p. 316; *Course*, pp. 230–1.
39. *Cours*, p. 263; *Course*, p. 192.
40. Léopold de Saussure, *Psychologie de la colonisation française*, p. 179.
41. *Cours*, p. 267; *Course*, p. 195.
42. See John E. Joseph, 'The Colonial Linguistics of Léopold de Saussure', in *History of Linguistics 1966: Selected Papers from the Seventh International Conference on the History of the Language Sciences*, (eds) David Cram, Andrew Linn, and Elke Nowak, John Benjamins, Amsterdam, 1999, pp. 7–8.
43. *Cours*, p. 279; *Course*, p. 204.
44. *Cours*, p. 306; *Course*, p. 223.

45. Linda Colley, *Britons: Forging the Nation, 1707–1837*, Yale University Press, New Haven, CT, 1992.

Chapter 5: Unspeakable Histories

1. See especially Bryan Cheyette and Laura Marcus (eds), *Modernity, Culture and 'The Jew'*, Polity, Cambridge, 1998.
2. Dissenting perspectives on hybridity have been compiled in Pnina Werbner and Tariq Modood (eds), *Debating Cultural Hybridity: Multi-cultural Identities and the Politics of Anti-racism*, Zed Books, London, 1997. This contains observations from Nikos Papastergiadis, 'Tracing Hybridity in Theory', which are exemplary in their lack of historical curiosity.
3. Enoch Powell was a prominent British politician of the Conservative Right who, from the mid-1960s, mobilized a powerful white populism under the banner of exclusive affiliation to the protocols of English civilization. His most notorious speech was delivered in April 1968, in which he foresaw (as he put it), 'the River Tiber foaming with much blood', by which he meant bloody racial war.
4. Bill Schwarz, 'Actually Existing Postcolonialism', *Radical Philosophy*, 104, November/December 2000, pp. 16–24.
5. Sigmund Freud, 'The Uncanny', in *The Standard Edition of the Complete Psychological Works of Sigmund Freud. Vol. XVII. An Infantile Neurosis and Other Works*, Hogarth Press, London, 1978, p. 245.
6. Tom Stacey, *Immigration and Enoch Powell*, Tom Stacey Books, London, 1970, p. 16.
7. Anthony Smith's theorization of the nation is couched entirely in these terms. He argues that the most important function of national identity is 'to provide a satisfactory answer to the problem of personal oblivion' (*National Identity*, Penguin, Harmondsworth, 1991, p. 16).
8. Patrick Cosgrave, *The Lives of Enoch Powell*, Pan, London, 1990, pp. 254–5.
9. Simon Heffer, *Like the Roman: The Life of Enoch Powell*, Weidenfeld and Nicolson, London, 1998, p. 450.
10. The reference is to Powell's speech of April 1968. See Bill Smithies and Peter Fiddick (eds), *Enoch Powell on Immigration*, Sphere, London, 1969, p. 43.
11. James Baldwin, Colin MacInnes and James Mossman, 'Race, Hate, Sex and Colour', transcribed and reproduced in *Encounter*, July 1965, p. 57.
12. James Baldwin, *The Fire Next Time*, Penguin, Harmondsworth, 1964, pp. 16–17.
13. Stuart Hall, 'Minimal Selves', in *Identity: The Real Me*, ICA documents 6, Institute of Contemporary Arts, London, 1987, p. 44.
14. Advocacy of contemporary nomadism can be found in, for example, Alberto Melucci, *Nomads of the Present: Social Movements and Individual Needs in Contemporary Society*, Hutchinson, London, 1989. The philosophical origins of these readings reach back to Heidegger's renowned phenomenological ruminations on the necessary homelessness of the modern subject.
15. Stuart Hall, 'The Formation of a Diasporic Intellectual: An Interview with

Kuan-Hsing Chen', in David Morley and Kuan-Hsing Chen (eds), *Stuart Hall: Critical Dialogues*, Routledge, London, 1996, p. 502. Hall's position accords, I think, with Jacqueline Rose's scepticism towards a fashionable postmodernism in which belonging is both everywhere and nowhere. As Rose suggests, this never sounds right, 'bereft of history and of passion'. Rose, *States of Fantasy: The Clarendon Lectures in English Literature 1994*, Clarendon Press, Oxford, 1996, p. 2.

16. Hall, 'Formation of a Diasporic Intellectual', pp. 485–9.
17. The arrival of the ship *Windrush* in June 1948, bringing some 400 West Indian immigrants to the UK, is conventionally taken as signifying the beginning of the post-war phase of mass immigration.
18. Hall, 'Formation of a Diasporic Intellectual', pp. 491–2.
19. C.L.R. James, 'Africans and Afro-Caribbeans: A Personal View', *Ten.8*, vol. 16, 1984, p. 55.
20. Derek Walcott, *What the Twilight Says*, Faber and Faber, London, 1998, p. 62.
21. C.L.R. James provides a very clear picture: 'We lived in two worlds. Inside the classrooms the heterogeneous jumble of Trinidad was battered and jostled and shaken down into some sort of order', *Beyond a Boundary*, Hutchinson, London, 1986, p. 34.
22. Mike Phillips and Trevor Phillips, *Windrush: The Irresistible Rise of Multi-racial Britain*, HarperCollins, London, 1997, p. 66.
23. Ibid., pp. 65–6.
24. Sam Selvon, *The Lonely Londoners*, Longman, London, 1986, pp. 23, 84–5.
25. Stuart Hall, 'Politics, Contingency, Strategy: An Interview with David Scott', *Small Axe*, vol. 1, 1997, p. 142. It was common in Britain in the 1950s for all West Indians, regardless of their provenance, to be described as Jamaicans.
26. See Horace Ove's film, *Baldwin's Nigger* (1969).
27. Stuart Hall, 'Postscript', *Soundings (Special Windrush Issue)*, vol. 10, 1998, p. 190.
28. Mary Chamberlain, *Narratives of Exile and Return*, Macmillan, London, 1997, pp. 74–5.
29. Hall, 'Formation of a Diasporic Intellectual', p. 490.
30. Thomas Holt, *The Problem of Race in the Twenty-First Century*, Harvard University Press, Cambridge, MA, 2000, p. 122.

Chapter 6: Race, Colonialism and History

1. For more on this, see Rebecca E. Karl, 'Staging the World in Late-Qing China: Globe, Nation, and Race in a 1904 Beijing Opera', *Identities*, vol. 6, no. 4, 2000, pp. 551–606.
2. For this 'othering' approach to 'race', see Frank Dikötter, *The Discourse of Race in Modern China*, Stanford University Press, Stanford, CA, 1992; and the various essays on China in Dikötter, (ed.), *The Construction of Racial Identities in China and Japan*, University of Hawaii Press, Honolulu, 1997.
3. This is James Pusey's argument, in *China and Charles Darwin*, Harvard University Press, Cambridge, MA, 1983.

4. For food metaphors in Chinese political and philosophical discourse, see Gang Yue, *The Mouth That Begs: Hunger, Cannibalism, and the Politics of Eating in Modern China*, Duke University Press, Durham, NC, 1999.
5. Ato Sekyi-Otu, *Fanon's Dialectic of Experience*, Harvard University Press, Cambridge, MA, 1996, p. 72. As Sekyi-Otu makes clear in an explicit argument against many postcolonial versions of Fanon, this spatialized system of radical irreciprocity cannot be accessed through analysis of the slippages in the language and discourse of colonial texts alone, but rather must be accessed through analyses of historical experience.
6. Clearly, there were also sub-national spatialities of region, district, language group, and so on, some of which were tied to divisions of labour within economic sectors and some to other historical factors. I will not be overtly concerned in this chapter with those issues, although my analyses are not antithetical to problems of sub-national 'race' – usually labelled 'ethnicity'.
7. Gilles Deleuze and Félix Guattari, *A Thousand Plateaus: Capitalism and Schizophrenia*, trans. Brian Massumi, University of Minnesota Press, Minneapolis, 1987, pp. 456–7.
8. Ibid., p. 456. For a slightly differently emphasized elaboration of this view of nationalism, see Rebecca E. Karl, *Staging the World: Chinese Nationalism at the Turn of the Twentieth Century*, Duke University Press, Durham, NC, 2002, Chapter 1.
9. For more on immanence and immanentism, see Deleuze and Guattari, *A Thousand Plateaus*, *passim*; also Michael Hardt and Antonio Negri, *Labour of Dionysus: A Critique of the State-Form*, University of Minnesota Press, Minneapolis, 1994, Chapter 7.
10. On 'appropriation' see Sekyi-Otu's discussion in *Fanon's Dialectic*, pp. 184–211 and *passim*:

    > Appropriation . . . would be the activity of coming into one's own when there is no primal self to return to, no inviolate native essences to recapture; consequently, the enterprise of transforming into one's own tradition of possibilities an imposed order of practices and thereby overcoming their violence. (p. 184)

    This meaning derives from Martin Heidegger.

    On 'desire', Foucault figures it as a regulatory discourse (*History of Sexuality*, vol. I, Vintage, New York, 1985). Yet, as Ann Laura Stoler points out, in a colonial context, 'desire' must also include its manufacture and not only its regulation and release (*Race and the Education of Desire: Foucault's History of Sexuality and the Colonial Order of Things*, Duke University Press, Durham, NC, 1995, p. 167). 'Desire' is here understood in the dialectical sense of what desire produces and what is productive of desire.
11. On 'ethnos' in Japan, see Naoki Sakai, *Translation and Subjectivity: On 'Japan' and Cultural Nationalism*, University of Minnesota Press, Minneapolis and London, 1997; for China, see Karl, *Staging the World*, Chapter 5. I take 'ethnos' to be different from 'ethnicity', insofar as 'ethnicity' – at least in the Chinese case – derives from a prior concept of the 'ethnos' and is thus rendered an instrumentalized category of differentiation. A different way of putting this might be that 'ethnicity' is about populations, whereas 'ethnos' is about peoples. For 'ethnicity' in China in its anthropological–sociological

sense, see the various essays in Stevan Harrell (ed.), *Cultural Encounters on China's Ethnic Frontiers*, University of Washington Press, Seattle, 1995.

12. See Neil Lazarus, *Nationalism and Cultural Practice in the Postcolonial World*, Cambridge University Press, Cambridge, 1999, p. 25: '(capitalist) modernity is characterized by unevenness: that is, by the dynamics of development and underdevelopment, autocentricity and dependency, the production and entrenchment of localisms . . . within larger processes of globalization, incorporation, and homogenization'.
13. Here, I borrow Jacques Rancière's notion of 'names of history', as that which is 'the very disruption of the relations between names and states of affairs'. Rancière, *The Names of History: On the Poetics of Knowledge*, trans. Hassan Melehy, University of Minnesota Press, Minneapolis, MN, 1994, p. 93.
14. On 'packaging,' see Theodor W. Adorno, 'Bourgeois Opera', in *Sound Figures*, trans. Rodney Livingstone, Stanford University Press, Stanford, CA, 1999, p. 16. On language, see Fredric Jameson, *The Prison-House of Language*, Princeton University Press, Princeton, NJ, 1972.
15. It is clear that, in the context of overseas Chinese – in South-east Asia or elsewhere – or of Chinese intellectuals residing in Japan, or yet in the treaty ports, whose socio-political organization was based upon imperialist racialisms, 'race' was indeed a potent lived experience for many Chinese. Particularly in the latter context, it would be interesting to investigate the ways in which Manchu/Han separation in urban spatial design and Western/Chinese separation in urban treaty port design were similarly or differentially understood; these topics, however, fall outside the parameters of the current chapter.
16. Stoler, *Race and the Education of Desire*, pp. 68–9.
17. For the renarration of the Manchu Qing deposing of the Ming through a colonial paradigm, see Rebecca E. Karl, 'Creating Asia: China in the World at the Beginning of the Twentieth Century', *American Historical Review*, vol. 103, No. 4 (October 1998), pp. 1096–118.
18. For a suggestive discussion of this issue for post-dynastic, pre-Communist China, see Joseph Levenson, *Revolution and Cosmopolitanism*, University of California Press, Berkeley, CA, 1971, pp. 6–11.
19. See Karl, *Staging the World*.
20. The title is also translated as *A Discourse on the Grand Unity*. Kang's book was written between 1884 and 1902. It began with the title *Universal Principles of Mankind* [*Renlei gongli*] and ended up as *One World Philosophy* [*Datong shu*]. The book was finished during Kang's sojourn in Darjeeling, India, where, among other places, he resided after being forced into exile after the 1898 reform movement. The book was only published in full after 1911. For more on the history of the book, a brief biographical sketch of Kang, and a full translation of the text, see Laurence G. Thompson, *The One World Philosophy of K'ang Yu-wei*, George Allen & Unwin, London, 1958.
21. See Lionel M. Jensen, *Manufacturing Confucianism: Chinese Traditions and Universal Civilization*, Duke University Press, Durham, NC, 1997, Chapter 3.
22. For more on Kang, see Hsiao Kung-ch'uan, *A Modern China and a New World: K'ang Yu-wei, Reformer and Utopian*, University of Washington Press, Seattle 1975; Tang Zhijun, *Kang Youwei yu wuxu bianfa* [Kang Youwei and the Wuxu Reforms], Zhonghua shuju, Beijing, 1984; Li Zehou, *Zhongguo jindai sixiangshi*

lun [*Essays on Modern Chinese Intellectual History*], Renmin chubanshe, Beijing, 1986, pp. 92–181.

23. Hao Chang, *Chinese Intellectuals in Crisis: Search for Order and Meaning*, University of California Press, Berkeley, CA, 1987, p. 25.
24. Ibid., p. 57.
25. Ibid., pp. 56–65.
26. Thompson, trans., *The One World Philosophy of K'ang Yu-wei*, pp. 84–5.
27. On this distinction in a different context, see D.R. Howland, *Borders of Chinese Civilization: Geography and History at Empire's End*, Duke University Press, Durham, NC, 1996, pp. 4, 177.
28. As Hao Chang notes (*Chinese Intellectuals in Crisis*, p. 62), unlike many utopias from both Chinese and other traditions, which 'feature the negation of government and authority as such, Kang's utopia is a politically organized universal state'.
29. As Lutz Niethammer summarizes pre-Second World War notions of 'posthistoire' in European thought: 'these authors see themselves facing anonymous structural processes before which individuals feel so powerless that they endow them with omnipotence . . . These processes are endowed with . . . a capacity to dissolve cultural values in non-temporal randomness.' (*Posthistoire: Has History Come to an End?*, Verso, London, 1994, p. 57).
30. Niethammer, *Posthistoire*, p. 17. Niethammer adds, this type of posthistoire – characteristic of the European nineteenth century – 'did not contain the frustration of cultural pessimism, but rather the hope that the chaos of history . . . might finally be overcome' (p. 18).
31. As he notes, white and yellow peoples are more similar in colour and intelligence, and thus, the amalgamation of these is relatively easily accomplished, which leaves 'brown and black . . . [who are] so distant from the white people [that they] will be really difficult to amalgamate'. His solution is to encourage miscegenation between white women and coloured men – where women are understood as the bearers of race – so as to produce successive generations of lighter offspring; and to encourage blacks and browns to move to northern climes (for example, Africans to Sweden) where darker colours will, over time, naturally fade. See Thompson, trans., *The One World Philosophy of K'ang Yu-wei*, pp. 140–8. Dikötter (*The Discourse of Race in Modern China*, p. 90) asserts that Kang's racial assimilationism is merely a transformation of 'the traditional concept of cultural absorption into a vision of physical amalgamation'. This, it seems to me, is only a superficial reading.
32. Thompson, trans., *The One World Philosophy of K'ang Yu-wei*, p. 143.
33. The sex boundary between man and woman could be dealt with, according to Kang, by abolishing the institution of marriage and its links to private property, restructuring society so that all were equally responsible for the raising of children, and degendering clothing.
34. Thompson, trans., *The One World Philosophy of K'ang Yu-wei*, p. 144. Kang had been several times to the United States, where he had witnessed the treatment of black Americans in the West and the north-east; he also sojourned in India, the treaty ports of China, Hong Kong, and south-east Asia, where Indians served as soldiers and servants to British colonials and settlers.
35. *Wenming* in this period can be understood either as civilization as a behavioural

norm or as modernity, or being modern. *Wenhua* is an older civilizational notion that carries with it a certain set of references to education in the classics and Confucian normativity; as a concept, it was also at just this time beginning to take on the meaning of 'national culture'. For more on the latter issue, see Lydia Liu, *Translingual Practice: Literature, National Culture, and Translated Modernity*, Stanford University Press, Stanford, CA, 1995, Chapter 9.

36. On *wen* as 'civilization' see Howland, *Borders of Chinese Civilization*. On 'civilizing missions' in China *vis-à-vis* non-Han peoples in the empire and on its fringes, see Stevan Harrell, 'Civilizing Projects and the Reaction to Them', in *Cultural Encounters on China's Ethnic Frontiers*, pp. 3–36.

    Kang was also, however, one of the major proponents of tying a formerly universalist Confucian civilizational topos to a national cultural realm, particularly in his later efforts to specify a religious content to Confucianism and to promote Confucianism as the religion of China. On this aspect, see Li Zehou, *Kang Youwei yu Tan Sitong sixiang yanjiu* [*A Study of the Thought of Kang Youwei and Tan Sitong*], in *Zhongguo jindai sixiangshi lun* [*Essays on Modern Chinese Intellectual History*], Renmin chubanshe, Beijing, 1986; also Jensen, *Manufacturing Confucianism*, Chapter 3.
37. Thompson, trans., *The One World Philosophy of K'ang Yu-wei*, pp. 140–1.
38. Hu Fengyang and Zhang Wenjian, *Zhongguo jindai shixue sichao yu liupai* [*Trends and Schools in Modern Chinese Historiography*], Huadong shida chubanshe, Shanghai, 1991, pp. 240–4.
39. Yu Danchu, 'Zhongguo jindai aiguo zhuyi de '*wangguo* shijian' chukao' ['Preliminary Investigation into Modern Chinese Patriotic "Mirrors on the History of Perished States"'], *Shijie lishi*, vol. 1, 1984, pp. 23–32; citation from p. 23.
40. Liang Qichao, 'Dongji yuedan' ['A Critique of Japanese Booklists'], in Liang Qichao, *Yinbingshi wenji* (*Collected Essays from the Ice-Drinker's Studio*], *juan* 4, p. 102.
41. Wu Tingjia, *Wuxu sichao zongheng lun* [A Complete Discussion of Intellectual Trends in the *wuxu* period], Renmin chubanshe, Beijing, 1988, p. 96. Liang's 1902 essay, *Xin shixue* [*New Historiography*], is generally considered the first attempt to write a national history of China; at the same time, Chen Fuchen [Jieshi], less a new-style journalist/intellectual (such as Liang) than an old-style scholar-literatus, also wrote an outline piece entitled *Dushi* [*Independent History*] that articulated guidelines for a new type of historical practice. Liang's *Xin shixue* was published serially in the middle of 1902 in *Xinmin congbao* [*New People's Miscellany*]; Chen's *Dushi* was published at the end of 1902 in *Xinshijie xuebao* [*New World Scholarly Journal*].
42. Liang Qichao, 'Xiaweiyi youji' ['Diary of Travel to Hawaii'], *Yinbingshi zhuanji*, vol. 7, pp. 149–60; citation from p. 160.
43. With this turn, the previous instances of a non-Han dynasty taking over from a Han Chinese dynasty – for example, the Mongol Yuan over the Song, the Manchu Qing over the Ming – were reinterpreted as colonizations, rather than as changes in dynasty.
44. The American Revolution was understood as both anti-colonial and anti-monarchical. The Mexican Revolution, begun in 1910, was the first seen as a peasant revolution of a different type altogether. But, because China's Repub-

lican revolution erupted in 1911, commentaries on Mexico – which had been numerous in 1910 – ended; Mexico was brought up again only in the 1920s, when a new wave of revolutionary theorizing got under way in China.

45. Indeed, the paradigm of colonialism was extended backwards to stand in for all occurrences of dominance of one state over another people or state. For more on the specific revolutionary movements at the turn of the century and how they were interpreted and appropriated in China, see Karl, *Staging the World*.
46. Kauko Laitinen, *Chinese Nationalism in the late-Qing Dynasty: Zhang Binglin as Anti-Manchu Propagandist*, Curzon, London, 1990, p. 24.
47. Anon., 'Yue Fei Zhuan' ['Biography of Yue Fei'], *Jinye xunbao* [*The Struggle*], vols 5–7, 8–9 (1906 and 1907). Also see Anon., 'Zhongguo minzu zhuyi diyi ren Yuefei zhuan' ['Biography of China's First Ethno-nationalist, Yue Fei'], *Hubei xuesheng jie* [*Hubei Student World*], 4–5 (April–May 1903), among others.
48. See, for example, 'Zhongguo aiguozhe Zheng Chenggong zhuan' ['Biography of the Patriot, Zheng Chenggong'], *Zhejiang chao*, vol. 4 (1903); 'Zheng Chenggong zhuan' ['Biography of Zheng Chenggong'], *Jiangsu*, vol. 3 (1903).
49. For a list with publication details, see Yu Danchu, 'Xinhai geming shiqi de minzu yingxiong renwu shijian chukao' ['Preliminary Investigation on National Heroes, Personnages, and their Times during the Xinhai Revolutionary Period'], *Jindaishi yanjiu*, vol. 6 (1991), pp. 34–52.
50. Tang (1871–1940) came from mean circumstances, even though his father had been a lower-level official in the Qing bureaucracy; yet, after his father's death, Tang had been brought up by his poverty-stricken uncle in a rural town in Zhejiang province, and after years of informal schooling, only at age 22 did he begin to attend a formal school in Hangzhou. After the 1911 revolution and many years of study in Japan, Tang became a prominent medical scholar and co-founded several of China's first comprehensive medical schools; in the late 1930s, Tang worked in the fields of medicine and education with the Japanese occupation government in Peking. He died in 1940. For an exonerating biography by Tang's son, see [Tang] Yousong, *Tang Erhe xiansheng* [*Mr Tang Erhe*], Zhonghua shuju, Beijing, 1942.
51. Vincent Raphael, 'Nationalism, Imagery, and the Filipino Intelligentsia in the Nineteenth Century', *Critical Inquiry*, vol. 16 (Spring 1990), pp. 591–611.
52. Benedict Anderson, *Imagined Communities*, Verso, London, 1991.
53. Tang Tiaoding, 'Feilübin haojie zhuan' ['Biographies of Heroes of the Philippines'], *Xinshijie xuebao* [New World Scholarly Journal] vol. 10 (12 February 1903), p. 10.
54. There was a certain trend at the time in Japan to claim that the Filipinos and Japanese were related, because of the widespread intermarriage on certain of the Philippines islands to which a number of Japanese had previously emigrated. See Lydia N. Yu-Jose, *Japan Views the Philippines, 1900–1944*, Ateneo de Manila University Press, Manila, 1992.
55. Hansheng, 'Feilübin wangguo canzhuang jilue' ['A Brief Outline of the Tragic Colonization of the Philippines'], *Hubei Xuesheng jie* [*Hubei Student World*], vol. 7.
56. Tang, 'Feilübin haojie zhuan', p. 11. I should note in passing that it was only

in these first years of the twentieth century that novels were beginning to be recognized by elite intellectuals as a viable form of writing. Indeed, only a few months earlier, in late 1902, Liang Qichao had called for the development of the political novel as a specific form of national literature in his *Xin xiaoshuo* [New Fiction]. This recognition of political novels was tied to the rise of political novels in Japan at the time. For more, see Xia Shaohong, *Jieshi yu chuanshi: Liang Qichao de wenxue daolu* [*Enlightenment and Eternity: Liang Qichao's Literary Path*], Renmin chubanshe, Shanghai, 1991.

57. Ma Junwu, 'Feilübin zhi aiguozhe' ['A Filipino Patriot'], *Xinmin congbao* [*New People's Miscellany*], vol. 27 (12 March 1903); reprint *Xinxuejie congbian* [*Compendium of New Learning*], vol. 8, *juan* 13, part 2, 4b–5b. These recitations were almost certainly provided by Mariano Ponce, delegate from the revolutionary Philippine Republican government to Japan, 1900–3. For more on the Chinese and Ponce in Japan, see Karl, *Staging the World*, Chapter 4.
58. Tang Tiaoding, 'Feilübin haojie zhuan', *Xinshijie xuebao*, vol. 10, p. 1.
59. Ibid., p. 6.
60. The People's Republic of China moved for four decades away from this *minzu* discourse to a more racially/ethnically neutral, albeit super-politically charged discourse of the *renmin* (the masses). However, since the 1980s, the *minzu* focus has become much more pronounced, in official and unofficial discourse alike.
61. Sekyi-Otu, *Fanon's Dialectic of Experience*, p. 11.

Chapter 7: Ethnicity and Species

1. For instance, *Naisen ittai no rinen oyobi sonogugen housaku yôkô* (The Idea of Japanese–Korean Synthesis and its Policies), Defense Headquarters, Korean League for the Total Mobilization of the Nation, 1941. For the Japanese–Korean synthesis, see S. Miyata, I. Kim and T. Ryao, *Sôshi Kaimei* (*The Creation of Surname and the Change of First Name*), Akashi Shobô, Tokyo, 1992.
2. For instance, Watsuji Tetsurô, *Fûdo*, Iwanami Shoten, Tokyo, 1934 (English translation, *Climate and Culture*, trans. Geoffrey Bownas, Japanese Ministry of Education, Tokyo, 1961); or his *Ethics II*, Iwanami Shoten, Tokyo, 1942 (reprinted in *Watsuji Zenshû*, vol. 11. See also Naoki Sakai, *Translation and Subjectivity: On 'Japan' and Cultural Nationalism*, Chapters 3 and 4, University of Minnesota Press, Minneapolis and London, 1997, pp. 72–152.
3. In his *Philosophy of Primordial Subjectivity* (*Kongen-teki shutai-sei no tetsugaku*), originally published in 1940, Nishitani Keiji stressed the purity of race and advocated the introduction of the Hitlerian spirit to Japan. *Philosophy of Primordial Subjectivity* is reproduced in Nishitani Keiji Chosakushû, Sôbunsha, Tokyo, 1986. For his involvement in Nazism, see its first volume, pp. 144–50, in particular.
4. For instance, Tomoo Odaka, *Kokutai no hongi to naisen-ittai* (*The Essence of Nationality and the Japanese–Korean Synthesis*), Defense Headquarters, Korean League for the Total Mobilization of the Nation, 1942; Kôsaka Masaaki,

Nishitani Keiji, Kôyama Iwao and Suzuki Shigetaka, *Sekaishi-teki tachiba to nihon* (*The Standpoint of World History and Japan*), Chûôkôron, January 1942.

5. See Oguma Eiji, *Tan'itsu minzoku shinwa no kigen* (*The Origins of Monoethnic Myth*), Shinyô-sha, Tokyo, 1995. For a critical review of Oguma's theoretical sloppiness, see my 'Introduction' to T. Iyotani, B. deBary and N. Sakai (eds), *Nashonarithi no datsukôchiku* (*Deconstruction of Nationality*), Shinyôsha, Tokyo, 1996 (English translation forthcoming in Cornell East Asia Monographs Series).
6. The philosophy department at Kyoto Imperial University was recognized as one of the intellectual centres in Japan from the 1920s until the early 1940s. The department developed under the leadership of Nishida Kitarô (1870–1945). In the 1910s, when Tanabe Hajime (1885–1962), who taught philosophy of science and mathematics (Whitehead, Frege, modern mathematics, quantum mechanics, theory of relativity, in addition to Neo-Kantianism) at Tôhôku University, joined the faculty at Kyoto, the philosophy department began to attract many talented students, who would later form the leading intelligentsia of the Japanese public sphere in the 1920s and 1930s. They included Miki Kiyoshi, Tosaka Jun, Tsuchida Kyôson, Nakai Masakazu and Hanada Kiyoteru (Hanada was in the English Department at Kyoto), Kuno Osamu and others. Included in the faculty were Tomonaga Sanjûrô, Hatano Seiichi, Watsuji Tetsurô (who taught at Kyoto for a short period of time, and moved to Tokyo Imperial University in 1934), Kuki Shûzô, Kôsaka Masaaki and Kôyama Iwao. In the 1920s Nishida published a series of articles in which he began to conceptualize the notion of *mu no basho* (the place of nothingness). Around the same time, Tanabe became interested in the ontology of social being and began to write about Kant's *Third Critique*, Bergson's social philosophy, Hegelian dialectic in reference to modern mathematics, particularly Riemann geometry and Minkovsky's theory of space and time. See *Shu no ronri* (*Logic of Species*).
7. Murayama Michio, *Daitôa Kensetsu-ron*, Shôkô Gyôsei-sha, Tokyo, 1943. Murayama was the secretary to the Governmental Planning Agency headed by Kishi Nobusuke, the Minister of Commerce and Industry in the Tojô Hideki cabinet (from 18 October 1941 until 18 October 1943) and then one of the ministers of the newly formed Ministry of the Great East Asia (from 18 October 1943 until 22 July 1944). From 1936, Kishi was *de facto* the chief administrator for the construction of Manchûkuo. After the defeat of Japan, Kishi was arrested as an A-class war criminal by the Allied Powers, but in 1948 he was released from prison; through the enthusiastic endorsement of the United States, he became the Minister of Foreign Affairs in the Ishibashi Tanzan cabinet (23 December 1956 until 25 February 1957), and then formed his own cabinets for two successive terms (25 February 1957 until 19 July 1960). He is known for his work as the political collaborator of US policies in East Asia. Kishi's case, as well as the case of the Kyoto School philosophers of world history, Kôsaka Masaaki, Kôyama Iwao, Nishitani Keiji, and Suzuki Shigetaka, who wrote vehemently in support of the US collective security policies in Asia during the 1950s and early 1960s, strongly suggest the continuity of pre-war/wartime Japanese imperial nationalism and post-war American imperial nationalism.

8. Its outline was published in *Kyoto Teikoku Daigaku Shinbun* (*Kyoto Imperial University News*) on 5 June 1943. See 'Shi Sei' ('Death and Life'), in *Tanabe Hajime Zenshû*, vol. 8, Chikuma Shobô, Tokyo, 1964.
9. 'Shi Sei', p. 261.
10. Maruyama Masao, 'Chûsei to hangyaku' ('Loyalty and Rebellion'), in *Chûsei to hangyaku* (*Loyalty and Rebellion*), Chikuma Shobô, Tokyo, 1992 [1960], pp. 3–109.
11. The notion of the individual had undergone a theoretical revision with Tanabe's mentor, Nishida Kitarô. Normally, in Japanese philosophical discourse of the 1920s and 1930s, the term *kobutsu* or *kotai* is a translation of 'the individual', but the original's sense of indivisibility or *individuum* is not necessarily emphasized. Nishida conceptualized *kobutsu* or singular-individual thing as that which is in a discontinuous relationship with any generality. For this reason, I translate his *kobutsu* into the individual-singular thing. Tanabe adopts the term *kotai* instead of Nishida's *kobutsu*. *Kotai* is still closer to the individual, yet Tanabe is aware that *kotai* or individual is not a generality or the most particular of generality: it is discontinuous with any generality, so it cannot evade being something like a singular point in mathematics.
12. For correlations between the concept of race and natural history, see Michel Foucault, *Les Mots et les choses*, Gallimard, Paris, 1966, pp. 137–76; George L. Mosse, *Toward the Final Solution: A History of European Racism*, University of Wisconsin Press, Madison WI, 1978, pp. 1–34; Mary Louise Pratt, *Imperial Eyes: Travel Writing and Transculturation*, Routledge, London and New York, 1992. From the outset, *Logic of Species* is aware that the taxonomy of natural history is utterly irrelevant in the discussion of the social. In this sense, Tanabe was most interested in the destructive effects of Darwin's *On the Origin of Species* with regard to the classical Linnaean taxonomy and Aristotelian logic of creatures. Tanabe attempted to conceptualize the species in the aftermath of Darwinian critique (see Kôyama Iwao's testimony, in the monthly supplement to *Tanabe Hajime Zenshû*, July 1963, pp. 3–4). In this respect, *Logic of Species* is most critical of the classical and static notion of race which Darwin's evolutionism effectively undermined. As goes without saying, it is hardly possible to dissociate the disintegration of the static taxonomy of creatures from the constant rearrangement of social relations by capitalism. There is no doubt that *Logic of Species* was a philosophical response to the development of Marxist scholarship on Japanese capitalism in the 1920s and 1930s. It is important to keep in mind that Japanese imperial nationalism also transformed itself in producing an argument to destroy the static concept of race. Yet, we must also remember that there is a racism with universalistic orientation which differentially reproduces a racial hierarchy by constantly rearranging static racial categories. It is from this perspective that racism in *Logic of Species* must be investigated, and as long as we continue to regard the Kyoto School philosophy as an ideology for particularistic ethnic nationalism, we will never be able to expose the racism inherent in it. For an attempt to analyse relationships between 'race' and colonialism from a dynamic viewpoint, see Robert Young, *Colonial Desire: Hybridity in Theory, Culture and Race*, Routledge, London and New York, 1995.

13. Tanabe Hajime, 'Shu no ronri to sekai zushiki', in *Tanabe Hajime Zenshû*, vol. 6, Chikuma Shobô, Tokyo, [1935] 1963, p. 185.
14. Tanabe insists that the essentially dialogical structure of inference haunts all logical argumentation: just as every enunciation is inevitably open to another enunciation, a proposition is intelligible only insofar as it is in relation to another proposition. What he pursues in the logic of species, therefore, must be located in the chain of inference and cannot be contained within a proposition or the synthetic unity of apperceptive predication. On the contrary, hermeneutics confines its investigation of *understanding* within a proposition, within a synthesis of predication, totally ignoring the inferential dimension of philosophical demonstration. From this observation, Tanabe concludes that hermeneutics (the zenith of which Tanabe found in his contemporary, Martin Heidegger) lacks the fundamental aspect of social praxis. Just as every proposition is open to another proposition in inference, the logic of species must be the logic of mediation in which an enunciation constitutes itself in relation and opposition to another. However, this process of mediation cannot be complete since every enunciation is always open to an additional enunciation. Hence, Tanabe argues that the logic of social praxis must be absolutely endless, and this absolutely endless nature of the logic of social praxis he called 'absolute mediation'. In the sense that there cannot be a terminal point or an end to mediation, the logic of species must be the logic of absolute mediation. See 'Shu no ronri to sekai zushiki'.
15. 'We are born into a society where already many maxims regulate the will and action of the individual, so we regulate our own will and action according to the generally accepted maxims before we experience our action and its consequence.' 'Hegeru tetsugaku to benshôhô' ('Hegelian Philosophy and Dialectic'), in *Tanabe Hajime Zenshû*, vol. 3, Chikuma Shobô, Tokyo, 1963 [1931], p. 214. However, Tanabe argues, following Kant, that those maxims cannot be moral maxims for the individual. Moral maxims are moral laws only for the autonomous subject who legislates these laws by itself (ibid. pp. 195–210).
16. Jacques Maritain, *Man and the State*, University of Chicago Press, Chicago, 1951, p. 16. This corporatist notion of the body politic is inherently incompatible with the modern notion of equality:

> Whatever may be said about it, Rousseau's reference to a 'moral and collective body composed of as many members as there are votes in the assembly, produced by the act of association that makes a people a people,' is not the *revival* but the *antithesis* of the corporatist idea of the *corpus mysticum* (theologians have never been fooled on this point). The 'double relationship' under which the individual's contract also has the effect of forbidding the fusion of individuals in a whole, whether immediately or by the mediation of some 'corporation.' (Etienne Balibar, 'Citizen Subject', trans. James B. Swenson Jr, in Eduard Cadava, Peter Connor and Jean-Luc Nancy, eds, *Who Comes After the Subject?*, Routledge, New York and London, 1991, p. 52, italics in the original).

17. See Claude Lefort, 'The Logic of Totalitarianism', and 'The Image of the Body and Totalitarianism', trans. Alan Sheridan, in his *The Political Form of*

Modern Society, ed. John Thompson, MIT Press, Cambridge, MA, 1986, pp. 273–306.

18. As to continuity and discontinuity, see Nishida Kitarô, 'Sekai no jiko-dôitsu to renzoku' ('The Self-identity of the World and Continuity'), in *Nishida Kitarô Zenshû*, vol. 8, Iwanami Shoten, Tokyo, 1965 [1935], pp. 7–106. Although Nishida Kitarô differentiates generality (*ippan-sei*) from universality (*huhen-sei*), Tanabe adopts Hegelian terminology which does not distinguish generality from universality. This is rather odd, as, being a philosopher of mathematics himself, Tanabe's argument owes much to modern mathematics, particularly Riemann geometry – subsequently also to Neo-Kantians and Bergson who philosophically responded to the emergence of the notion of discontinuity and infinity in nineteenth-century mathematics – and the issues of singularity and universality with regard to discontinuity occupy central positions in his philosophy. So, I introduce the terms generality and universality here as they are distinguished from one another and conceptualized by Gilles Deleuze.
19. Tanabe Hajime, 'Shakai sonzai no ronri' ('The Logic of the Social Being'), in *Tanabe Hajime Zenshû*, vol. 6, Chikuma Shobô, Tokyo, 1963 [1934–5], pp. 55ff.
20. The most important aspect of totemic belief is that it consists of a set of generalities according to which members of a tribe are classified and determined as particulars. What is most clearly demonstrated by the example of the totemic belief is that the basic mode in which the social group such as the state rules its members is reducible to the logical relation of the general and the particular, a relation in which the general subsumes the particular under it. Ibid. pp. 53–6.
21. Tanabe, 'Shakai sonzai no ronri', pp. 74–128; 'Rinri to ronri' ('Ethics and Logic'), in *Tanabe Hajime Zenshû*, vol. 7, Chikuma Shobô, Tokyo, 1963 [1940] pp. 173–209.
22. Alexander Kojève's reading of Hegel, with its emphasis on negativity, is well known. Almost simultaneously in two places, Paris and Kyoto, Hegel was read in a characteristic way. For negativity and mediation in Hegel, see Alexander Kojève, 'L'Idée de la mort dans la philosophie de Hegel', in *Introduction à la lecture de Hegel*, Gallimard, Paris, 1947, pp. 529–75.
23. Tanabe, 'Zushiki "jikan" kara zushiki "sekai" e' ('From schema "time" to schema "world") in *Tanabe Hajime Zenshû*, vol. 7, Chikuma Shobô, Tokyo, 1963 [1940], pp. 25–8.
24. Ibid. pp. 11–18. Tanabe believes that Heidegger's reading of Kant successfully captured the aspect of the individual's indebtedness to the species as part of *Dasein*'s thrownness. However, he claims, the Heideggerian *Entwurft* lacks a practical aspect and essentially remains speculative, since Heidegger failed to recognize the spatiality of social practice. To overcome this shortcoming, Tanabe proposes to introduce the schema of the world. A similar critique of Heidegger was offered by Watsuji Tetsurô about Heidegger's neglect of spatiality, but Watsuji's reading, where the temporality of *Dasein* is completely eliminated, is no match for Tanabe's in terms of rigour, and these two critiques of Heidegger's *Kant Book* must not be confused. This explains why Watsuji's static conception of the national community could legitimate post-war Japanese

cultural nationalism successfully, whereas Tanabe's social ontology was fast forgotten after the loss of the Japanese Empire in 1945.

25. Tanabe, 'Shakai sonzai no ronri', p. 69.
26. Here we might note that Nishida Kitarô, for example, tried to introduce two different conceptions of universality: *fuhen*, in the sense of the universality of the Kantian idea, and *ippansha*, generality in the sense of the universality of the Kantian concept.
27. Tanabe, 'Shi Sei', p. 261.
28. Tanabe, 'Shu no ronri to sekai zushiki', p. 198.
29. Tanabe, 'Hegeru tetsugaku to benshôhô', p. 124.
30. For the distinction between differenciation and differentiation, see Gilles Deleuze, *Difference and Repetition*, trans. Paul Patton, Columbia University Press, New York, 1994.
31. The term *mu* was introduced by Nishida Kitarô in the context of the ontology of self-awareness or *jikaku*. It has often been translated as 'nothingness'. But it primarily designated the undecidability of the transcendental subject in opposition to the decidability of the empirical ego in the Kantian formula. See Nishida Kitarô, 'Basho', in *Nishida Kitarô Zenshû*, vol. 4, Iwanami Shoten, Tokyo, 1965 [1926], pp. 208–89; and *Mu no jikaku-teki gentei* ('Self-determination of Mu'), in *Nishida Kitarô Zenshû*, vol. 6, Iwanami Shoten, Tokyo, 1965 [1930–2].
32. The most obvious case is Watsuji Tetsurô, who followed Tanabe's argument in his *Ethics* to a great extent, but he deliberately eliminated negativity between the individual and the state, so that the state is positively immanent in the individual. In other words, the nation is continually the state without the mediation of the individual's negativity. In this respect, in Watsuji's *Ethics*, the state does not guarantee the individual's right of refusal to accept the dictates of a given community. See Naoki Sakai, 'Return to the West/Return to the East', in Masao Miyoshi (ed.), *Boundary 2*, vol. 18, no. 3, Fall 1991, pp. 157–90; also in *Translation and Subjectivity*.
33. Tanabe explains this relationship between the subject and the Subject in reference to Pure Land Shin Buddhism established by Shinran (1173–262). Perhaps the most explicit reference to Shin Buddhism can be found in his 'Zangedô no tetsugaku', *Tanabe Hajime Zenshû*, vol. 9, Chikuma Shobô, Tokyo, 1963 [1946] (English translation, *Philosophy as Metanoetics*, trans. Takeuchi Yoshinori, Valdo Viglielmo and James W. Heisig, University of California Press, Berkeley, CA, 1986).
34. G.W.F. Hegel, *Phenomenology of Spirit*, trans. A.V. Miller, Oxford University Press, Oxford, 1977 [1807], p. 213.
35. Ibid. For a detailed account of work and individuality in Hegel, see Jean Hyppolite, *Genesis and Structure of Hegel's Phenomenology of Spirit*, trans. Samuel Chernick and John Heckman, Northwestern University Press, Evanston, IL, 1974, pp. 296–318.
36. Cf. Hegel's *Philosophy of Right*, trans. T.M. Knox, Oxford University Press, Oxford, 1967, p. 279.
37. Tanabe repeatedly referred to the Holy Trinity in order to explain schematically the relationship between the individual, the species and the genus. See, for instance, his 'Kokka sonzai no ronri' ('The Logic of the State Being'), in

Tanabe Hajime Zenshû, vol. 7, pp. 42–4. For a critique of Tanabe's obsession with Christianity, see Tosaka Jun, 'Gendai yuibutsu-ron kôwa' ('Lectures on Today's Materialism'), in *Tosaka Jun Zenshû*, vol. 3, Keisô Shobô, Tokyo, 1961 [1936], p. 309.

38. Hegel called this work 'spiritual essence as ethical substance.' See *Phenomenology of Spirit*, p. 264.
39. 'Shakai sonzai no ronri', p. 157.
40. Ibid. p. 155.
41. One has to be extremely sensitive to the political function of an ethnic identity. The ethnic identity must not be essentialized or spatialized, but it is very important to note that, in certain contexts, it might be the only means to resist the imperialist manoeuvre. In this respect, we find the most rigorous critic of Tanabe's logic of species in Takeuchi Yoshimi, who valued the significance of *minzokushugi* or ethnic nationalism as an indispensable means by which to resist imperialisms, but who endorsed it only as an inevitable moment in imperialist domination, a moment which would be utterly meaningless outside an imperialist hegemony although he could not totally avoid the essentialization of ethnic identity in ethnic nationalism. See Takeuchi Yoshimi, 'Kindai towa nanika' ('What is Modernity?'), in *Takeuchi Yoshimi Zenshû*, vol. 4, Chikuma Shobô, Tokyo, 1980 [1948].
42. Tosaka Jun, for example, criticizes Nishida Kitarô's philosophy as a typical form of bourgeois idealism. Yet his critique of Nishida seems to coincide with Tanabe's critique of him in many respects. Tosaka was very sympathetic to Tanabe's *Logic of Species* except for Tanabe's emphasis on religions and, particularly, Christianity. See his *Nihon ideologî-ron*. For Tanabe's political activities in the 1930s and early 1940s, see Ienaga Saburô, *Tanabe Hajime no shisô-teki kenkyû*, Hosei University Press, Tokyo, 1974.
43. 'Shakai sonzai no ronri', p. 160, my emphasis.
44. Ibid.
45. 'The nation-state contains within it the conquering ethnos [*shuzoku*] and the conquered ethnos', ibid.

Chapter 8: On Chineseness As a Theoretical Problem

1. An earlier version of this chapter was published as the introduction to a special issue of *Boundary 2*, vol. 25, no. 3, Fall 1998. This special issue has since been expanded and published as Rey Chow (ed.), *Modern Chinese Literary and Cultural Studies in the Age of Theory: Reimagining A Field*, Duke University Press, Durham, NC, 2000.
2. A short (and incomplete) list of scholarly works (in English) by single authors published in the 1990s includes, for instance, Michelle Yeh, *Modern Chinese Poetry: Theory and Practice since 1917*, Yale University Press, New Haven, CT, 1991; David Der-wei Wang, *Fictional Realism in Twentieth-Century China: Mao Dun, Lao She, Shen Congwen*, Columbia University Press, New York, 1992; Yvonne Sung-sheng Chang, *Modernism and the Nativist Resistance: Contemporary Chinese Fiction from Taiwan*, Duke University Press, Durham, NC, 1993;

Sheldon Hsiao-peng Lu, *From Historicity to Fictionality: The Chinese Poetics of Narrative*, Stanford University Press, Stanford, CA, 1994; Xiaomei Chen, *Occidentalism: A Theory of Counter-Discourse in Post-Mao China*, Oxford University Press, New York, 1995; Lydia H. Liu, *Translingual Practice: Literature, National Culture, and Translated Modernity – China, 1900–1937*, Stanford University Press, Stanford, CA, 1995; Tonglin Lu, *Misogyny, Cultural Nihilism, and Oppositional Politics: Contemporary Chinese Experimental Fiction*, Stanford University Press, Stanford, CA, 1995; Jing Wang, *High Culture Fever: Politics, Aesthetics, and Ideology in Deng's China*, University of California Press, Berkeley and Los Angeles, CA, 1996; Yingjin Zhang, *The City in Modern Chinese Literature and Film: Configurations of Space, Time, and Gender*, Stanford University Press, Stanford, 1996; Ban Wang, *The Sublime Figure of History: Aesthetics and Politics in Twentieth-Century China*, Stanford University Press, Stanford, CA, 1997; David Der-wei Wang, *Fin-de-Siècle Splendor: Repressed Modernities of Late Qing Fiction, 1849–1911*, Stanford University Press, Stanford, CA, 1997; Xudong Zhang, *Chinese Modernism in the Era of Reforms: Cultural Fever, Avant-Garde Fiction, and the New Chinese Cinema*, Duke University Press, Durham, NC, 1997; Sally Taylor Lieberman, *The Mother and Narrative Politics in Modern China*, University Press of Virginia, Charlottesville, VA, 1998.

3. For an informed overview of Western scholarship, including feminist scholarship, on Chinese women, see Jinhua Emma Teng, 'The Construction of the "Traditional Chinese Woman" in the Western Academy: A Critical Review', *Signs*, vol. 22, no. 1, Autumn 1996, pp. 115–51. For an argument about a predominant mode of literary representation of women – through recurrent tropes of hunger – in modern Chinese literature, see David Der-wei Wang, 'Three Hungry Women', in *Modern Chinese Literary and Cultural Studies in the Age of Theory*. For arguments about how the curiosity about Chinese women as exotica is part and parcel of a long-standing Orientalist fascination with China, see Dorothy Ko, 'Footbinding and Fashion Theory', in *Modern Chinese Literary and Cultural Studies in the Age of Theory*.
4. Naoki Sakai, *Translation and Subjectivity: On 'Japan' and Cultural Nationalism*, foreword by Meaghan Morris, University of Minnesota Press, Minneapolis, 1997, p. 61.
5. A discussion that has been helpful to my formulation of ethnicity here is Stuart Hall, 'New Ethnicities', in *Black Film, British Cinema*, ICA Documents, London, 1988, pp. 27–31. Referring to the black experience in Britain, Hall writes:

> The struggle to come into representation was predicated on a critique of the degree of fetishization, objectification and negative figuration which are so much a feature of the representation of the black subject . . . The cultural politics and strategies which developed around this critique had many facets, but its two principal objects were: first the question of *access* to the rights to representation by black artists and black cultural workers themselves. Secondly the *contestation* of the marginality, the stereotypical quality and the fetishised nature of images of blacks, by the counter-position of a 'positive' black imagery. (p. 27; Hall's emphases)

6. See the section 'Chinese Film in the Age of Interdisciplinarity' in my *Primitive Passions: Visuality, Sexuality, Ethnography, and Contemporary Chinese Cinema*, Columbia University Press, New York, 1995, pp. 26–8.
7. For a more sustained discussion of this point, see Rey Chow, 'King Kong in Hong Kong: Watching the "Handover" from the USA', *Social Text* 55, Summer 1998, pp. 93–108.
8. As Naoki Sakai reminds us, this tendency toward self-referentiality on the part of modern non-Western cultures should be understood as always already operating in a *comparative* framework in what he refers to alternately as a 'schema of cofiguration' or 'regime of translation'. See, in particular, Chapter 2 of *Translation and Subjectivity*, 'The Problem of "Japanese Thought": The Formation of "Japan" and the Schema of Cofiguration', pp. 40–71.
9. See Song Qiang *et al.*, *Zhongguo keyi shuo bu* (*China Can Say No*), Ming Pao, Hong Kong, 1996; and *Zhongguo haishi neng shuo bu* (*China Can Still Say No*), Ming Pao, Hong Kong, 1996. For a discussion of the ramifications of such sinochauvinism, especially as it has surfaced in theoretical debates among contemporary PRC scholars, see Michelle Yeh, 'International Theory and the Transnational Critic', in *Modern Chinese Literary and Cultural Studies in the Age of Theory*. See also (in the same volume) Chris Berry, 'If China Can Say No, Can China Make Movies? Or, Do Movies Make China?', which discusses the related problem of theorizing collective agency in the case of contemporary Chinese cinema.
10. Etienne Balibar, 'Is There a "Neo-Racism"?' trans. Chris Turner, in Etienne Balibar and Immanuel Wallerstein, *Race, Nation, Class: Ambiguous Identities*, Verso, New York, 1991, pp. 21–2, Balibar's emphasis. Balibar is making his arguments primarily from the perspective of a culturally hegemonic post-war France, but they are also applicable to the attitudes typical of sinochauvinism. For another major discussion of the 'new racism' (this time in contemporary Britain) that is based less on biological essentialism than on the notion of a pure and homogeneous cultural and national identity, see Paul Gilroy, *There Ain't No Black in the Union Jack*, Routledge, London, 1991. For an example of a collective attempt, prior to the introduction of post-structuralism, to rethink anthropology as a Western, in particular a post-Second World War, phenomenon, see some of the essays in Dell Hymes, (ed.), *Reinventing Anthropology*, Pantheon, New York, 1969.
11. David Yen-ho Wu, 'The Construction of Chinese and Non-Chinese Identities', *Daedalus* 120, no. 2, Spring 1991, pp. 159–79; Ien Ang, 'On Not Speaking Chinese', *New Formations* 24, Winter 1994, pp. 1–18; Allen Chun, 'Fuck Chineseness: On the Ambiguities of Ethnicity as Culture as Identity', *Boundary 2*, vol. 23, no. 2, Summer 1996, pp. 111–38. For a related discussion of the way the governments in mainland China and the Chinese overseas have interacted during alternating periods of strength and weakness in the Chinese polity, see Wang Gungwu, 'Greater China and the Chinese Overseas', in David Shambaugh (ed.), *Greater China: The Next Superpower?*, Oxford University Press, Oxford, 1995, pp. 274–96.
12. Hall, 'New Ethnicities', p. 29, Hall's emphasis.
13. The best example in this regard is the use of feminist theory. One reason investigations of women are so popular in the China field, I think, is that

gender serves in effect as a smokescreen, which enables Western women scholars to be both orientalist *and* politically correct at once – precisely by studying Chinese women – without having to come to terms with the exploitative implications of their own undertakings. While there is an abundance of research on ancient and modern Chinese women (ranging from wives and widows to maids and concubines or from writers and revolutionaries to factory workers and prostitutes), therefore, there is also a noticeable lack of inquiry into the racial and ethnic implications of the subjective structuring of these investigations.

14. See the essay by Stanley K. Abe, 'No Questions, No Answers', in *Modern Chinese Literary and Cultural Studies in the Age of Theory*, for a critical reading of the orientalism prevalent in certain instances of Western appreciation of Chinese art and calligraphy.
15. John DeFrancis, *The Chinese Language: Fact and Fantasy*, University of Hawaii Press, Honolulu, 1984, p. 39.
16. See DeFrancis, *The Chinese Language*, pp. 54–7, for a discussion of the controversy over the classification of different varieties of spoken Chinese, a controversy that constitutes part of the global problem of the relationship between dialect and language.
17. The devaluing of Chinese in Hong Kong continues in the post-British period. An ongoing controversy after 1 July 1997, for instance, has to do with the Hong Kong government's attempt to implement the use of Cantonese (the mother tongue of the overwhelming majority of the population) as the medium of instruction in the local education system. This has been met with severe criticism and opposition from large sectors of Hong Kong's Chinese population, who prefer to retain English as that medium. For a discussion of the inferior cultural position occupied by colonial Hong Kong *vis-à-vis* both mainland China and Britain, especially as this position is negotiated in fictional writing and literary criticism, see Leung Ping-kwan, 'Two Discourses on Colonialism', in *Modern Chinese Literary and Cultural Studies in the Age of Theory*.
18. It should be pointed out that those who are considered 'inauthentic' Chinese are often discriminated against in other major ways as well. For instance, in South-east Asian countries such as Indonesia and Malaysia, where anti-Chinese sentiments are traditionally strong, Chinese people are discriminated against by not being allowed to *forget* that they are Chinese, even when their families have lived in those countries for generations and they do not speak Chinese languages at all. For a moving discussion of this vast historical scenario relating to what are known as the Peranakan Chinese, see Ien Ang, 'On Not Speaking Chinese'; see also Ang's essay 'Can One Say No to Chineseness?' (in *Modern Chinese Literary and Cultural Studies in the Age of Theory*) for a critique of the recent discourse of 'cultural China', which, despite its seeming openness, is in the end still deeply China-rooted and hence unable to address such issues of Chineseness as those constitutive of the diasporic experiences of the Peranakan Chinese populations.
19. Even though it is not my main concern, a third set of questions around language can presumably be developed around the age-old myth of Chinese as an 'ideographic' language. For an authoritative discussion that dispels this

myth, see DeFrancis, *The Chinese Language*, pp. 133–48. 'Chinese characters are a phonetic, not an ideographic, system of writing . . . There never has been, and never can be, such a thing as an ideographic system of writing', DeFrancis writes. 'The concept of Chinese writings as a means of conveying ideas without regard to speech took hold as part of the chinoiserie fad among Western intellectuals that was stimulated by the generally highly laudatory writings of Catholic missionaries from the sixteenth to the eighteenth centuries' (ibid., p. 133). Considering the centrality of the early work of a scholar such as Jacques Derrida for post-structuralist studies in general, and remembering how that work invokes Chinese 'ideographic' writing as *the* metaphor for difference from 'Western' phonocentrism – the heart of Derrida's critique – the implications of DeFrancis's assertion are staggering. For an analysis of the power-ridden relation between Chinese speech and Chinese writing in post-British Hong Kong, see Kwai-cheung Lo, 'Look Who's Talking?', in *Modern Chinese Literary and Cultural Studies in the Age of Theory*.

20. I borrow the term *fictive ethnicity* from Etienne Balibar, 'The Nation Form: History and Ideology', in Balibar and Wallerstein, *Race, Nation, Class*, pp. 86–106; see, in particular, the discussion on p. 96.
21. In his study of Japan, Naoki Sakai perceptively calls this kind of effort to promote an ethnic culture 'mimetic': 'The desire to identify either with Japan or the West is . . . invariably a mimetic one, so that the insistence on Japan's originality, for instance, would have to be mediated by the mimetic desire for the West' (*Translation and Subjectivity*, p. 52). As my arguments show, this mimeticism fundamental to modern East–West relations is further complicated in the China situation by sinologists' (ideological) insistence that classical Chinese writings are, in and of themselves, nonmimetic in nature.
22. For an informative discussion of the intellectual problems generated by such arguments in the field of ancient Chinese poetry and poetics, see Yong Ren, 'Cosmogony, Fictionality, Poetic Creativity: Western and Traditional Chinese Cultural Perspectives', *Comparative Literature* 50, no. 2, Spring 1998, pp. 98–119. In his well-known essay 'White Mythology', Jacques Derrida, explaining the classical Western philosophical tradition, has suggested that, for a major philosopher such as Aristotle, mimesis 'belongs to *logos*' itself and is 'tied to the possibility of meaning and truth in discourse' in general. Accordingly, mimesis is considered:

> proper to man. Only man imitates properly. Man alone takes pleasure in imitating, man alone learns to imitate, man alone learns by imitation. The power of truth, as the unveiling of nature (*physis*) by *mimesis*, congenitally belongs to the physics of man, to anthropophysics. Such is the natural origin of poetry, and such is the natural origin of metaphor. (*Margins of Philosophy*, trans. with additional notes, by Alan Bass, University of Chicago Press, Chicago, 1982, p. 237)

Because my purpose here is to foreground the problem of ethnicity as it relates to literature (rather than the generality of mimesis [in writing] *per se*), a fully-fledged discussion of the implications of Derrida's reading of Aristotle will have to be taken up on a different occasion.

23. Haun Saussy, *The Problem of a Chinese Aesthetic*, Stanford University Press, Stanford, CA, 1993, pp. 27, 31. Saussy offers an informed discussion of the views that sinologists doing 'comparative poetics' typically advance to support the claim that Chinese literature is nonmimetic and nonallegorical. See, in particular, Chapter 1, 'The Question of Chinese Allegory'.
24. A good analogy here is Julia Kristeva's 'positive' and laudatory reading of Chinese women by way of the psychoanalytic notions of pre-Oedipality, motherhood, the semiotic, and so forth, in *About Chinese Women*, trans. Anita Barrows, Marion Boyars, London, 1977. For an incisive recent critique of this kind of essentialist reading of 'ethnic' cultures by critics following theorists such as Kristeva, see Tomo Hattori, 'Psycholinguistic Orientalism in Criticism of *The Woman Warrior* and *Obasan*', in Sandra Kumamoto Stanley (ed.), *Other Sisterhoods: Literary Theory and U.S. Women of Color*, University of Illinois Press, Urbana, IL, 1997, pp. 119–38.
25. Ien Ang, 'The Differential Politics of Chineseness', *Communal/Plural* (Research Centre in Intercommunal Studies, University of Western Sydney, Nepean) 1, 1993, p. 25.
26. Balibar, 'Is There a "Neo-Racism"?', pp. 21–2.
27. R.H. Van Gulik, *Sexual Life in Ancient China* (1961), reprint, Brill, Leiden, 1974.
28. 'The juxtaposition of Eastern and Western poetics outlined by these critics seems to involve hypotheses inimical to their conclusions' (Saussy, *The Problem of a Chinese Aesthetic*, p. 34).
29. One such form is, I think, the genre known as reportage, which, as Charles Laughlin argues, should be dated from the 1930s rather than the more recent Chinese Communist period. See his 'Narrative Subjectivity and the Production of Social Space in Chinese Reportage' (in *Modern Chinese Literary and Cultural Studies in the Age of Theory*) for the intricate relations between style (narrative subjectivity) and politics (the production of social space) in modern Chinese literature since the early twentieth century.
30. Edward Gunn, *Rewriting Chinese: Style and Innovation in Twentieth-Century Chinese Prose*, Stanford University Press, Stanford, CA, 1991.
31. Gunn writes:

    > 'the new political cohesion in China required predictability in language and writing to build the nation . . . Style was fixed largely as it existed in politically acceptable works of the late 1940s . . . In stabilizing writing style to such a degree and greatly expanding the literacy rate, the PRC had to sacrifice the aesthetic value of the unpredictable, whether in the language-specific, metonymic range of regional vocabulary and grammar, or in the more metaphorically charged range of cohesion and disjunction'. (*Rewriting Chinese*, p. 56)

32. For a related discussion, see, for instance, Anthony Kane, 'The Humanities in Contemporary China Studies: An Uncomfortable Tradition', in David Shambaugh (ed.), *American Studies of Contemporary China*, Woodrow Wilson Center Press, Washington, DC, 1993), pp. 65–81. Kane recapitulates the idealistic manners in which American China scholars in the early 1970s tried to defend the noble 'difference' of PRC literature and art. What these scholars were really defending, he writes,

> was the *politics* of contemporary Chinese literature and art while simply positing the existence of the literature and art itself. In the years since the death of Mao and the fall of the Gang of Four, the false optimism of the early 1970s has become the cause of much soul-searching and embarrassment, acknowledged and unacknowledged. Why, many wonder, were many in the field so determined to defend something that in retrospect seems so completely indefensible? . . . The mistake was not in trying to avoid being culture-bound; rather it was that in the process scholars suspended their disbelief to a point where they lost the ability to analyze critically. (p. 69; Kane's emphasis)

33. The best example of the use of New Criticism to interpret modern Chinese literature remains C.T. Hsia's *A History of Modern Chinese Fiction*, Yale University Press, New Haven, CT, 1971, (2nd edn). Apart from the convention of Hegelian intellectual history, New Criticism is arguably still the predominant mode of analysis in modern Chinese literary studies today.
34. Gunn, *Rewriting Chinese*, pp. 148–9.
35. See, for instance, Gunn's suggestive discussion of the renowned Taiwan author Bai Xianyong:

> Taken as stories of the older generation of mainland émigrés, comprising its elite, Bai's portraits placed them, through his idealized style, in a museum of their own nostalgia, within the approved grammatical structures and lexical relics associated with that past and, more to the point, with *the* past. Just as their objective significance in society is displaced by the narratives to a focus on their subjective experience, so the style encases the characters in an ideal of prose features and associations recognized as signs of their archaism. Displaced from the center of an objective social reality, the émigré characters are gently set aside in a museum of prose that was both a tribute and an elegy . . . *[I]t is critical to the appreciation of Bai's style that it rests on a mimetic foundation, that it serves to authenticate both the existence of a social group and its retirement to a museum.* (*Rewriting Chinese*, pp. 149–50; first emphasis is Gunn's, second emphasis mine)

Gunn's description, which captures the sociological pathos of a non-Western literary modernism, can also be used on numerous other novelistic treatments of the lives of Chinese people who moved from Taiwan to the United States (for example, in the works of the woman author Yu Lihua). For another reading of the non-Western modernism occurring in Taiwan, see Christopher Lupke, 'Wang Wenxing and the Loss of China', in *Modern Chinese Literary and Cultural Studies in the Age of Theory*. See also Sung-sheng Yvonne Chang, 'Beyond Cultural and National Identities' (in the same volume), for a discussion of the legacy of Japanese colonialism that constitutes an important part of Taiwan's modern literary historiography.

36. In recent years, we have witnessed the emergence of another type of Chinese writing in exile – the genre of the post-Cultural Revolution confession/memoir, which is regularly read in the West as an authentic, factographic record of the monstrosities that took place in the PRC during the turbulent Cultural Revolution period. I am indebted to Christopher Lee for this argument.
37. Another familiar example along the same lines would be the attempts by critics (in Chinese studies as much as in other fields) to read writings by women by

identifying feminine characteristics. Once identified in the mimeticist mode, however, such feminine characteristics are often judged to be a limitation. They are, accordingly, what make it impossible for women writers to attain the broad, universal visions found in the works of men.

38. For a sustained critique of the institution of area studies, in particular as it pertains to Asian studies, see H.D. Harootunian, 'Tracking the Dinosaur: Area Studies in a Time of "Globalism"', in his *History's Disquiet: Modernity and Everyday Life*, Columbia University Press, New York, 2000. For discussions of related interest, see Harry Harding, 'The Evolution of American Scholarship on Contemporary China', and Richard Madsen, 'The Academic China Specialists', both in *American Studies of Contemporary China*, pp. 14–40 and pp. 163–75 respectively.
39. Ang, 'On Not Speaking Chinese', p. 16.

Chapter 9: Race and Slavery

1. See the report by Chris McGreal, 'Turning Racism on its Head', at http://www.guardian.co.uk/Archive.
2. I do not include Guyana among the post-slavery societies because of its specific formation: the importance of native groups; its marginal position as a slave society; and the presence of a greater pro-independence sentiment than in the Creole societies to which I refer.
3. Although it is always problematic to speak of 'the West'. It performs a totalizing gesture that marginalizes the critical traditions of Europe.
4. Tzvetan Todorov, *Mémoire du mal, tentation du bien*, Robert Laffond, Paris, 2000, p. 3.
5. This refers to remarks made in an informal discussion with Margalit.
6. François Flahault, *La méchanceté*, Descartes & Cie., Paris, 2000, p. 13.
7. Rony Brauman, Postface to *L'industrie de l'holocauste: Réflexions sur l'exploitation de la souffrance des Juifs*, La Fabrique, Paris, 2000; Peter Novick, *The Holocaust in American Life*, Houghton Mifflin, New York, 1999; Norman Finkelstein, *The Holocaust Industry: Reflections on the Exploitation of Jewish Suffering*, Verso, London, 2000.
8. Elie Wiesel, *All Rivers Run to the Sea : Memoirs*, Schocken Books, New York, 1996. Cited in Novick, *The Holocaust in American Life*, p. 274. Novick remarks also on the relation between Wiesel's words and certain aspects of doctrinal Christianity.
9. See, for example, John and Jean Comaroff, 'Millennial Capitalism: First Thoughts on a Second Coming', *Public Culture*, vol. 12, no. 1, 2000, pp. 291–343, and 'Alien Nation: Zombies, Immigrants and Global Capitalism', *CODESRIA Bulletin*, 3/4, 1999, pp. 17–28.
10. Achille Mbembe, 'Cosmopolitanism from the Margins', unpublished lecture at the Patna Conference on 'Cosmopolitanism and the Nation-State', 22–26 February 2001.
11. See my 'Colonizing Citizenship', *Radical Philosophy* 95, May/June1999.
12. I discuss the relation between the abolitionist doctrine and contemporary

humanitarian causes in more detail in my *Abolir l'esclavage: une utopie coloniale. Les ambiguïtés d'une politique humanitaire*, Albin Michel, Paris, 2001.

13. Though feminist historians and critics have, of course, long questioned the 'masculinity' of the French Republic.
14. For more details see Chapter II of my *Monsters and Revolutionaries: Colonial Family Romance and Métissage*, Duke University Press, Durham, NC, 1999; and 'Colonizing Citizenship'.
15. Albert Memmi, *The Colonizer and the Colonized*, trans. Howard Greenfeld, Orion Press, New York, 1965, p. 151.
16. Frantz Fanon, *Black Skin, White Masks*, trans. Charles Lam Markmann, Grove Press, New York, 1967, p. 226.
17. Vergès, '"I am Not the Slave of Slavery": The Politics of Reparation in (French) Postslavery Communities', in Alexander Alessandri (ed.), *Frantz Fanon: Critical Perspectives*, Routledge, London, 1999, pp. 258–75.

Chapter 10: Rewriting the Black Subject

1. In this chapter, I am interested in the political effects of the deployment of the concept of the racial, as an abstract construct manufactured to apprehend particular 'empirical' processes. However, just as the term 'race' appears in constructs such as 'race prejudice' and 'race consciousness', the term 'racial' also appears in constructs such as 'racial politics' and 'racial discrimination' because that is how both appear in the literature under discussion.
2. While the later phase of the pan-African project combined a recognition that the continent and the diaspora shared a common destiny, this commonality was premised on a critique of race subjection which privileged the political and economic structures underlying race relations in the US and European imperialism. Penny von Eschen in *Race Against Empire*, Cornell University Press, Ithaca, NY, 1997, offers an interesting examination of the Pan-African movement highlighting its emphasis upon anti-imperialism and anti-racist and anticapitalist struggle by concentrating on African-American involvement in the movement.
3. For example, Tricia Rose, *Black Noise: Rap Music and Black Culture in Contemporary America*, Wesleyan University Press, Middletown, 1994.
4. For example, Paul Gilroy, '"After the Love Has Gone": Bio-politics and Ethopoetics in the Black Public Sphere', *Public Culture* 7, 1994.
5. For example, Hazel Carby, *Race Men*, Harvard University Press, Cambridge, MA, 1998; Robin Kelley, *Yo' Mama's DisFUNKtional*, Beacon Press, Boston, 1997. Hence, authenticity (and essentialism) appear here complicated by the effective way in which corporations have been able to transform (and control the transformation of) once rebellious cultural products and the meanings they communicate into valuable commodities (See Gilroy, '"After the Love Has Gone": Bio-politics and Etho-poetics in the Black Public Sphere'). I exclude interventions such as Henry Louis Gates and Cornel West's *The Future of the Race*, Alfred A. Knopf, New York, 1996, which seems to yearn for a different kind of articulation of blackness, one that privileges (US) intellectual projects

and conceives of the conditions in which black urban culture emerges as problematic. I also exclude crucial contributions such as that of Wahneema Lubiano's 'Black Nationalism and Black Common Sense', in *The House That Race Built*, Vintage Books, New York, 1998, who correctly points to how these cultural products can convey rather conservative views of urban blacks conditions.

6. With the notion of 'the veil', Du Bois describes black consciousness under segregation as an alienated (mediated) condition.

> [T]he Negro is a sort of seventh son, born with a veil, and gifted with second sight in this American world – a world which yields him no true-self-consciousness, but only lets him see himself through the revelation of the other world. It is a peculiar sensation, this double-consciousness, this sense of always looking at one's self through the eyes of the others, of measuring one's soul by the tape of a world that looks on in amused contempt and pity. (W.E.B. Du Bois, 'Of Our Spiritual Strivings', in *Writings*, The Library of America College Editions, New York, 1996, p. 364).

   Underlying this construction, which is also present in Fanon, is nostalgia for transparency, the desire to write an unmediated black consciousness. See Frantz Fanon, *Black Skin, White Masks*, trans. Charles Lam Markmann, Grove Press, New York, 1967 (first published 1952).

7. As it is formulated, for example, by Hegel in *The Philosophy of History*, Willey Book Co., New York, 1900.
8. In *The Black Atlantic: Modernity and Double Consciousness*, Harvard University Press, Cambridge, MA, 1993, Paul Gilroy advances a view of black diasporic culture and politics as emerging out of the journeys, displacements, and migrations which have marked the history of black people in the West. Reading earlier African American intellectuals, he highlights their contradictory impulses towards the projects of modernity, both embracing and rejecting it. According to Gilroy, the culture and politics of the black Atlantic is an 'expression of and commentaries upon the ambivalence generated by modernity and their [black Atlanticists'] location within it' (ibid., p. xx).
9. According to Gilroy, the ambivalence of a placing articulated as racial terror enables three impulses characterizing black diasporic culture and politics. In black cultural expression, he argues, there is an impulse toward the liberation of the body in the slave songs, the liberation of culture, where language becomes a 'means of self-creation', and the liberation of music itself, which rather than being understood as a commodity is reclaimed as a 'means of communal self-development'. In black political expression, on the other hand, emancipation has taken two key forms: the attainment of citizenship within a specific nation–state and the movement towards racial exclusiveness, self-government.
10. See Franz Boas, *The Mind of Primitive Man*, Macmillan, New York, 1911; Johannes Fabian, *Time and the Other: How Anthropology Makes its Objects*, Columbia University Press, New York, 1983.
11. He says, for example, of soul in Harlem in the 1970s:

> As debates over the black aesthetic raged, the concept of soul was an assertion that there are 'black ways' of doing things, even if those ways are contested and

> the boundaries around what is 'black are fluid' . . . *soul* was a euphemism or a creative way of identifying what many believed was a black aesthetic or black style, and it was a synonym for black itself or a way to talk about being black without reference to color, which is why peoples of other ethnic groups could not have soul. (Kelley, *Yo' Mama's DisFUNKtional*, pp. 25–6)

12. The earliest sociological formulation of this perspective – that black consciousness reflects social conditions – can be found in Robert E. Park, 'Negro Consciousness as Reflected in Race Literature', in *Race and Culture*, The Free Press, Glencoe, IL, 1950 (first published 1923). Du Bois, however, seems to have been the first to formulate a conception of black consciousness along the lines of Hegel's account (in *The Philosophy of History*) of self-consciousness as the moment in which the I recognizes itself in its determined forms.
13. The term 'racial knowledge' refers to projects such as the nineteenth-century science of life and the science of man, twentieth-century sociology of race relations, as well the critical racial studies that emerged in the 1980s, such as Black British cultural studies, African-American, Asian American and Chicano Studies, and comparative ethnic studies.
14. Something similar, perhaps, to what Judith Butler, in *Bodies That Matter*, Routledge London, 1993, identifies with the notion of 'zones of inhabitability', which are necessary to define the boundaries and limits of the gendered subject constituted within the heterosexual matrix.
15. See, for example, Carlos Hasenbalg, *Discriminação e Desigualdades Raciais no Brasil*, Graal, Rio de Janeiro, 1979; Michael Hanchard, *Orpheus and Power*, Princeton University Press, Princeton, NJ, 1994.
16. See, for example, G. Reid Andrews, *Blacks and Whites in São Paulo*, University of Wisconsin Press, Madison, WI, 1992.
17. See, in particular, Hanchard, *Orpheus and Power*.
18. See, for example, Gunnar Myrdal, *An American Dilemma*, Harper & Row, New York, 1962 (first published 1944).
19. See, for example, Oliver C. Cox, *Caste, Class, and Race*, Doubleday, Garden City, NJ, 1948.
20. See Stuart Hall, 'Race, Articulation and Societies Structured in Dominance', in Houston Baker Jr. *et al.*, (eds), *Black British Cultural Studies: A Reader*, University of Chicago Press, Chicago, 1996; Michael Omi and H. Winant, *Racial Formation in the United States*, Routledge and Kegan Paul, New York, 1986.
21. This argument is further elaborated in Denise Ferreira da Silva, 'Toward a Critique of the Socio-Logos of Justice: The Analytics of Raciality and the Production of Universality', *Social Identities*, vol. 7, no. 3, 2001, pp. 421–54, and Denise Ferreira da Silva, *Race and Nation in the Mapping of the Modern Global Space: A Critique of Sociology of Race Relations*, Duke University Press, Durham, NC, forthcoming.
22. For a discussion of the argument concerning hybridity and miscegenation see Robert Young, *Colonial Desire*, Routledge, London, 1995.
23. See Denise Ferreira da Silva, 'Facts of Blackness: Brazil is not (Quite) the United States . . . and Racial Politics in Brazil?', *Social Identities*, vol. 4, no. 2, 1998, pp. 201–23.

24. In *Race and Nation* (forthcoming) I discuss the two versions of the hegemonic Brazilian text in detail. Briefly, the initial version, whitening, drew on the nineteenth century biological construction of race, which assumed (i) a natural connection between body, place of origin, and form of consciousness; and (ii) that the Caucasian body indicated the type of people whose consciousness naturally expressed the cultural principles able to fulfil the political and material projects of modernity. Brazilian intellectuals involved in this whitening project appropriated this argument to produce the Brazilian subject as a European subject, who, though always already *mestiço*, constituted an American manifestation of the European spirit: see, for example, Sylvio Romero, *Historia da Literatura Brasileira*, Garnier, Rio de Janeiro, 1888; Oliveira Vianna, *A Evolução do Povo Brasileiro*, Cia Editora Nacional, São Paulo, 1938; Paulo Prado, *Retrato do Brasil*, José Olympio Editora, Rio de Janeiro, 1962 (first published 1926); Raymundo Nina Rodrigues, *As Raças Humanas e a Responsabilidade Penal no Brasil*, Livraria Progress, Salvador, 1957 (first published 1894); Raymundo Nina Rodrigues, *O Animismo Fetichista dos Negros Bahianos*, Civilização Brasileira, Rio de Janeiro, 1935 (first published 1900). The second, and still prevailing version of the Brazilian text, race democracy, would resignify miscegenation as the constitutive attribute of a Brazilian spirit, seeing the social problems entailed by the co-existence of individuals from different races in the same social space (problems of, for example, prejudice and conflict) as an obstacle to the institution of a social form ruled by abstract and egalitarian principles. The racial democracy thesis appropriated race-mixture as a proof that, from the outset, the Brazilian soul expressed the democratic, egalitarian principles organizing modern conditions. See, for example, Gilberto Freyre, *Casa Grande e Senzala*, José Olympio Editora, Rio de Janeiro, 1987 (first published 1933) and Gilberto Freyre, *Novo Mundo nos Trópicos*, Cia Editora Nacional, São Paulo, 1969.
25. See, for example, Maria Ercilia do Nascimento, 'A Estratégia da Desigualdade: O Movimento Negro dos Anos 70', unpublished MA thesis, Pontifícia Universidade Católica, São Paulo, 1989; Hanchard, *Orpheus and Power*; Andrews, *Blacks and Whites in São Paulo*.
26. 'The MNU . . . represents a moment of political advancement, as the political discourse about racism, particularly the Brazilian racial problem, saw class exploitation as the fundamental explanation for racial discrimination' (Nascimento, *A Estratégia da Desigualdade*, p. 15, my translation).
27. See, for instance, Carlos Hasenbalg, 'O Negro nas Vésperas do Centenário', *Estudos Afro-Asiáticos*, no. 13, 1987, pp. 79–86.
28. The meeting brought together activists representing various black Brazilian organizations. Their interventions, published in the journal *Estudos Afro-Asiáticos*, no. 8/9, 1983, communicate what would be the 1980s' black movement agenda. The strategies they highlighted would reappear in documents by activists throughout the decade.
29. Centro de Cultura Negra do Maranhão, São Luiz, Maranhão, *Estudos Afro-Asiáticos*, no. 8/9, 1983, p. 38.
30. Núcleo Cultural Afro-Brasileiro, Salvador, Bahia, *Estudos Afro-Asiáticos*, no. 8/9, 1983, p. 55.
31. Elsewhere, I have examined the gendered effects of the hegemonic Brazilian

narrative. The silencing of female black subjectivity in this reading reflects the general strategy of the black Brazilian movement in this period. Like other emancipatory projects, this narrative also assumed masculinity as an immediate signifier of black desire.

32. Instituto de Pesquisa das Culturals Negras, Rio de Janeiro, *Estudos Afro-Asiáticos*, no. 8/9, 1983, p. 173.
33. See Andrews, *Blacks and Whites in São Paulo.*
34. The documents released by various institutions in the period between 1978 and 1989 suggest the centrality of sociological formulations in black political demands. This period was characterized by an exchange between Brazilian social scientists and black activists, an exchange that has been identified as crucial by most of those involved in this phase of the black Brazilian movement. See Helene Monteiro, 'O Resurgimento do Movimento Negro na Década de 70', unpublished MA thesis, Universidade Federal do Rio de Janeiro, 1991.
35. Movimento Negro Unificado, Belo Horizonte, Minas Gerais, *Estudos Afro-Asiáticos*, no. 8/9, 1983, p. 27. Sociological formulations became such an important part of the rhetoric of the movement that in their interventions in meetings which were not necessarily academic in character activists used the results of sociological (usually quantitative) researches to back up their critique of the Brazilian society.
36. Centro de Cultura Negra do Maranhão, São Luiz, Maranhão, *Estudos Afro-Asiáticos*, no. 8/9, 1983, p. 45.
37. See Peter Fry, *Para Ingles Ver*, Zahar, Rio de Janeiro, 1982.
38. Since the turn of the century, Brazilian anthropologists and cultural analysts – such as Nina Rodrigues (see note 24), Arthur Ramos (*O Negro Brasileiro*, Civilização Brasileira, Rio de Janeiro, 1934; *O Folclore Negro do Brasil*, Casa do Estudante do Brasil, Rio de Janeiro, 1935), and Edison Carneiro (*Ladinos e Crioulos*, Civilização Brasileira, Rio de Janeiro, 1964; *As Religiões Negras/Negros Bantos*, Civilização Brasileira, Rio de Janeiro, 1981) – have participated in the construction of an authentic African culture that could be found with some degree of 'purity' in black Brazilian cultural products. While these anthropological formulations actually enabled the appropriation of these products to specify Brazilian culture, they also highlighted the harms these 'primitive cultural elements' entailed, and advocated their study in order to facilitate their elimination. By the 1970s, however, the culture of resistance literature created the possibility for a reclaiming of African cultural products by their producers (see, for example, Yvonne Maggie, *Medo do Feitiço: Relações entre Magia e Poder no Brasil*, Arquivo Nacional, Rio de Janeiro, 1992).
39. See Monteiro, *O Resurgimento do Movimento Negro na Década de 70.*
40. See Silva, *Race and Nation.*
41. See Gayatri Spivak, 'Can the Subaltern Speak?', in Patrick Williams and Laura Chrisman (eds), *Colonial Discourse and Post-Colonial Theory*, Columbia University Press, New York, 1994.
42. This formulation can be found in Du Bois's *Writings*, and it was later appropriated in Robert E. Park's examination of black consciousness in *Race and Culture*. For a fuller elaboration of this argument see Silva, *Race and Nation.*
43. The appropriation of this line as an empirical point of departure in the

examination of black conditions can be seen in the first formulation of race as a sociological category in Park's essays 'The Bases of Race Prejudice' and 'The Etiquette of Race Relations in the South', from 1928 and 1937 respectively (both in *Race and Culture*), and in later formulations such as that of Myrdal (*An American Dilemma*), Cox (*Caste, Class, and Race*); Philip Mason (*Race Relations*, Oxford University Press, Oxford, 1970; *Patterns of Dominance*, Oxford University Press, Oxford, 1970); and Franklin Frazier (*Race and Culture Contacts in the Modern World*, Beacon Press, Boston, 1965 (first published 1957); *On Race Relations*, University of Chicago Press, Chicago, 1968).

Select Bibliography

Anderson, Benedict. *Imagined Communities: Reflections on the Origin and Spread of Nationalism*, Verso, London, 1991 (revised and expanded edition).

Anderson, Benedict. *The Spectre of Comparison: Nationalism, Southeast Asia and the World*, Verso, London and New York, 1998.

Appiah, K. Anthony. *In My Father's House: Africa in the Philosophy of Culture*, Oxford University Press, Oxford, 1992.

Appiah K. Anthony, and Gutmann, Amy. *Color Conscious: The Political Morality of Race*, Princeton University Press, Princeton, NJ, 1996.

Babbitt, Susan E. and Campbell, Sue (eds), *Racism and Philosophy*, Cornell University Press, Ithaca, NY, and London, 1999.

Balibar, Etienne and Wallerstein, Immanuel. *Race, Nation, Class: Ambiguous Identities*, Verso, New York, 1991.

Bernasconi, Robert (ed.), *Race*, Blackwell, Oxford, 2001.

Bernasconi, Robert and Lott, Tommy (eds), *The Idea of Race*, Hackett, Indianapolis, 2000.

Bhabha, Homi. *The Location of Culture*, Routledge, London, 1994.

Bhatt, Chetan. *Liberation and Purity: Race, New Religious Movements and the Ethics of Postmodernity*, UCL Press, London, 1997.

Boxill, Bernard (ed.), *Race and Racism*, Oxford University Press, Oxford/New York, 2001.

Dikötter, Frank. *The Discourse of Race in Modern China*, Stanford University Press, Stanford, CA, 1992.

Dikötter, Frank (ed.), *The Construction of Racial Identities in China and Japan*, University of Hawaii Press, Honolulu, 1997.

Eze, Emmanuel (ed.), *Race and the Enlightenment: A Reader*, Blackwell, Oxford, 1997.

Gates, Henry Louis and West, Cornel. *The Future of the Race*, Alfred A. Knopf, New York, 1996.

Gilroy, Paul. *There Ain't No Black in the Union Jack*, Routledge, London, 1991.

Gilroy, Paul. *The Black Atlantic: Modernity and Double Consciousness*, Verso, London, 1993.

Gilroy, Paul. *Between Camps: Race, Identity and Nationalism at the End of the Colour Line*, Allen Lane/Penguin, London, 2000.

Goldberg, David Theo. *Racist Cultures: Philosophy and the Politics of Meaning*, Blackwell, Oxford, 1993.

Goldberg, David Theo. *The Racial State*, Blackwell, Oxford, 2001.

Gordon, Lewis R. (ed.), *Existence in Black: An Anthology of Black Existential Philosophy*, Routledge, New York and London, 1993.

Hannaford, Ivan. *Race: The History of an Idea in the West*, Johns Hopkins University Press, Baltimore, 1996.

Harootunian, Harry D. *History's Disquiet: Modernity and Everyday Life*, Columbia University Press, New York, 2000a.

Harootunian, Harry D. *Overcome by Modernity: History, Culture and Community in Interwar Japan*, Princeton University Press, Princeton, NJ, 2000b.

Karl, Rebecca E. *Staging the World: Chinese Nationalism at the Turn of the Twentieth Century*, Duke University Press, Durham, NC, 2002.

Mills, Charles W. *Blackness Visible: Essays on Philosophy and Race*, Cornell University Press, Ithaca NY, 1998.

Morley, David and Chen, Kuan-Hsing (eds), *Stuart Hall: Critical Dialogues*, Routledge, London, 1996.

Omi, Michael and Winant, Howard. *Racial Formation in the United States from the 1960s to the 1980s*, Routledge, New York and London, 1994.

Said, Edward. *Orientalism*, Penguin, Harmondsworth, 1995 (expanded edition).

Sakai, Naoki. *Translation and Subjectivity: On 'Japan' and Cultural Nationalism*, University of Minnesota Press, Minneapolis and London, 1997.

Spivak, Gayatri C. *A Critique of Postcolonial Reason*, Routledge, London, 1999.

Ward, Julie K. and Lott, Tommy, (eds), *Philosophers on Race: Critical Essays*, Blackwell, Oxford and Malden, MA, 2002.

West, Cornel. *Keeping Faith: Philosophy and Race in America*, Routledge, New York and London, 1993.

Young, Robert. *White Mythologies: Writing History and the West*, Routledge, London, 1990.

Young, Robert. *Colonial Desire: Hybridity in Theory, Culture and Race*, Routledge, London and New York, 1995.

Index